D1030934

SETON LLOYD

EARLY ANATOLIA

THE ARCHAEOLOGY OF ASIA MINOR
BEFORE THE GREEKS

*

With a Note on the Anthropology of the
Ancient Inhabitants of Anatolia by

DR MUZAFFER ŞENYÜREK

PENGUIN BOOKS

Penguin Books Ltd, Harmondsworth, Middlesex

U.S.A.: Penguin Books Inc., 3300 Clipper Mill Road, Baltimore 11, Md

CANADA: Penguin Books (Canada) Ltd, 178 Norseman Street,
Toronto 18, Ontario

AUSTRALIA: Penguin Books Pty Ltd, 762 Whitehorse Road,
Mitcham, Victoria

SOUTH AFRICA: Penguin Books (S.A.) Pty Ltd, Gibraltar House,
Regent Road, Sea Point, Cape Town

—

First published 1956

DS
46
L55

Collogravure plates by Harrison & Sons Ltd
Made and printed in Great Britain
by The Whitefriars Press Ltd
London and Tonbridge

CONTENTS

List of Plates

1 Diagrammatic view of the excavations at Mersin, showing objects found at various levels (Prof. J. Garstang, C.B.E., and the Oxford University Press)

2 (a) and (b) Gold head-dresses and subsidiary jewellery from Schliemann's 'Treasure of Priam': actually belonging to the final phase of the Second Settlement (IIg) and dating from the late third millennium B.C. (Hubert Schmidt, *Trojanische Altertümer*, Georg Reimer, Berlin, 1902. Beilage I)

3 Mrs Schliemann wearing the Trojan jewellery (Picture Post Library)

4 A group of copper 'standards' from the 'Copper-age' tombs at Alaja, at present dated to the second half of the third millennium B.C. (Dr Hamit Z. Koşay)

5 Metal objects from the tombs at Alaja: Terminal figure of a steer in copper with silver inlay, Gold jar with fluted ornament, Gold drinking-cup, Gold jug, Elaborate copper 'standard' with stag and steers (Dr Hamit Z. Koşay and the Turkish Tourist Dept)

6 (a) One of the houses of the Assyrian merchants at Kültepe, in which the tablets were found; two rooms leading off a passage and an open court with baking-oven beyond (Prof. Tahsin Özgüç and Dr Nimet Özgüç)

  (b) In one of the houses of the *karum* at *Kültepe*; a shaped hearth of baked clay and pottery still in place (Prof. Tahsin Özgüç and Dr Nimet Özgüç)

7 From the Assyrian *karum* at Kültepe; clay tablets and tablet-envelopes bearing the impression of cylinder seals: (*upper left*) A seal in the 'Old Babylonian' style; (*upper right*) Impressions of two seals, above in the 'Syro-Cappadocian' and below in the 'Anatolian' styles; (*lower left*) Impressions of two seals in the 'Anatolian' style; (*lower right*) A seal-impression in the 'developed Anatolian' stype (Dr Nimet Özgüç)

8 Four characteristic red burnished vessels of the 'Hittite' class from the *karum* at Kültepe (Middle Bronze Age) (Prof. Tahsin Özgüç and Dr Nimet Özgüç)

vii

LIST OF PLATES

LIST OF PLATES

List of Figures

Commentary on Figures 2, 3, and 4

illustrating chronology of pottery and small objects

The Chalcolithic

Alaja and Gülüjek have the finely incised pottery now associated with the name of the latter: squares and triangles filled with cross-hatching or dots and the curious motifs perhaps representing the stitching of a leather object. There are 'fruitstands', sometimes with pierced foot and more elaborate shapes with handles surmounted by ornamental knobs. There are also the first examples of matt white paint on a black slip.

Incised pottery from Alishar has only a distant resemblance and more typical are fruitstands and other large vessels with polished black or grey slip. Simple copper objects are in evidence and the first button-seals with geometric ornament.

At Troy this period is described as Early Bronze and represented by the first settlement. Among the vessels illustrated perhaps the most typical are the carinated bowl with pierced tubular lugs beneath the rim and squat jars, jugs, etc., supported on three legs. These are mostly black or brown with a burnished slip.

Contemporary at Mersin in Cilicia is the latest phase only of the local Chalcolithic. There are survivals of Al'Ubaid motifs in painted ornament, such as 'swags' and 'meanders', still combined with local variations in shape: plain grey bowls, with moulded rims of the Uruk type and the peculiar 'flint-scraped' bowls, first found at Grai Resh. Finally there are examples of bell-shaped bowls and chalices in the black burnished ware ornamented with matt white paint.

Early Bronze II (Copper Age)

Here at Alaja are the famous tombs with their content of precious metal objects. Among these are features useful for dating: a stone battle-axe like the one found in Troy II: double-spiral ornaments and 'Cypriot daggers' with two holes pierced in the blade, also having parallels at Troy. The pottery, too, all typical Copper Age, has squat jugs like Ahlatlibel and (top right) a *depas amphikypellon*.

Polatli has its small jugs and bowls in polished, red-slipped ware, decorated with horizontal fluting or incisions beneath the slip. There are also examples of white paint on a polished slip and one wheel-made *depas*. Copper, which is plentiful, includes a jug-shape typical of the period and in clay there are incised spindle-whorls and a characteristic figurine.

Alishar repeats many of the features already mentioned and has examples both of stamp- and cylinder-seals, the latter perhaps imported from further south.

Ahlatlibel is characterized by innumerable small saucers with a single loop handle and grotesque little jugs, all with a burnished slip, but here predominantly black rather than red. There are examples of dark-on-light painted ornament, and again much copper.

At Troy this period is represented by the second settlement, which produced the various 'treasures' of metal objects: tassel ornaments, elaborate hair-pins, ear-rings and gold or silver vessels. Among the pottery, bowls and jars still tend to have legs, but there are also the first 'face-urns', *depas* and *askoi* (large flask-shaped water jars).

At Tarsus and Mersin in Cilicia there are also vessels resembling the *depas*, side by side with multiple jars and tall-spouted jugs. One group of pottery from Mersin including such shapes falls indeterminately between this period and the next (Early Bronze III).

Early Bronze III

This period is typified at the plateau sites by the appearance of the exotic 'Cappadocian' and Alishar III polychrome painted pottery, and ends both there and in the maritime provinces with the curious phenomenon known as the red-cross bowl. In Cilicia, as at Troy, the plain pottery is mostly a direct development from the previous period, which it closely resembles.

Middle Bronze

This is the period of the Assyrian colony at Kültepe, with its tablets, metal figurines and animals modelled in clay. It is also the time of the finest and most characteristic Anatolian pottery; the polished red-slip vessels with elaborately graceful shapes, first known under the designation 'Alishar II'. Long beak-spouts, channel-spouts with strainers, basket-handles, tea-pots and lentoid flasks are typical shapes and there are occasional examples of a polished golden slip which is as attractive as the red.

At Troy it is the earlier part of the sixth settlement and pottery is beginning to show Aegaean influence in chalices and high-handled cups.

In Cilicia, on the contrary, relations can be seen with Syria and quite un-Anatolian painted pottery, light-on-dark, is common. A peculiar jug, with a bird's-eye painted beneath the rim, found always in association with small painted bowls standing on a solid foot, is interesting as both types are represented in the form of imports among the indigenous pottery of the *karum* at Kültepe.

Late Bronze

It must be remembered that this period includes both the Old Hittite Kingdom and the Hittite Empire. During the former, the elegant red burnished pottery of Alishar II was still in use and even improved in refinement. It is to this early half of the Late Bronze

Age that most of the types illustrated under Alaja belong. The pottery of the Hittite Empire is much less well-represented in Turkish museums. It is in any case greatly inferior in quality to that of the preceding periods. The shapes are often decadent and the ware coarse. Some typical shapes here from Polatli, Kusura ('C') and Boghazköy include jugs with narrow neck and vertical spout, crude chalices on stems, lentoid flasks, carinated bowls with vertical loop-handles starting at the carination, basket-handles, etc. Ring-shaped pot-stands are common and a simple funnel. From the Hittite capital there are both human and animal figurines of metal.

At Troy this is the period which ends with the Homeric episode. The pottery in the last half of the sixth settlement and beginning of the seventh, is increasingly Aegean, while both here and at Tarsus in Cilicia there is considerable importation of Mycenaean painted wares. Among bronze implements, perhaps the most characteristic of the period is the so-called 'lugged-axe', which had a wide distribution at this time.

Editorial Foreword

BY

PROFESSOR M. E. L. MALLOWAN

*Professor of Western Asiatic Archaeology,
University of London*

MR SETON LLOYD, since many years Director of the British Institute of Archaeology in Ankara, has travelled widely in Asia Minor and is able to give a first-hand account of its ancient sites and their setting. Anatolian archaeology is therefore enlivened by one who has himself dug in the country and, particularly at Beycesultan, has made discoveries which have a direct bearing on Homer, the Hittites, Troy, and other topics – Assuwa and Arzawa – less well known but no less intriguing.

The gradual process of Anatolian discovery conveys to us a cumulative excitement as bit by bit we see taking shape before our eyes the richly coloured picture of the ancient civilizations which arose in this well-defined part of western Asia. There is much that must attract our attentions: the gold-laden tombs of Alaja Hüyük; the Assyrian merchants who in their colonies at Kanesh and elsewhere traded in lead and fine clothing, and the carefully kept accounts of their transactions which have survived upon sealed clay tablets for 3,700 years. The two sites at which these things have been found are, together with Karatepe, sources of the remarkable work recently achieved by Turkish scholars who in addition to their digging have also contributed greatly to kindred subjects so varied as Hittite art, and linguistics. Dr Muzaffer Şenyürek, a distinguished Turkish authority in the field of anthropology, has written a valuable appendix on the skeletal remains.

Seton Lloyd's book is a companion volume to the Pelican by Dr O. R. Gurney entitled *The Hittites*, for it traces the archaeological developments which preceded and succeeded them, and brings the story to a close with a description of the dramatic monuments and remains of the Phrygians, a people about whom future discovery has much to reveal.

NOTE

Modern Turkish spelling has been standardized for proper names, except in a few cases where this might introduce problems of pronunciation (e.g. *Alaja* for *Alaca*) and others where pre-Republican transliteration remains more generally familiar (e.g. *Carchemish* for *Gargamis*).

S. L.

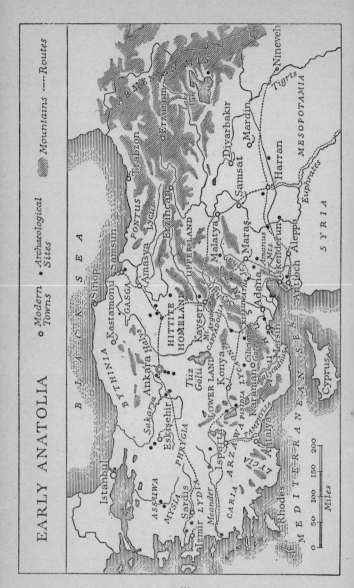

EARLY ANATOLIA

○ Modern Towns · Archaeological Sites Mountains ---- Routes

Map showing names of archaeological sites

NEW TERMINOLOGY			SITES			OLD TERMINOLOGY
			SOUTH	PLATEAU	WEST	
Neolithic		5th mill.	Mersin: 'Lower' xxxiii–xxvii 'Upper' xxvi and xxv / Tarsus / Sakjegözü			Same
Chalcolithic	Early	3800?	Mersin: 'Early' xxiii–xx / Tarsus / Sakjegözü			Same
	Middle	3600?	Mersin: 'Middle' xix–xvii / Tarsus / Sakjegözü			Same
		3000	Mersin: 'Late' xvi–xiiiB	Alishar 19–15 ('O') / Gülücek	Kumtepe / Fikirtepe	'Plateau Chalcolithic' 'Alishar Chalcolithic' etc.
	Late		Mersin xiiA / Tarsus (Transitional)	Alishar 14–12 ('O') / Gülücek / Alaja 14–9 (iv)	Troy I / Thermi / Yortan / Kusura A	
Early Bronze	TWO	2600	Mersin xi? / Tarsus (Middle Phase)	2900 — Early Bronze ONE — Polatli I / Alishar I / Many other Plateau sites ROYAL TOMBS	Troy II / Yortan / Kusura B	'Copper Age' 'Early Metal Age'
	THREE	2300	Mersin xi / Tarsus Last Phase	Cappadocian / Alishar III / Boghazköy v / Polatli II	Troy III, iv, v / Kusura B/C — Destruction	'Cappadocian' 'Early Bronze Age'
Middle Bronze		1900	Mersin xi / Cilician Middle Bronze	Alaja 4 (ii) / Kültepe karum / Polatli III / Alishar II / Boghazköy iv	Troy vi 'Early' and 'Middle'	'Küttepe' 'Old Hittite' 'Cilician Hittite' etc.
		1600				
Late Bronze		1200	Mersin x and ix / Tarsus 'Old Kingdom' and 'Empire'	Alaja 3b, 3a, 2 (ii) / Polatli iv / Boghazköy iii: Old Kingdom, Hittite Emp.	Troy vi and viiA / Kusura C	'Old Kingdom' or 'Hittite Empire'; 'Middle Hittite' or 'Late Hittite'

CHAPTER I

Introductory

ANATOLIA is not an old name by the standards of antiquity
to which one becomes accustomed in dealing with West
Asiatic countries. It first appears in the works of a tenth-cen-
tury Byzantine writer, who uses it as an alternative designation
for the country which in his time had already been known for
five hundred years as Asia Minor. In more recent times, the
Turkish form of the name, Anadolu, has come to be applied
rather loosely to the entire Asiatic territory of the Turkish
Republic, including the mountainous provinces east of the
Euphrates, which early writers would have referred to as
Armenia.* Anadolu, therefore, or Turkey within its modern
frontiers, has acquired in our day an ethnic as well as a political
unity, unparalleled at any other period in its long history. If
the reason is to be sought for the disunity of this land in the
past, we must first examine its most distinctive physical
character.

In considering Anatolia, we are dealing above all with a
land of conspicuous contrasts. Geographical contrasts between
plain and mountains are supplemented by seasonal contrasts of
climate, and parallel disparities in agricultural economy. There
are the alpine landscapes of the eastern provinces, where
beasts can graze only during the short summer months; semi-
tropical forests above Trebizond, on the mountain-sides facing
the Black Sea; steppe-country on the central plateau, resembling Central Asia (of which it is in fact an extension); tem-
perate valleys with vineyards and olive-groves in the Aegean
provinces; and coastal plains facing the Mediterranean, rich in
citrus-fruit and cotton-plantations. It has in fact been observed
that a Scotsman, an African, a Swiss, a Russian, or a Neapo-
litan, could any one of them find in some part of Asiatic

---

* The name Armenia is in fact used elsewhere in these pages in this
same historical sense, for want of an alternative geographical designation.

Turkey living conditions approximating to those with which he was most familiar. A brief geographical survey of the country, as it appears on the standard wall-map in a Turkish primary school, will very easily explain this situation.

The Armenian mountains, which reach a maximum height in the twin peaks of Mount Ararat, 17,000 feet above the sea, are really a westward extension of the great Elburz chain, whose northern slopes face the Caspian Sea. The chain ends in a confusion of watersheds around the sources of the Euphrates, and the upper reaches of that river can in fact be conveniently considered as the eastern limit of Anatolia proper. From here, a new dual system of mountain ranges begins. Diverging to the north-east and south-west, like arms embracing the high central plateau, their elbows are thrust out into the Black and Mediterranean seas, and their extremities return inland to complete the gesture of encirclement. The northern system consists of the so-called Pontic arc, which follows the shore-line of the Black Sea from Trebizond to Sinope, and terminates in the Ilgas Dagh south of Kastamonu. It is interrupted only by occasional deep gorges, through which the rivers of the plateau escape seawards. Its southern counterpart is Taurus, which through its southward drainage has created the coastal plain of Cilicia. Between these two systems of geologically 'newer' folds, the plateau is based upon a core of ancient rocks lying in almost horizontal strata. But this is not apparent. What the traveller sees is an austere upland, arid and thinly populated, inhospitable in character by comparison with the natural amenities of the coastal fringe. To the latter he may descend only after negotiating the peripheral barrier of mountains. Westward of the central basin, however, he will find the monotony of the tableland varied by a pattern of lakes and rivers. On this side there is no direct descent to the sea, for the peninsula terminates in a series of parallel mountain ridges thrust out like fingers of a hand towards the Aegean. These are aligned with ranges on the Greek mainland beyond, of which they are indeed a prolongation, as is shown by lines of islands intermittently emphasizing their submerged continuity.

The diversity of climate in Anatolia, to which we have already referred, is inherent in this spectacular distribution of mountains and in their relation to the sea. The Armenian winter is of more than alpine severity and makes road-communication impracticable for many months in the year. The plateau suffers more from contrasting extremes of temperature; a prevailing absence of moisture in the late summer and long winter months under snow. The Black Sea provinces are still partly and in the past were heavily afforested; they tend to an excess of summer moisture; while the Mediterranean and Aegean littorals approximate closely to the climate of the French Riviera. As a final contrast, there is the piedmont country on the southern border between the Tigris and Euphrates, overwhelmed in summer by the intolerable heat of the Mesopotamian desert and dependent on a precarious winter rainfall.

By now it may be realized that the most superficial description of Anatolian geography is impracticable without the use of place-names, and that some of those already used have an historical flavour. We are therefore reminded that, if the details are now to be filled in, some ruling must be made on the subject of topographical terminology. For modern Turkish cities and administrative districts, it may sometimes be convenient to substitute names which are more historically familiar to the Western ear, in order to obtain the full benefit of their traditional associations. In doing so, it will be difficult always to maintain consistency, and minor anachronisms will accordingly have to be forgiven.* The archaeological period which we are about to consider is poorly documented. No place-name is satisfactorily authenticated until the beginning of the second millennium B.C. Hittite geography, as a study, is still in its infancy, and hardly a dozen towns and provinces have till now been irrefutably identified, while fewer still can be expected to be familiar outside specialist circles. The Greek cities, on the other hand, and the divisions of Asia Minor in classical times are comparatively well known, and their names

* E.g. mention of a road leading 'from Isparta (modern Turkish) to Pamphylia (Greek)' on p. 9.

have an evocative quality which can be helpful in creating a geographical picture. It will not therefore be surprising if we find ourselves sometimes employing Greek or Roman names in preference to more up-to-date designations.

Yet the Hittites, having once been mentioned, can no longer be ignored. In the whole panorama of centuries, from the arrival of the first human settlers in Anatolia to the foundation of the Greek cities, the central historical fact is the existence for several centuries in the late second millennium of a great imperial power, centred on the plateau, but extending its influence over much of the peninsula. Its military and economic requirements gave new significance to physical aspects of the country, such as the disposition of mountains and rivers, which had till then been regarded merely as creating fortuitous barriers between the primitive states or communities into which the land was divided. Hittite communications and trade routes knitted the country together into a coherent pattern and established strategic and political principles, which have remained unchallenged by their successors. It is the Hittite horizon, therefore, which may be most conveniently adopted as a base-line for a more particularized survey of Anatolian topography.

A salt lake (Tatta or Tuz Gölü) some fifty miles wide, lying in a shallow basin of very barren country indeed, provides a navel for the plateau. But historically the focus of interest is slightly off-centre. It is in the natural province of moderately fertile hills and valleys, enclosed by the vast, sickle-shaped curve of the Halys (Kizil Irmak), a stream nearly 600 miles long, which rises in the Armenian watershed and discharges eventually into the Black Sea. This was the homeland of the Hittites, whose great capital city, Hattusas (Boghazköy), occupied a dominating central position, radiating lines of political influence over well-guarded military routes. In the near foreground, beyond the Halys, were contiguous provinces, controlled by or closely associated with the homeland itself. To the south-east, for instance, and most closely affiliated, was Cappadocia, with its farthest limit on the Euphrates. Included within its boundaries are virtually all the

imperial cities which have been satisfactorily identified, outside the actual Halys 'bend'. Mazaka (now Kayseri), its capital,
lay in the shadow of an extinct volcano, Mount Argaeus,
which has a crater 13,000 feet above the sea. To the south,
Cappadocia was strictly confined by the great sweep of the
Taurus mountains, so that Cilicia, which lay beyond, was
accessible only through the famous pass known as the Cilician
Gates (Gülek Boghazı). But since it was traversed by the vital
highroad to north Syria, Hittite control over the coastal plain
can rarely have been relaxed, and Cilicia must be considered
as one of the 'home provinces'. Girt around with high mountains, it is for the most part flat and easily cultivated, being
irrigated, like a miniature Garden of Eden, by two fine rivers,
the Sarus and Pyramus (Seyhan and Ceyhan) and a smaller
stream, the Tarsus Chay. Another inland province, west of
Cappadocia, we may call Lycaonia-Pisidia, in order to include
the 'lake district' centred around modern Isparta, which was
already so prolifically inhabited in the third millennium B.C.
and clearly of great interest to the Hittites. North again is
Galatia, approximately the modern Vilayet of Ankara, whose
name reflects a strange migration of Europeans in the third
century B.C. This embraces the upper tributaries of the
Sangarius (Sakarya) the second largest river in Anatolia
which, like the Halys, also flows northwards to the Black Sea.
With its bare hills and water-courses deeply embedded in
vegetation, it may be regarded as some of the most typical
plateau-country. North of the 'homeland', the rivers Lycus
and Iris make an independent system of waterways within the
curve of the Halys. This, in classical times, was the heart of
the Pontic kingdom which drew its wealth from these fertile
valleys as well as from the timber and minerals which were so
abundantly available in the coastal mountain range. In the
second millennium it must have been the home of the Kaska
tribes who were so often to be found in opposition to the
Hittite kings.

All those parts of central Anatolia, upon the early history
of which the Hittite texts have thrown some light, are thus
accounted for, and we must turn now to the remoter districts,

including the maritime provinces, where such light is scanty and archaeology is the major source of information.

First, then, in the extreme north-west there is Bithynia, lying along the Black Sea coast and extending to the Asiatic shores of the Bosphorus and Marmara. Bithynia, unfortunately for our own purpose, can be dismissed in a few words, since archaeology has so far contributed little and the texts nothing to our knowledge of its pre-classical past. Phrygia also, to the south, acquired importance only in the early first millennium B.C., when a newly immigrant people replaced the Hittites as the central authority in Anatolia. The province which still bore their name in Roman times is broken country more wooded than the plateau and full of strange geological formations which the Phrygians exploited as a setting for their own curious sculptured monuments. It is interposed between the tableland to the east and the western provinces bordering the Aegean, which are familiar under the Greek names, Mysia, Lydia, and Caria. Here are the river valleys running outwards to the deeply indented coast; the Caycus, Hermus, Cayster, and Maeander, whose estuaries the Greeks chose as sites for their most illustrious cities. From the earliest times these lands developed idiosyncrasies and affiliations which segregated them from the eastern parts of the peninsula. Their orientation was towards Europe and their earliest cultural development seems to have marched in step rather with the islands and lands beyond the Agean than with the interior of the plateau. Troy, in its small marshy plain near the entrance to the Hellespont, was an integral part of the Aegean world, and its archaeology has at present to serve as a criterion for the whole composite province. Here the first historical associations are established by the legends of Greece rather than by the Hittite texts.

A knot of rugged mountains forms the south-west extremity of the peninsula (Lycia). Between this and the returning curve of Taurus, Pamphylia lies flat against the sea, a 'riviera' country of scrub-oak and sand dunes with some important areas of cultivation. For the rest, the Mediterranean coast, westwards of the Cilician plain, has a rugged aspect and few agricultural possibilities. Everywhere the high mountains descend almost vertically into the sea; access to the interior is difficult and coastwise communications mainly by boat. It is perhaps for this reason that human occupation of these parts seems to have been so long delayed, and no traces are to be found of any considerable early settlements.

Now, therefore, the eye must move eastwards to the lands bordering Syria and the Mesopotamian desert, which we shall find already to have been affected by the earliest developments in world-civilization, at a time when the greater part of the peninsula was virtually uninhabited. Here, west of the Euphrates, was Aleppo and the plain of Antioch (Amuq) with its great central swamp. This was already farmland in the fourth millennium B.C., and in later times divided into city-states ruled by Amorites or Aramaeans. Far eastwards again, Assyria lay astride the upper Tigris, and between the two, where cornlands and rising pastures prefaced the ascent to the Armenian massif, was Mitanni, which became a powerful political entity at the time of the Hittite Empire. In Armenia itself we must also not omit to mention Lake Van, since upon its eastern shore was centred in the early first millennium the outlandish kingdom of Urartu, whose contacts with Assyria are made historical by the cuneiform inscriptions carved on the rocks of its capital city.

Having drawn in a light geographical framework for the picture of Anatolia which we are endeavouring to create, we must now consider the process by which it originally became populated, and various lines of approach by which the first immigrants may have arrived.

The function of the peninsula as a 'land-bridge' between Europe and Asia is obvious. There can be little doubt that from the earliest times there were intermittent movements of peoples from Europe and south-west Russia eastwards across the Bosphorus or Hellespont. But the alternative approach from the Caucasus or Caspian, westwards through the Armenian mountains is one which has not until recently been fully considered. Here, in fact, the deep alpine valleys have a predominantly east-west orientation and, whereas the corresponding mountain ridges have throughout history made the region unapproachable from the south, they have also pointed the direction of trade and presented little obstacle to invasion from the east. While, therefore, we should expect to find peoples ultimately of European origin predominating in the western part of the plateau, we should also be prepared to recognize a more easterly affiliation, for instance with the Caucasus, in some of the earliest arrivals on the Anatolian plateau. In the days when, it may be suspected, primitive methods of navigation made any large-scale movement by sea impracticable, the only remaining line of approach was northwards through Syria and Mesopotamia. This would for the most part have been by way of the two great river-valleys which penetrate deeply into the highlands; but a third alternative was the natural high road, to which we have already made reference, leading across the Amanus mountains to Cilicia and by the Taurus passes to the heart of the plateau.

These geographical approaches bring us naturally to the problem of communications in general, since the channels through which immigration is effected afterwards become the trade routes of an established people.

It should be said at once that only approximate itineraries can be reconstructed from the historical movements and campaigns of the Hittite kings. The earliest road systems in Anatolia are therefore still a subject for speculation. It is well known, however, that roads are features of antiquity which give the measure of man's essential conservatism, and indeed their direction is generally dictated by unchanging geographical circumstances, which even the modern engineer can hardly afford to ignore. Much, therefore, is to be learnt from a study of the arterial routes of later times. Undoubtedly the most famous of these is the so-called Royal Road of the Persian kings, which led, in the sixth century B.C., from their capital at Susa across northern Mesopotamia and eventually to the old Lydian capital at Sardis east of Smyrna. Long before the ruins at Boghazköy had been identified as those of the Hittite capital, Sir William Ramsay had been the first to point out a significant deviation in the course taken by this route across Anatolia. He showed that, whereas the direct line from Sardis to the Cilician Gates should pass south of the Salt Lake through Pisidia and Lycaonia, according to Herodotus, the road must in fact first have taken a north-easterly direction towards modern Ankara, and then have passed through the centre of the Halys 'bend' before finally returning southwards through Cappadocia to the pass. He argued from this the existence in pre-Persian times of some important political centre, perhaps to be identified with the Boghazköy ruins, towards which an earlier road system must have been oriented. There can in fact be little doubt that the road from the Halys to the Aegean coast was a reality in Hittite times, and must have been rivalled in importance only by that leading southwards to Cilicia, which provided direct access to north Syria.

Other routes generally used by the Greeks and Romans can be justifiably recognized as survivals from a much earlier age. One road leading north-eastwards from Hattusas, passed through Amasya, and then, disdaining the circuitous valley of the Iris river, struck out northwards again across the mountains to reach the Black Sea at Amisus (Samsun). Where the southern highway reached Mazaka, after crossing the upper Halys, there was an important junction with two roads leading more directly to Mesopotamia. One of these crossed the Anti-Taurus by devious ways to Marash and eventually Aleppo; the other ran east to Malatya and the Euphrates crossing at Samosata (Samsat); then due south, cutting across the great eastward bend of the river, to rejoin it at Nicephorium (Rakka) and continue in the direction of Babylon. At Harran it crossed the Royal Road, with which it had parted company at Mazaka, here to be found skirting the northern fringe of the desert from Aleppo to Nineveh. If we add the minor roads, leading southwards from the plateau to the coast, from Isparta to Pamphylia or from Laranda (Karaman) to the lower valley of the Calycadnus river, we shall have completed a skeleton of communications upon which the early inhabitants of Anatolia must have been continually dependent.

The physical aspect of the country, as it must have appeared to its first human inhabitants, begins now to make a coherent picture, and it becomes possible to anticipate some influences which it might exert upon their choice of a home and subsequent social development. Climatically, in the fourth millennium B.C., the plateau may have been even less inviting to potential farmers than it must appear to-day to its hardy Turkish cultivators. At all events the prehistoric villagers, whoever they may have been, who first braved the rigours of its long winter, were late-comers. In lands further to the south, food production had already replaced the old food-gathering economy, and the entire 'fertile crescent' had been populated for many centuries with agricultural communities of increasing sophistication. Through the evidence of archaeology we shall be able to trace the northward thrust of these earlier farmers into Cilicia and up the great river valleys, and shall have to decide whether or not it was they who eventually populated the plateau. If the answer appears to be negative, we must consider the alternative of a westward migration from the Caucasus or Caspian regions, spreading across Anatolia. In this case we shall have also to observe the simultaneous population of the region bordering the Aegean by westerners of quite different heredity, with whom the new-comers could none the less contrive a long period of peaceful co-existence.

TERMINOLOGY

But before proceeding to discuss the sequence of discoveries which have done so much to illuminate these and other problems of Anatolian antiquity, the subject of terminology must again be mentioned in connexion with the labelling of archaeological periods.

It will be noticed that the word 'prehistoric' has already been used in reference to the earliest human settlements. As a term it is subject to widely different interpretations and its employment here cannot be allowed to pass without some comment. It will be understood that if, in its accepted archaeological sense, it is to refer to a period before written history, it must be used only in relation to a specified country. In Mesopotamia, for instance, it will end at the beginning of the third millennium, whereas in Greece it will still be applicable

2,000 years later. If, however, this local particularization be agreed upon, it will remain a convenient word to describe the sequence of developments and changes in human behaviour, which preceded the definition of actual events in written records. For our own purpose, it will also serve to distinguish an epoch during which our knowledge of the past must depend mostly on the results of excavations and the interpretation of material remains. Directly the point is reached where such evidence can be supplemented by the testimony of contemporary inscriptions, the whole focus of archaeology changes, and the picture becomes expanded in the light of written records. We may start therefore with the prehistoric or 'pre-textual' phase of antiquity in Anatolia and consider its accepted subdivisions.

First, then, there is the Palaeolithic period. In Turkey, as elsewhere in the mountainous fringe of the 'fertile crescent' – in Palestine, Iraqi Kurdistan, and Iran – traces are to be found of palaeolithic man, both in caves and open stations. The terminology of these remains is too well authenticated to present any difficulty. But in our area the earliest traces of settled communities and the practice of agriculture herald the beginning of the 'new stone age', which is not always so clearly defined. The best course will perhaps be to adopt the convention on which local excavators are in general agreement, and apply the term 'Neolithic' to a period, perhaps in the fifth millennium B.C., represented by the deepest levels at certain sites such as Mersin, Tarsus, and Sakjegözü, all of which occupy geographical situations where conditions would be similar to those in the 'fertile crescent', and which may therefore be regarded as a northward extension of it. We shall then also be justified in giving the name 'Chalcolithic' to a succession of 'cultural periods', whose chronological succession and general characteristics have become familiar, pre-eminently as the result of excavations in North Syria and Mesopotamia. But the name Chalcolithic must then also be extended to include the earliest settlements on the plateau and in the Aegean provinces to the west; to the oldest remains at sites like Alaja and Alishar and to the first settlement at Troy.

The phase represented by these latter, we should perhaps refer to as 'late' Chalcolithic, for it can hardly be dated earlier than the final centuries of the fourth millennium and must have continued into the earliest centuries of the third.

We have now reached the final phases of the prehistoric era, and terminology assumes a more controversial aspect. The remainder of the third millennium is characterized on the plateau by the strangely consistent relics of a single culture, showing the rigid conservatism usually to be associated with a period of political tranquillity, and few signs of technological progress. Only the smelting of metal, which had indeed already been achieved in the Chalcolithic period, was now abundantly practised; and, perhaps for this reason, the period has come to be known (particularly in Turkish archaeological circles) as the 'Copper Age'. There have been objections to the use of this term, first on the ground that it was unjustified by the chemical analysis of the metal most generally in use; and secondly because of its inconsistency with the terminology currently accepted in neighbouring countries such as Syria, Cyprus, and the Aegean, with which in their 'Early Bronze Age' it might be expected to have connexions, through intermediate stations, say in Cilicia or at Troy. These are indeed valid objections; but such terms, once they are in common use, become difficult to eliminate from one's vocabulary. For the purpose of the present work, therefore, the writer has felt it best to retain the name 'Copper Age', at least when dealing with the antiquities of the Anatolian Plateau, but with all diffidence to submit a simplified system of terminology, which would more adequately satisfy present requirements, and not, to the best of his belief, be unacceptable to his principal colleagues (see diagram, page xx).

Apart from the semi-legendary accounts of the campaigns of Mesopotamian kings the earliest texts to throw any light on the history of Anatolia are a collection of cuneiform tablets from Kültepe, an ancient site near Mazaka (Kayseri) in Cappadocia. They are for the most part the business documents of an Assyrian commercial colony, functioning as a trade centre on a caravan route whose importance, at the period in the nineteenth century B.C. from which they date, must have been considerable. From the names of people and places which they record and from their contents generally, the first picture emerges of life on the plateau, at a time when it was just beginning to be dominated by the people we know to-day as the Hittites. Almost all political details are however lacking, and the history of the following four centuries, during which Hittite authority was substantiated by the establishment of a ruling dynasty, can be reconstructed only from archives compiled in the fourteenth century and found in the ruins of their later capital at Boghazköy. They had by then established an empire, which lasted until the end of the thirteenth century, ending in some upheaval sufficiently formidable to drive them from the plateau. The two principal phases of Hittite history, the 'Old Kingdom' and the 'Empire', correspond approximately to the 'Late Bronze Age', for instance in Syria, and their archaeological remains are accordingly sometimes labelled in this way. The fall of the Hittite empire can be conveniently equated with the beginning of the 'Iron Age'.

The period between 1200 B.C. and the conquest of Anatolia by the Achaemenian Persians, in the sixth century B.C., accounts for the remainder of the periods with which we are concerned. After a 'dark Age' of some three centuries, during which little is known of events or conditions in Anatolia, the Phrygians replaced the Hittites as the predominant power and were themselves replaced by the Lydians. Neither phase is documented by intelligible inscriptions, and the historian must rely on the retrospective accounts of Greek writers and on the somewhat scanty evidence of archaeology, supplemented by brief references in Assyrian and Achaemenian records.

During these early centuries of the first millennium, the Hittites themselves again reappear in small city-states east of Taurus and in North Syria, at one time mere colonies of the motherland from which they had been ejected. This Indian summer of their existence, whose remains chanced to become the preoccupation of archaeologists at a time when little was yet known of their earlier history, has bequeathed a legacy of monuments and inscriptions to which the terms 'Syro-Hittite' or 'Neo-Hittite' are usually applied, to distinguish them from the relics of the Old Kingdom and Empire.

EARTHQUAKES*

No physical description of Asia Minor could create an adequate background to its history, without some reference to the earthquakes, which have so persistently interfered with the security of its inhabitants and devastated their monuments. In a recent work on the archaeological stratigraphy of Western Asia,* a contemporary French scholar has attempted to account for gaps in the sequence of civilizations at various periods within the third and second millennia, and movements of peoples, by a series of major seismic upheavals; a task which was considerably complicated by their obvious frequency. He was dealing, of course, with primarily archaeological evidence dating from the first, second, and third millennia before Christ; but history shows an increase rather than a diminution in the frequency of these catastrophes during our own era. Hardly fifteen years have elapsed since the winter's night on which the modern town of Erzinjan was razed to the ground, and during the very days on which these words are penned, some hundreds of Turkish peasants have lost their lives and many more have been rendered homeless in the neighbourhood of Homeric Troy, whose ancient peace was so often disturbed by 'the Earth-shaking son of Chronos'.

In antiquity, a common epicentre seems to have affected Palestine and Syria. This would have accounted for instance for the upheaval in 763 B.C. which brought down the roof of the temple at Jerusalem and started a huge landslide on the Mount of Olives. It seems also to have rendered precarious the situation of Antioch in the alluvium of the Orontes valley, for the city was almost totally demolished in 184 B.C. and damaged no less than ten times in the first six centuries of our era. But unhappily, more frequently affected than almost any other Mediterranean lands were the western provinces of Asia

* C. Schaeffer, *Stratigraphie comparée et chronologique de l' Asie Occidentale.* Oxford, 1948.

Minor. From Lycia in the south to the Troad and the shores of the Hellespont, the Aegean littoral seems to have been a natural seismic area. The river valleys with their elegant Greek cities suffered repeated tremors, and their horrors were augmented by the disastrous effect of tidal waves. Phrygia too was in continual danger, and a vulnerable line of country where a volcanic rift runs diagonally across the plateau towards Trebizond. The whole peninsula was more or less affected, and building methods were adapted to the prevailing danger. Nevertheless, any attempt to visualize for instance the classical monuments of Anatolia as they would have appeared to-day had they been spared the destructive effects of earthquakes, must fill an antiquarian with feelings of regret, which their value as stratigraphic evidence can hardly modify.

For it should be added that Schaeffer's interpretation of such evidence has been received with a certain scepticism. It is in fact difficult to admit the theory which he proposes that so many centres so far removed from one another were affected at one and the same time. It is generally known that the force of an earthquake diminishes proportionately to the distance from the epicentre. His hypothesis would accordingly postulate some extraordinary seismic phenomenon without parallel in the known periods of history.

CHAPTER 2

The Sequence of Discoveries

BEARING in mind the important role which chance has played in the direction of archaeological research during the last hundred years, we should hardly expect to find the resulting pattern of discovery related in any way to actual historical chronology. It is accordingly the more interesting to notice that, in some areas at least, priority of attention seems to have been conferred on the historical periods in the reverse order of their chronological succession. A glance, for instance, at the archaeology of Mesopotamia, will show how the discovery of the late Assyrian palaces in the middle of the last century led logically to the investigation of earlier remains in Babylonia, and how these in turn aroused interest, first in the Sumerians and then in their Chalcolithic predecessors. Similarly in Egypt, the attention of excavators was not directed towards the proto- and pre-dynastic sites till after many important historical cities had been extensively dug.

In Asia Minor, organized journeys of exploration, beginning with those sponsored by the Dilettante Society as early as 1764, gave priority of interest to the Greek and Roman ruins of the Aegean provinces; with the result that, a century later, the cities of Ionia, Mysia, and Caria (whose date places them outside the scope of this particular work), were the scene of some of the earliest excavating activity. But it is in this area also that we encounter the first notable exception to the general rule. For Schliemann's excavations at Troy, which began in 1870, brought him at once into contact with a civilization at whose prodigious antiquity he could only guess; indeed, the significance of its remains, for lack of comparable criteria, was to remain unappreciated for several generations. We are thus presented with a new line of reflection; for it may be realized from Schliemann's bewilderment and the unprofitable process of guessing to which it led him, that a more gradual recession in the focus of historical interest was in fact desirable; that progress from the known to the unknown through orderly intermediate stages has something to recommend it; and that comprehension of each increasingly remote phase of antiquity can be facilitated by some preliminary knowledge of that which immediately succeeded it. In spite of this, Troy must here be made to serve as a point of departure for our narrative of Anatolian excavations. And indeed so much ground has been dug since Schliemann's time, that what were dark periods to him have become to us a more open book.

TROY (see also pp. 39, 85, 101 and 149)

Schliemann's personal story is one of the great romantic epics of archaeology, and as such, too well-known to require more than summarizing in this context. The clergyman's son and sometime grocer's assistant, with his great talent for languages and instinctive business acumen, which made him a millionaire at the age of forty, must have been an impressive figure even in the decade following the Crimean war, when such fortunes were made and lost almost overnight. A more remarkable feature of his case was his decision in 1863 to wind up his business for good, and to devote both life and fortune to the gratification of a youthful ambition; in a word to test by actual excavation the correctness or otherwise of certain private theories about Homeric geography. The first of these was his preference for the mound called Hissarlik, near Çanakkale, as the most probable site of Homeric Troy, at a time when the greatest contemporary scholars, if conceding its existence at all, would probably have placed it at the summit of Balidagh, near Punarbashi. The spring of 1870 saw him installed in a village near Hissarlik and ready to face the beginning of an enterprise whose complexity he can have had no means of understanding. Two years later, the most sceptical of professional antiquarians were compelled to take notice of his discoveries and to consider the revision of their views about Punarbashi. He had found, not a single fortress but the superimposed remains of a whole series of walled enclosures. This in itself seemed a new and remarkable phenomenon, at a time when stratification and the composition of mounds were less familiar to archaeologists than they have become to-day, and the actual size of the enclosure (whose diameter at its greatest extent measured hardly more than two hundred yards), did not deter him from describing them as 'cities'. For Schliemann, in fact, it was Troy; and Troy it has remained until the present day, having survived a storm of debate in the lifetime of its discoverer and the most methodical scrutiny of which modern science has been capable in more recent times. Only, during those early years, Schliemann's selection of a building period to equate with the Homeric city led him disastrously into error, for it resulted in his underrating the antiquity of the famous 'Treasure of Priam' by a matter of more than ten centuries.

Apart from intervals during which his attention was diverted to Mycenae and other sites on the Greek mainland, Schliemann worked alone at Troy until 1878. In view of the criticism to which his methods of excavating had been subjected, and the reluctance of some to accept his own unsupported testimony as to the context in which his finds were made, he thereafter willingly accepted the collaboration, first of Virchow and Burnouf and afterwards of Dörpfeld, who shared the direction of the excavations for the last season before his death (1890) and himself resumed them later (1893-4). Schliemann had recognized seven 'cities', a number which was subsequently increased by Dörpfeld to nine; and nine primary occupation levels were retained as a basis of stratigraphical numbering by the American expedition to whose work at the site in more recent times we shall presently have occasion to refer in detail. Schliemann had associated the second, then on second thoughts the third 'city' with the Homeric period, though both of these levels date actually from the third millennium B.C. His earliest 'city', a primitive fortress hardly a hundred yards across and built directly on virgin rock, we now equate with some of the earliest settlements on the plateau, in the late Chalcolithic period. The smallest of his finds in these deepest levels have therefore acquired for ourselves a much greater significance than they would have possessed had they, as he supposed, been associated with the Mycenaean period, which is to-day well documented, and easily recognized by its characteristic remains.

But for the great amateur of the 1870s, the attribution of even approximate dates to his successive buildings presented overwhelming difficulties. It was beyond his powers at the time, for instance, to know that six of his 'cities' must already have fallen when contemporaries of the Achaeans constructed a new fortress on the Trojan mound, or to discover that when Alexander, in pious regard for Homeric tradition, refounded Ilion, the summit of the same mound was levelled to provide an emplacement for municipal buildings, with disastrous results to the remains of the sixth and seventh 'cities'. It is not by these unavoidable shortcomings that Schliemann is to be judged. The personal quality which immortalized his name was the devout and childlike faith with which, in spite of all ridicule, he clung to an actual historic foundation for the Homeric poems and the Trojan war, and which was in the end victorious over the accumulated scepticism of those more erudite than himself. The scene in Schliemann's excavating headquarters, where innumerable guests would be patiently entertained, in the absence of their father, by the two children, Andromache and Agamemnon, or by their distinguished Greek mother (who would occasionally appear herself wearing a headdress assembled from the contents of 'Priam's Treasure' (Plate 3), makes a pleasant curtain-raiser to the story of Anatolian archaeology, and his own books about Troy must receive a place of honour, beside Dörpfeld's *Troja und Ilion*, in any bibliography on the subject.

HITTITE DISCOVERIES

While Schliemann at Troy was absorbed in his search for remains of the second millennium B.C. and unconsciously in contact with those of the third, discoveries in North Syria were pointing the way to the investigation of a comparatively more recent epoch in Anatolian history. Stones found at Hama and Aleppo, inscribed in an unknown form of pictographic writing, had begun to be compared with similar pictographs, carved on natural rock-faces, which had been reported by travellers in remote parts of Asia Minor. In 1876 Sayce was able to propose the association of this form of writing with the Hittites of the Old Testament and the 'Kheta' of the Egyptian hieroglyphic texts. French and German as well as British archaeologists responded to this interesting suggestion by revisiting rock-reliefs and ancient sites on both sides of Taurus, at which traces of 'Hittite' inscriptions had been found, sometimes in association with crudely sculptured reliefs, which had evidently once ornamented the walls of buildings. In this way many new items were added to the growing catalogue of known 'Hittite' antiquities. But excavations at such sites had yet to begin.

CARCHEMISH

The year 1876 found George Smith of the British Museum 'prospecting sites in West Asia with a view to possible excavations', and one of those which he visited was the great mound at Jerablus on the Turco-Syrian frontier; where the modern railway crosses the Euphrates. He recorded in his diary: 'Grand site: vast walls and palace mounds: 8,000 feet round: many sculptures and monoliths with inscriptions; site of Karchemish.' He made sketches of the sculptures and copied some of the 'Hittite' inscriptions before continuing his journey towards Iraq. His summary identification of the site, though contrary to the opinion of some earlier visitors, proved correct, and one of the results of his journey (which ended in his death on the road from Mosul to Aleppo later in the year), was the first excavations at Carchemish, sponsored by the British Museum in 1878 and 1881. The work was still of the 'quarrying' type which had characterized the excavation of the Assyrian palaces during the previous quarter of a century, but it brought to the British Museum the first representative collection of late Hittite sculptures and hieroglyph inscriptions. The excavations were not resumed on a scientific basis until the years immediately preceding the first World War, and the antiquities which had been left exposed suffered much damage as a result.

SINJERLI (see also p. 161)

The next comparable enterprise was undertaken between 1888 and 1892, this time by the German Orient Society. The leaders of the expedition (among them Robert Koldewey, who subsequently became famous as the excavator of Babylon), chose a site far to the north in the foothills of Anti-Taurus. From the Plain of Antioch a wide valley runs north-eastwards into the mountains in the direction of Marash, skirting the eastern flank of the Amanus range. It is at Fevzi Pasha on the west side of this valley that the railway emerges, after crossing the Bahche Pass from Cilicia and is joined by a branch-line coming west from Malatya before continuing on its way to Aleppo. Beyond Fevzi Pasha there is a shallow lake and near to its western shore is the site called Sinjerli, which was the ancient city of Sam'al. By a curious chance, the German archaeologists could hardly have chosen a city which corresponded more closely in historical associations and ancient status with Carchemish. Both were townships with an obscure background in the Bronze and earlier ages and appear to have acquired city status as dependencies of the Hittite Empire. They had prospered as independent states in the early centuries of the first millennium, when the Anatolian homeland had been abandoned; and they suffered an aftermath of subjection to the Assyrians in the eighth and seventh centuries. Neither showed signs of extensive occupation after the fall of Assyria.

The Germans found a walled citadel, conforming to the oval shape of a mound whose summit it occupied and approached by a formal gateway on the south side. The space within the citadel was again partitioned by fortress walls into several compartments, and contained two notable buildings with columned porticos, designed according to the formula which afterwards became known to the Assyrians as *bit-hilâni*. Beyond the limits of the citadel mound, the city itself had been enclosed, perhaps in the days of the Empire, by an exactly circular wall, 11 feet thick, with projecting towers. In the Assyrian period this had been duplicated at a distance of a few yards by a second, similar wall. At three points in the circumference there were fortified gateways affording admission to the enclosure through both enceintes. These gateways, like that of the citadel and the buildings within, had been lavishly ornamented with sculptured reliefs, which again showed the intricate pattern of the then incomprehensible Hittite hieroglyphs. The ancient identity of the city was revealed by a stela set up by the Assyrian king Esarhaddon in 670 B.C. to commemorate victories over the kings of Egypt and Tyre.

THE PLATEAU

Knowledge of these late 'Hittite' states and their historical background was now rapidly increasing. Furthermore, it was already beginning to be suspected that they were survivors of a more ancient imperial organization, to which they had originally been related in a provincial or colonial capacity. Speculation in regard to the habitat or geographical centre of this earlier power pointed towards the Anatolian plateau. In this area excavations had hardly begun. In 1889 a mound on the Sakarya river had been tentatively identified as the site of ancient Gordium and two Germans, the Körte brothers, had made soundings in search of Phrygian remains. But they had become involved with overlying strata of a later period, which more recent researches have shown to be of a formidable character, and eventually abandoned the project. At the same time, much had been learnt from the exploratory journeys and patient study of remains above ground, undertaken by a succession of distinguished scholars. Much earlier in the day Texier (1839) and Hamilton (1842) had already reported on the site called Boghazköy, in the centre of the Halys 'bend', where the walls and sculptured gateways of a vast fortified city could easily be recognized. They had also visited the curious shrine, called Yazılıkaya, occupying a cleft in the rocks of an adjoining valley, whose fascinating and extraordinary sculp-

tured reliefs alternated with groups of 'Hittite' hieroglyphs.
They had found similar monuments and again traces of a city
at Gâvur (Giaour) Kalesi, south of Ankara. In the closing
years of the century their work was resumed and extended by
explorers such as Humann, Ramsay, Hogarth, and Chantre,
all of whom contributed records of new monuments, many of
them on the plateau, to the corpus which was published by
Messerschmidt in 1900. In that year also, a new form of
evidence began to be available. The first collections of cuneiform tablets appeared in the hands of antique dealers, purporting to be derived from sites in central Anatolia.

The First Texts

One group of these documents which were in the Akkadian
language, commonly used for commercial purposes by the
Assyrians and Babylonians, had begun to appear as early as
the year 1880, but their source could only now be positively
identified as a mound called Karahüyük near the village of
Kültepe, some twenty miles north of Mazaka (Kayseri). The
source of the second group had been known since 1893 to be
the site of Boghazköy itself. These latter were also inscribed
in the familiar Babylonian cuneiform script, but in an incomprehensible language known only from its occasional occurrence in the famous 'Amarna' correspondence between an
eighteenth dynasty Pharaoh and his asiatic contemporaries.
Clearly the time had come for Anatolian sites to be excavated,
and in 1906 the initiative was taken at Boghazköy by Winckler,
on behalf of the German Orient Society. Chantre, in the same
year, made soundings at various points in the Kültepe mound,
but he failed for the present to discover the source of the
tablets.

At Boghazköy, after some preliminary work on temple
buildings in the lower part of the site, Winckler attacked the
high acropolis mound known to the villagers as Büyükkale.
Here his success was immediate and sensational. From a range
of ruined store-chambers, showing signs of having been
destroyed in some great conflagration, he recovered more
than 10,000 tablets, most of them kiln-baked or hardened by

the effects of the fire. He was conscious at once of having lit upon some official archive of great importance, and a further study of the documents confirmed this impression. The vast majority of the tablets were in the same unknown language as those previously obtained from dealers, but a few were in the more familiar Akkadian. Reference was made in these to a country called the 'Land of Hatti', and of this land the capital city was clearly represented by the ruins of Boghazköy. Winckler's subsequent campaigns, which continued, latterly in collaboration with the Turkish archaeologist, Makridi Bey, until 1912, also revealed the architecture and fortifications of this gigantic metropolis with its temples, palaces, monumental gateways and sculptured ornaments. There could be no doubt about their implications. As they stand to-day, revealed by the excavations, their ruins are easily recognized as the monuments of a great imperial people.

The impression which they make on the most casual modern visitor may be summed up in the words of an English writer who recently saw them for the first time. 'It is easy', he says, 'to think of the Hittites, as I had, only as an obscure and tiresome little tribe of Biblical Bedouin, of no more importance than the Hivites or Girgashites. These colossal works of sophisticated masonry, these accomplished sculptures, not only made them real but brought alive a civilized and powerful empire comparable to Babylon and Egypt.' *

CARCHEMISH AGAIN (see also p. 160)

The remaining years before the outbreak of the first World War saw further discoveries in the field of Hittite archaeology; but the purpose which they served was mainly to amplify existing knowledge of the Syro-Hittite culture in the early centuries of the first millennium. In 1911 the excavations at Carchemish were resumed by the British Museum with a formidable team, directed first by Campbell-Thompson, then by Hogarth, and finally by Woolley, with Lawrence ('of Arabia') as assistant. The excavations were now done systematically, and much was learnt about the general lay-

* A. Grant, *Geographical Magazine*, November, 1952, p. 351.

out and character of the city. Like Sinjerli, it had a fortified citadel, occupying the summit of a mound, which in its turn represented the accumulated remains of prehistoric and Bronze Age settlements. The mound in this case sloped steeply down on one side to the banks of the Euphrates. In Empire days it had served as an acropolis for a considerable walled city with the usual monumental gateways. But at some time early in the first millennium the enclosed area had proved inadequate and an extension to the west and south had again been protected by a polygonal fortress wall. The excavator's attention was concentrated mostly on the gateways in the town walls, which were lavishly ornamented with sculptures, and at the approach from the inner town to the citadel, where traces were found of a temple and palace, though their complete plans were not recovered. Some other isolated buildings were investigated, and the prevailing impression gained from Woolley's plans is that many more remain to be discovered. The volume of Hittite sculptures and inscriptions which came to light was immense, and all of it of the greatest possible interest. A part was transported to the British Museum; but unfortunately, when the work was interrupted by the outbreak of war in 1914, a very large group of the sculptures had still not been moved, and these remained during the years which followed lying unprotected on a railway siding. The damage which they suffered can be gauged from their appearance to-day in the Archaeological Museum at Ankara.

Woolley and Hogarth both made attempts to examine the earlier strata of the citadel mound, by means of a cutting in the steep eastern flank, which sloped down to the river. As with Schliemann at Troy, this brought them into contact with the remains of periods whose interrelation was at that time totally unfamiliar. It led them to the postulation of a 'Bronze Age', which they also associated with 'cist' graves found in the cemeteries outside the town walls. The excavation of one of these cemeteries near the little village called Yunus also resulted in the discovery of a group of kilns, from which a great quantity of painted pottery was recovered. This material, which Woolley provisionally labelled 'Neolithic', falls actually into the Chalcolithic category now known as 'Halafian', and dates from the early fourth millennium.

Nor was the attribution of dates to the main discoveries – to the various building periods and styles of art – a matter which could at once be decided. Hogarth himself and the French scholar, Pottier, who had made a stylistic study of the material, published simultaneously in 1926 proposals for dividing the finds into two main periods, one corresponding to the late Bronze Age, which we should now equate with the Hittite 'Empire', and the other to the 'Syro-Hittite' period in the early first millennium. But they could not agree as to whether any of the sculptures belonged to the first period. Woolley's appraisal, which came later, will be summarized in a later chapter.

SAKJEGÖZÜ

A newcomer to the field of Hittite studies during the years we are considering was J. Garstang, who had travelled widely in Anatolia at the beginning of the century, and in 1910 published a most comprehensive and readable account of the Anatolian monuments and their geographical background, under the title *Land of the Hittites*. Garstang's attention had been drawn to a pair of Hittite slab-reliefs in the Berlin Museum, purporting to come from a village called Sakjegözü on the road from Fevzi Pasha to Antep. Visiting the place, he traced their actual source to a mound called Jobba Hüyük, one of many similar landmarks in the valley to which we have already referred as providing a setting for Sinjerli. Excavations which he undertook here between 1907 and 1911 showed that the summit of the mound was occupied by a small fortified palace of the Syro-Hittite period, and a fine series of sculptured orthostats were again brought to light. Unfortunately no documentary evidence was found which could provide a clue either to the name of the city or the approximate date of the building. In an attempt to remedy this default by a study of stratigraphical evidence, a deep sounding was made beneath the foundations of the palace. This was, as it happened, a fortunate circumstance, since it revealed, in the deepest levels of the mound, traces of a Neolithic settlement whose antiquity is hardly exceeded by any more recent discoveries in the area which we are considering. In fact the finds from this shaft, combined with others discovered by the same excavator at Jericho in Palestine, long remained the only existing criteria by which the earliest stages in the evolution of human community life could be recognized.

THE VANNIC REMAINS (see also Chap. 10)

While following the course and development of Hittite research in the last century we have omitted to mention certain discoveries in a rather different field, which have remained outside our immediate line of vision. In one of the remoter eastern provinces of modern Turkey, in a shallow depression between the almost inaccessible Hakkiyari region on the one side and the Armenian alps on the other, lies the strange isolated lake called Van. Approximating in size to, say Lake Geneva, it is surrounded by mountains, including two extinct volcanoes, whose perpetual snows are reflected in its waters. Only from its eastern shore do the hills recede sufficiently to leave room for an area of agricultural land and pastures. Here, at the mouth of a stream which discharges into the lake, there is a great rock crowned by an ancient fortress, and at its foot the ruins of a Turkish city, for which, until quite recent years, it served as a citadel. The modern town is pleasantly situated among the fruit orchards further inland, and is itself dominated by a shoulder projecting from the hills behind, known as Toprakkale. The most striking feature of the citadel is the large areas of rock-face which have at some time been artificially smoothed and then incised with long inscriptions in the cuneiform script of old Babylonia. Amongst them are openings leading to a formal arrangement of rock-cut chambers.

As early as 1827 a young German professor of the name of Schulz was sent out by the French Government to examine these Vannic inscriptions. By a misfortune of a kind that is happily rare in the history of Anatolian exploration, he was murdered by Kurdish bandits two years later; but his papers were recovered and brought to Paris. The publication after a ten-years' interval of the memoir which they contained, together with Schulz's faithful copies of forty-two inscriptions, not one sign of which he could understand, created great interest and led to further visits to the site by Layard and others. But the language of the inscriptions appeared to be unrelated to those of Assyria and Babylonia, and it was not until the latter had been deciphered by Rawlinson and others, that its own interpretation in turn became possible. It was then found that one prominent inscription on the southern face of the rock was of later date than the others, having been placed there by the Achaemenian king, Xerxes; and the same formula was therefore repeated in three different languages, Assyrian, Old Persian, and the unknown language peculiar to Van. The work of decipherment was undertaken by Sayce and others, and by the final years of the century the contents both of these and other inscriptions afterwards discovered in the neighbourhood became universally known. It was then possible to understand that during the first half of the first millennium, if not before, Van had been the capital city of a considerable principality, called by the Assyrians Urartu, a name of which Ararat is a corrupt form. The inscriptions recorded also the names of its kings and their relations, often of an unfriendly nature, with their Assyrian neighbours, from whose own records they were already known during the ninth to seventh centuries B.C.

The first actual excavations at Van were undertaken for the British Museum by Hormuzd Rassam in 1879. (They indeed represented only one of several soundings of which he was at this time simultaneously responsible, at points between here and southern Babylonia.) Rassam directed his attention towards Toprakkale, where he located a temple built of good ashlar masonry. The most important find in this building was a number of bronze shields with cuneiform inscriptions, embossed and ornamented with figures of animals, some of which eventually reached the British Museum. The remainder, since the work was inadequately supervised, were disposed of by his workmen. Some order was brought to Rassam's excavations when they were resumed in 1898 by two German scholars, Belck and Lehmann-Haupt. More objects in silver, bronze, and iron were discovered, and from textual evidence they were able to show that Toprakkale had been adapted as an acropolis by a king called Rusas, probably after the destruction of the old city by Tiglath-Pileser III. Finally, in 1916, a Russian party under the leadership of Marr and Orbeli made excavations at the foot of the old citadel. They found an impressive temple cut into the base of the rock and an inscribed stela still standing intact and perfectly preserved in its ritual niche.

CHAPTER 3

Research Between Wars

THE war of 1914–18, in which Turkey was a belligerent, naturally put a stop for the time being to all excavating activity in Anatolia and created a five-year hiatus in the proper collaboration of European scholars. Nevertheless in Germany, where the great volume of texts from Boghazköy was now available, the new science of Hittitology made considerable strides. As early as 1915 the first sketch of Hittite grammar was published by Hrozný. It had now come to be known that the language of the Boghazköy tablets comprised an indigenous tongue and a variety of different dialects, imposed upon it by an immigrant Indo-European people soon after the beginning of the second millennium B.C. The indigenous people themselves, who were thereafter subjected or absorbed by the newcomers, seem previously to have been organized into a federation of small city states, one of which was known to them as the 'Land of the City of Hatti (Hattusas)'. It was this city which the newcomers eventually adopted as their capital, and from which the name 'Hittite' was later derived. Their subsequent history could be reconstructed in considerable detail from the state records found in the Boghazköy archives, and by 1918 it was possible even to produce a reasonably complete list of their kings covering a period of several centuries. Of the indigenous, non-Indo-European people, on the other hand, little was yet known. Only a single episode in their history had so far been found, recorded in a Hittite text of a later date; and though it gave the names of two petty kings and a list of city names including that of Hatti, as a document it seemed to be of doubtful authenticity. It was hoped therefore at this time that more information about them might be supplied by the records of the Assyrian colony at Kültepe, which appeared to have existed at a period before the Indo-Europeans assumed power. These hopes were now, as it proved, in some measure to be realized.

KÜLTEPE (see also pp. 47 and 116)

In 1906 a new attempt had been made by Winckler to locate the source of the Kültepe tablets; but this also had met with little success, and it had begun to be doubted whether the site itself had been correctly identified. When excavating once more became possible after the war the question clearly had to be settled one way or the other, and in 1925 a Czecho-slovakian expedition, led by B. Hrozný, went to Kültepe with this purpose in view. Hrozný, like his predecessors, cut his first trenches in the summit of the main mound, and spent several weeks in excavating what he considered to be a 'Hittite fortress', without coming upon any traces of tablets. It is a remarkable tribute to the purposeful reticence of the Kültepe villagers that they were now for the third time in succession able to watch a party of foreigners engaged in this particular form of wild goose chase. Since the sale of the tablets to dealers had recently proved a reliable source of income, there could be little point in revealing their actual whereabouts. This time however the peasants' luck did not hold. In addition to his great ability as a philologist, Hrozný was a good linguist and spoke excellent Turkish. Two of his employees were natives of Kayseri, where the situation at Kültepe had long been a standing joke, and by cross-questioning them he eventually arrived at the truth. The meadow to which they led him was hardly more than 100 yards distant from the foot of the main mound, but screened from it by a line of trees, and he could immediately see that its surface was disturbed by traces, only half-heartedly concealed, of amateur excavations on a considerable scale. His own labourers were at once directed to the locality, and during the weeks which followed his perseverance was rewarded by the recovery of more than a thousand 'Cappadocian' tablets and much valuable information regarding the setting in which they lay.

It was now clear that the main mound (Karahüyük), on which so much preliminary work had been wasted, repre-sented a walled city, inhabited at the beginning of the second millennium by the indigenous people of Anatolia. The fields where the tablets were found covered the remains of a cantonment, annexed to the city; a foreign commercial colony of the sort known to the Assyrians as a 'karum'. Its name was Kanesh. Together with other details of contemporary life, Hrozný was able to recover from the contents of the tablets the names of individual merchants and the complete records of their business over a long period. The settlement had in the end been destroyed by fire and its inhabitants having as is usual on such occasions, left in some haste, the contents of their houses had for the most part remained in place. Much pottery and a variety of domestic objects could therefore also be recovered, and to these a special significance was attached; for the tablets were exactly dated by the names of contemporary Assyrian kings, and objects found with them could from now onwards serve as chronological criteria for comparison with materials found at sites where no texts were available.

ALISHAR (see also pp. 88 and 192)

It was about this time that the Oriental Institute, founded by Rockefeller at Chicago University, had begun to take an active part in field-archaeology, and J. H. Breasted as director was engaged in the organization of large-scale excavations in several countries of the Middle East. In 1927 an Anatolian expedition was inaugurated and after a preliminary survey of archaeological sites in or near the Halys 'bend' and a tentative sounding at Gâvur Kalesi, a mound known as Alishar Hüyük, fifty miles south-east of Boghazköy, was selected as the scene of its operation. The work at this site was maintained from then onwards on an expensive scale until 1932, under the leadership of H. H. von der Osten and E. Schmidt. These operations were in a sense a new departure from previous archaeological practice, since the purpose was to submit this 100-foot accumulation of stratified occupational débris to a form of scrutiny which limited financial and technological resources had previously made impracticable for European excavators. In effect, its success was by no means unqualified.

In appraising the results of the Alishar excavation as they are published in five large volumes, lavishly illustrated and meticulously detailed, one immediately becomes conscious of a major disappointment with which the excavators must in the end have been faced. A central hope, often expressed in the early days of their work, was that of finding a Hittite city, perhaps like Boghazköy containing written archives, throwing further light on the history of the Empire. It is now known that by some irony of fortune, in the whole range of periods into which the history of the Anatolian plateau is divided, almost the only one which is not represented in the successive settlements at Alishar is that between the seventeenth and thirteenth centuries B.C., during which the old Hittite Kingdom and the later Hittite Empire flourished. The remains which in the publication are attributed to the 'Period of the Hittite Empires' in fact belong to the time of the Assyrian colony at Kültepe, when the Hittites were not yet established as a political power. Such tablets as were found in these levels at Alishar accordingly corresponded in date, as in fact they do in content, to those from Kültepe.

Schmidt and von der Osten were faced with other perplexities. This was the first stratigraphical test yet made on the plateau, and they had been conscious of the difficulties attendant upon a pioneer enterprise of the sort they were undertaking; the absence of comparable criteria for dating purposes and the danger of being influenced by preconceived ideas. Under the circumstances, Breasted's initial advice had been to content themselves with faithfully recording an archaeological sequence, as a framework into which isolated finds at other sites might afterwards be fitted. Even this did not prove easy. The Alishar 'hüyük' was asymmetrical, with a highest excrescence, afterwards known as the 'citadel mound', somewhat off-centre, and a lower shoulder or 'terrace'. It gradually came to be understood that the settlement had at certain times been confined to the citadel alone, while at others it had spread over the lower terrace, leaving the citadel itself unoccupied. The sequence of occupations revealed by soundings in the two different parts of the mound consequently bore little relation to one another, and it was difficult at first to find any system of numbering the 'levels', which would correctly reflect their chronological succession. The excavators' decisions in these matters, which appeared in their earlier reports, had frequently to be reconsidered and no definitive ruling could be made until the final publication was produced in the late 1930s. Even then the attribution of their levels to the accepted chronological periods remained controversial and widely different alternatives were suggested by various scholars such as Bittel and others, who had made subsequent examinations of the stratigraphical evidence. For our own purpose, therefore, it may be well to confine ourselves to the sequence of periods as they were eventually fixed in the final publication.

The remains at Alishar with which we are concerned were then broadly divided into five phases; and only the numbers by which they are known any longer reflect earlier uncertainties. Starting from the earliest occupation, there is a first phase numbered 'O', and called by the excavators 'Neolithic'. Only its lowest levels are now considered to antedate the beginning of the Copper Age. Phase 'I' represents the Copper Age itself, and here, as at many other plateau sites, there are signs that it can be separated into two sub-periods. Next comes the phase known as 'Alishar III', characterized by the sudden intrusion of brilliantly painted pottery, previously known as 'Cappadocian'. This is followed (not, as was first thought, preceded) by Phase 'II', where the beautifully shaped monochrome vessels have reverted to a simple polish more characteristically Anatolian. We have now reached the period of the Kültepe tablets, and it is followed by a hiatus of some centuries, during which the mound apparently remained unoccupied. Finally, Phase 'IV' is correctly described as 'Post-Hittite-Phrygian'.

No buildings of conspicuous size or interest were encountered at Alishar. The chalcolithic settlement had developed from a town with a citadel fortress in the first part of Phase I, to being a fortified city during the later part. After its temporary eclipse in Hittite times, it reappeared in the Phrygian period as a strong fortress on the citadel mound and a walled extension spreading down the side of the hill. The objects which the excavation contributed to Turkish Museums are distinguished by their number and variety rather than by fine workmanship or intrinsic value. But gratitude to their discoverers must always be felt by subsequent workers in the same field, on account of the characteristic thoroughness with which they were recorded and published.

TURKISH EXCAVATORS

During the years in which the American excavators were working at Alishar, Kemal Atatürk's Republic had developed from a brilliant conception to a formidable reality. The unabated interest which the great Turkish statesman had himself taken in this foreign enterprise was transferred to the encouragement of historical research in his own universities. As a result the 1930s were conspicuous mainly for the entry of Turkish archaeologists into the field of excavation. Great figures such as Makridi and Halil Edhem had not been lacking in the past; but their attention had of necessity been primarily directed towards standing monuments and museum organization rather than long-term archaeological projects. Following in their footsteps now came scholars such as H. Koşay, R. Arik, Sh. Kansu and a formidable team of younger men, whose local education had been supplemented by specialist instruction at home and abroad.

ALAJA (see also pp. 96 and 136)

One Turkish enterprise inaugurated during these years was to produce the most important single discovery of the whole decade; an archaeological event more sensational than any which had taken place since the finding of the Hittite archives. This was the excavation at Alaja Hüyük, a site rather more than twenty miles north-east of Boghazköy in the Halys 'bend'.

Already in the nineteenth century Alaja Hüyük had been visited and described by a succession of European travellers, in whose accounts of their journeys, through an eccentricity of transliteration, it usually appeared under the name 'Eyuk', (Alaja being the name of a market town some miles distant). They reported the existence of a low but extensive mound,

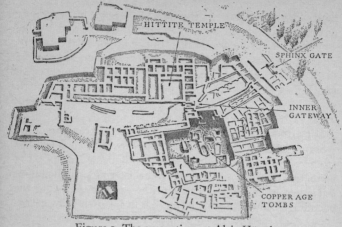

Figure 1. The excavations at Alaja Hüyük

partially covered by a modern village, and on its lower slopes, the survival above ground of two great stone sphinxes which clearly indicated the existence of a monumental gateway in the Hittite manner. In 1861 Perrot had even made some clearances in the vicinity of these sculptures and encountered traces of important stone buildings inside the enclosure. Excavations had afterwards been resumed sporadically by Chantre (1863), Winkler (1906), and finally under Makridi in 1907, by which time some parts of a large public building had been uncovered and a fine collection of sculptured reliefs brought to light. These, together with casts of the two sphinxes, are to-day to be seen in the Ankara Museum, and are known to date from the time of the Hittite Empire. The new Turkish expedition was organized in 1935 by the Turkish Historical Society under the leadership of Koşay and Arik. Their intention was for the first time to penetrate into the deeper levels of the mound and investigate its earlier occupations. The choice of a location for the sounding was dictated largely by the limited space available between the houses of the modern villagers and reluctance to expropriate or demolish their property. Under these circumstances their choice was favoured by fortune. After recording and removing walls dating from the

Hittite period and later remains, they encountered a deep layer of ash and burnt débris, signifying some cataclysm in which the settlement had been destroyed by fire. In and beneath this layer, at a depth of approximately 20 feet below the surface, they came upon the first three Copper Age tombs, which, multiplied to the number of thirteen in later seasons, were to make the site famous.

The nature and duration of the Copper Age on the Anatolian plateau was at that time known only from the results of excavations in the deeper levels of the mound at Alishar. There the picture had been created of a farming and trading settlement, whose unpretentious culture showed signs of peaceful continuity over a period of some centuries – perhaps during the greater part of the third millennium B.C. Here, suddenly revealed at Alaja, was a tantalizing vignette of the same civilization in its metropolitan aspect, showing evidence of moral advancement and technological accomplishment hitherto entirely unsuspected. The tombs were evidently those of priests or royalties, buried with considerable ritual among the valuable offerings and rich appointments of contemporary convention. Women were accompanied by their jewellery and toilet articles; men by their personal ornaments and weapons. In each grave the body was surrounded by elaborately wrought 'solar disks' and animal symbols, which had perhaps been carried as standards in their funeral processions, and a profusion of images, libation vessels and other cult objects. A very large proportion of these were of gold or silver, beautifully wrought in a technique which in some cases rivalled even the craft of the Sumerian metal-smiths at Ur. Other objects were of bronze, occasionally inlaid with more precious metals. There were dagger blades of iron.

As has already been mentioned, ten more of these tombs were discovered and excavated during the seasons 1937–9, and their contents have been completely published by Koşay, who was in sole charge of the excavation after the first season. The work has been periodically resumed since that time and preliminary reports show that the original sounding was afterwards carried down through remains of the Chalcolithic period to virgin soil, with results of the greatest interest. The phases of occupation are now divided into four main periods, of which the first and latest is a composite group of levels representing the more recent occupations of the mound after the end of the Hittite Empire. Phase II is 'Hittite', including a transitional stage corresponding to the Kültepe tablets, and three sub-phases more accurately called so. Phase III represents the Copper Age, including the famous tombs, and Phase IV the Chalcolithic. The dates attributed by the excavators to these periods at the time of their discoveries have stood up well to the fluctuations of scientific opinion in later years, and conform fairly closely to the evaluation which we ourselves shall presently be inclined to accept. The tombs themselves are almost certainly correctly placed in the later half of the third millennium B.C. Some light was thrown on the sub-divisions of the true Hittite period by the complete excavation and planning during the early seasons of the public buildings inside the sphinx gate, the largest of which had been several times rebuilt. It seemed likely to have been a temple or palace and was of great architectural interest.

BOGHAZKÖY (see also p. 130)

Temples like that just mentioned could now profitably be compared with those at Boghzaköy, where K. Bittel, as Director of the German Archaeological Institute in Istanbul, had in 1931 reopened the excavations. During the following eight years he exposed and planned the remains of many Hittite buildings, both in the city itself and at the neighbouring shrine of Yazılıkaya, where a complex religious edifice was found to have stood at the approach to the sculptured rock-sanctuaries. In general at Boghazköy, architecture and texts constituted the main results of the excavation, other finds being few in number and poor enough in quality to suggest a certain austerity in the standard of living at the Hittite capital. This applied equally to the remains of pre-Hittite occupation which Bittel investigated beneath the palace on the old citadel of Büyükkale, but these enabled him to trace the earlier history of the city from the Copper Age onwards.

Again there was an increasing range of comparison for this kind of prehistoric material. During the 1930s a succession of smaller Copper Age sites on the plateau were excavated by Turkish archaeologists. Ahlatlıbel (Koşay), Etiyokuşu (Kansu) and Karaoğlan (Arik), all in the vicinity of Ankara, yielded interesting collections of pottery and objects, while at others, such as Pazarlı (Koşay), the interest of the prehistoric levels was supplemented by a rich occupation in Phrygian times. Little remained to be learned about village life on the plateau in the late third millennium. The parallel development of the Aegean culture in the western part of the peninsula was also becoming increasingly well known.

BACK TO TROY (see also pp. 85, 101 and 149)

In 1932 the University of Cincinnati had decided on a long-term plan for re-excavating the Hissarlik mound at Troy. Since Dörpfeld's work came to an end in 1892 knowledge of pre-classical civilization in the eastern Mediterranean had greatly advanced. New discoveries in Crete, Cyprus, Macedonia, the Cyclades, and the Greek mainland had yielded a vast increment of detailed information and made possible the establishment of a comparative chronology for the various Aegean cultures. For this purpose Trojan analogies and comparisons had freely to be used; but the stratigraphical confusion of primary material during the early excavations at Hissarlik complicated the task of fitting Dörpfeld's nine 'cities' into the new scheme of dating. For this reason, in the words of C. Blegen, who led the new American expedition, 'it seemed desirable, timely, and worth while to return to Troy to undertake an exhaustive, painstaking re-examination of the whole site'. It was to be planned as 'a work of sober, serious research, and there was no compulsion to recover objects of startling or sensational character with high publicity value'. This statement set the tone of the whole enterprise. The excavations lasted for five years, during which preliminary communications were regularly made concerning its results. Of the final publication three finely produced volumes have now appeared, dealing with the first seven cities. They are admirably detailed and documented records, of the sort which no worker in the same field could fail to admire and appreciate. If they leave one with a regret, it is that professional caution and perfectionism have eliminated much of the interest for the layman, so that he may still be inclined to fall back on the accounts of Schliemann and Dörpfeld.

Blegen's policy in re-opening the excavation had been to approach its problems with an open mind, unprejudiced by the complicated and often conflicting inference of his predecessors in regard to stratification. His hope had been to attempt a new assessment of the stratified evidence, much of it unsatisfactory because of the difficulty of co-ordinating the finds with the sequent levels of occupation. With this end in view, the expedition was to examine the isolated 'islands' of unexcavated ground between their trenches and obtain from them groups of 'certified' objects and pottery, which could then form the basis of a new and reliable archaeological framework. In this he was eminently successful and the framework now exists; but it is based entirely upon his own finds and caution has again debarred him from any large-scale attempt to fit into it the great wealth of material unearthed by earlier excavation. Caution is also discernible in his reluctance to follow up analogies and comparisons with parallel finds elsewhere. The external relations of each material culture are touched on only in the most general terms, while dates in years are still only suggested as 'working hypotheses'. The overall results are accordingly by no means easy to summarize.

Dörpfeld's nine cities had become such an accepted principle of Trojan chronology that, with the minor reservation that their size alone made 'settlements' a more suitable word, Blegen decided to accept these as major historical divisions. But his own work enabled him to detect no less than forty-six sub-strata or building periods. (Troy I, for instance, is now divided into ten sub-periods lettered from 'a' to 'j'.) Broadly speaking, Settlements I–V represent a long period of cultural continuity corresponding to the Aegean Early Bronze Age in the third millennium B.C. Settlement VI accounts for the early and middle part of the second millennium and the first subdivision of Settlement VII (which is assumed to occupy the whole of the thirteenth century B.C.), is to be identified with 'Homeric' Troy. Settlement VIII covers the period of classical Greece and Settlement IX the Hellenistic and Roman period. The great conflagration of which Schliemann had found traces, still marks the end of Settlement II, and 'Priam's Treasure', together with most of the other similar groups of precious objects found by Schliemann are now dated to the last sub-phase of that period. Blegen's own uncertainty ('How long Troy III endured is a matter for conjecture', and 'How long Troy IV maintained its existence cannot be certainly determined') makes any attempt at more precise dating premature.

The character of the American excavations at Troy may perhaps be judged even from this brief intimation, and it will accordingly be the more easy to understand that the finds at this site still remain the principal criterion by which the archaeology of the Aegean provinces must be judged. Indeed very little other work had till then been done in that area. In 1901 French archaeologists at Yortan east of Pergamum had excavated finely made pottery comparable to that of Troy I and II; but this came from a cemetery and its chronological relations were doubtful. Minor finds have been made elsewhere in the Troad in recent times, but none of them seem likely to rival in importance a subsidiary sounding undertaken by the Americans themselves (on this occasion in collaboration with Koşay) at a small site called Kumtepe, where traces were for the first time found of a culture clearly earlier than Troy I. Its connexions with the deepest level at Alishar on the plateau we shall presently have to consider.

KUSURA (see also Chap. 7)

While Blegen's excavation was in progress some new light on relations between the Aegean province and the plateau was also thrown by the work of W. Lamb (the first lady archaeologist in the Anatolian field), at Kusura near Afyon Karahisar. Miss Lamb was well qualified to detect traces of Aegean connexions, having recently completed a masterly excavation at

Thermi on the island of Lesbos, where a succession of primitive settlements were revealed, corresponding approximately to the first phase at Troy. Kusura in fact, as might be expected from its geographical situation, produced an archaeological sequence of village settlements dating from the late Chalcolithic period to the early second millennium; its material appurtenances had much in common with those on the plateau, but were at the same time linked to the Aegean by the frequent occurrence of familiar Trojan types. This was a first step towards cross-dating between the two provinces. A second was taken by Bittel at a site called Demirci Hüyük west of Eskişehir with very similar results.

PREHISTORIC MERSIN (see also p. 75)

The year after that in which Blegen's work at Troy came to an end, excavations were begun in another peripheral region of Anatolia, against a totally different archaeological background. After a quarter of a century's absence, Garstang had returned to the Turkish field, intent upon investigating the pre-history of the Adana plain. After a preliminary survey, he selected a small but high mound called Yümüktepe, standing beside a clear stream on the outskirts of modern Mersin. In view of the extraordinary interest attaching to the results of this excavation, one must see in his choice an example of that peculiar 'flair', shared by him with certain other pioneers of his own generation, for no accumulation of stratified evidence could better have fulfilled his purpose. The expedition, sponsored by Liverpool University, was economically organized, but in four excavating seasons before and after the war, it achieved an almost complete cross-section of pre-classical archaeology in Cilicia. (Plate 1.)

Even the upper levels of Yümüktepe were of interest. Islamic and Byzantine occupations were succeeded by some Aegean remains and the huge chambered wall of a fortress belonging to the time of the Hittite Empire. Then came earlier Hittite and 'Kültepe' cultures, preceded by the Cilician equivalent of the Copper Age, all conveniently cross-dated by the intrusion of exclusively Syrian types of pottery. When the first Chalcolithic levels were reached, there were still Anatolian associations to be seen among the pottery, and one could visualize an epoch when the first settlements were appearing on the plateau to the north. But here in Cilicia, the same epoch marked not the beginning but the end of a long succession of brilliant cultures, and the excavator could note with satisfaction that almost 50 feet of stratified débris remained to be examined.

Now in succession came the well-known phases of Mesopotamian and Syrian pre-history, whose familiar wares lay side by side with the beautifully decorated products of local potters and more significant imports from regions beyond the Aegean. Three stages ('Early', 'Middle', and 'Late') in the evolution of the Chalcolithic settlement could be recognized, and the latest of these had more than the usual pottery and small objects to distinguish it. For here, at this remarkably early age, the settlement had been ingeniously fortified, and it was possible to examine in detail the surprisingly elaborate appointments of a quasi-military establishment of approximately 3500 B.C. with its defences, garrison quarters, and weapons.

After passing through a transitional or 'Proto-Chalcolithic' stage corresponding to that of Hassuna, which represents the earliest metal-using age in Mesopotamia, there were still 20 feet of earlier settlements to explore; and these were accounted for by a phase described as Neolithic in which weapons and implements were of flint or Anatolian obsidian, and primitive pottery, burnished rather than painted, like that in deep levels which Garstang himself had been the first to discover at Sakjegözü and at Jericho in Palestine. A conservative estimate for the date of the first Neolithic settlement on the banks of the little stream at Mersin would be the middle of the fifth millennium B.C.

Garstang has described the results of the Yümük Tepe excavations in a readable volume. His study of these very eloquent remains conveys to us a sense of logic in human evolution and progressive invention laboriously attained. Neolithic man, among his stone sheepfolds, finds an outlet for the craftsman's instinct in chipping black volcanic glass into purposeful shapes. Where he reaped wild barley, his descendants or successors scatter the seed grain which they have stored through the winter in stone silos, and weave garments of spun wool to replace his skin coverings. They hammer small implements out of unsmelted copper, and cover their domestic pottery with ingenious painted patterns. These changes are landmarks in a tranquil succession of generations, changed suddenly out of all recognition by the impulse to communal defence, symbolized by the Chalcolithic fortress. Then come many centuries of peace and continuity, corresponding to the Copper Age on the plateau and to the first five settlements at Troy. They are followed by a less well illustrated phase in the second millennium, which ends in another fortress, built this time to a scale commensurate with the requirements of Hittite imperialism and the dictates of Late Bronze Age technology.

TARSUS

Garstang's initiative in Cilicia had been to some extent anticipated by H. Goldman of Bryn Mawr, whose excavations in the mound called Gözlüküle in the suburbs of modern Tarsus had begun in 1934. Her work, which was largely concerned with periods outside the scope of this story, served most fortunately to supplement the finds at Yümük Tepe. Phases where the continuity of occupation seemed broken at one site proved conveniently rich at the other, and the combined stratigraphical evidence of the two sites has created a system of typology which is unlikely for the present to be superseded.

MALATYA (see also p. 168)

Of the major excavations in the period between the wars it remains only to mention the discovery of Hittite sculptures in the great mound called Arslantepe, near Malatya, which evidently represents the earliest capital of the province of that name. A part of these were recovered by von der Osten during the early explorations of the Chicago expedition in 1926 and have found a place in the Museum of Oriental Antiquities at Istanbul. The remainder, which ornament the Ankara Museum, are due to the excavations begun by L. Delaporte in 1932 and afterwards resumed by Schaeffer on behalf of the French Institute at Istanbul. Delaporte's finds include the colossal statue of a king, which now faces the entrance to the Museum. Malatya, owing to its position within the girdle of the mountains which enclosed the 'homeland', is likely to have been intimately associated with the history of the Hittite Empire. The remains of its occupation, which appears to continue well into the Syro-Hittite period, should therefore be expected to provide a stylistic link between the two epochs.

RECENT YEARS

By the outbreak of the second World War, Anatolian archaeology had become a subject of systematic study, and some order had finally been brought into the unbalanced pattern of chance finds upon which, a generation earlier, the pre-classical history of Asia Minor had rested. Much had been gained by improvements in excavating technique, and although during the six years which followed, actual digging could continue only on a small scale, the neutrality of the Republic enabled a new generation of Turkish scholars to contribute the results of individual research in several fields of archaeological study. Important results could be obtained by them from the proper study and correlation of excavations and epigraphical material; but such work also served to emphasize the magnitude and multiplicity of the lacunae which remained to be filled, and of the cardinal problems whose solutions could not be hoped for until full-scale excavations were resumed. One such enigma was the meaning and origin of the 'Hittite' hieroglyphs, which had for so long defied all attempts at decipherment. By a remarkable chance, this problem at least was partially solved by a discovery made in 1945, almost before the bombs had ceased to fall in Europe.

KARATEPE (see also Chap. 10)

In the autumn of that year a party of archaeologists from Istanbul University, led by H. Th. Bossert and H. Çambel, were exploring the outlying parts of the Adana province. At Kadırlı, a remote market town in the foothills of Taurus, the local schoolmaster, himself an adventurous spirit, told them of a hillock called Karatepe which he had discovered over-looking the Jeyhan (Turkish 'Ceyhan') river at a distance of about five hours on horseback to the south-east. Here he said he had seen a fallen statue covered with inscriptions, and other traces of early occupation. The following day the explorers were able to pay a short visit to the place and con-firm his story. Exposed above ground they found a sculptured base, on which two lions were held by a standing human figure; and beside it a statue lying on its face, whose exposed back was covered by a long inscription in what at first appeared to be old Aramaic. The remainder of the hill was encumbered with thick scrub, but from the bare patches they were able to recover fragments of sculptured reliefs and inscriptions in hieroglyphs, which convinced them that they had discovered a new Hittite city. It was not until 1947 that a fuller investigation could be made, but its results seemed sufficiently important to warrant the organization of an excavation, and in the following year this was undertaken by H. Th. Bossert and B. Alkim. The work both at Karatepe and at the twin site called Domuztepe on the other side of the river has been regularly resumed every summer since that time, and the results may be summarized as follows.

At Karatepe the remains appeared to date from the eighth century B.C. At that period the summit of the hill had been enclosed with a polygonal fortress wall, having twenty-eight rectangular towers, and there were an upper and a lower gate-way, each approached by ramps and guarded by towers. The gate chambers through which one passed on entering were lined with inscribed and sculptured slabs, many of them still excellently preserved and still held in their original position by the tie-stones between them which ran deep into the wall. These galleries of strange reliefs, almost grotesquely stylized and artistically inferior as they may at first seem, are of the greatest possible archaeological interest, if only on account of the real-life details accompanying the more formal votive and ritual scenes; a sea-battle with drowning sailors, various forms of sport, an orchestra of musicians, and many simpler episodes of contemporary domesticity. For the stylist there are links to trace both with Egyptian and Mesopotamian art, and for the technologist they offer many indications of the stone-cutter's technique. Even more interesting, when they came to be studied, were the inscriptions, both in Hittite hieroglyphs and a second language which proved to be a dialect of Phoenician. For it was not long before parallel versions could be identified of the same text written in both languages. Here then, at last was the long-awaited bilingual inscription which could provide a key to the decipherment of the hieroglyphs. This vital task has since fallen primarily to the lot of H. Th. Bossert himself. Now that his work is complete, the many documents in this language scattered throughout the museums of the world may finally be expected to yield up their secrets. Meanwhile the Phoenician inscriptions also have already produced important historical data about the inhabitants of Karatepe, now identified as the Danunians, a people whose name was already known from references in Egyptian and Assyrian records.

The only considerable building excavated within the fortress at Karatepe itself appeared to be a palace, incorporating the 'hilâni' portico, often associated with late Hittite architecture. Excavations at Domuztepe across the river also revealed buildings and some sculpture of a slightly earlier period.

RETURN TO KÜLTEPE (see also Chap. 7)

The next major Turkish excavation was concerned with a period nearly a thousand years earlier than that represented at Karatepe. In 1948 the Turkish Historical Society, which has its headquarters in Ankara University, decided to resume the excavation at Kanesh, the Assyrian cantonment at Kültepe, where the work of the Czech expedition had been abandoned twenty-two years ealier. As directors of the new enterprise, Tahsin and Nimet Özgüç, both of whom were fully qualified archaeologists, provided the first example of professional collaboration by a married couple. Their work, which has recently been prolonged into an eighth season, was phenomenally successful. Where Hroznỳ had placed the recovery of tablets above all other considerations, the Özgüçs were able more methodically to examine the setting in which they lay, and to disentangle the successive occupation of the settlement. The result was as fascinating as only the outcome of such careful work can be, quite apart from the tablets themselves, which have continued to accumulate at the rate of about a thousand pieces per season.

The Özgüçs were able to distinguish five separate building levels all dating approximately between 2000 and 1700 B.C. Of these the first and the last (Levels IA and IV) were of less importance archaeologically, since they appeared to represent, in the one case a period before the arrival of the Assyrian traders, and in the other a rebuilding of the settlement after their departure. In the three middle levels (IB – III) were the houses of the colonists themselves, and in each case there were signs that the cantonment had been destroyed by fire. Period II in particular had obviously ended in some overwhelming catastrophe. The fire had spread so rapidly that the inhabitants had no time to remove their belongings. The loss of the Assyrian merchants proved a gain to posterity, for, apart from the damage caused by heat and collapsing roof-timbers, their possessions remained intact and the orderly arrangement of the rooms could still be observed.

This was indeed a mine of archaeological information. For apart from the content of the tablets, which provided details of the merchandise, business procedure, and relations of the colonists with foreign countries, their mention of political events and persons in their native Ashur enabled the lifetime of their owners to be dated, not to a century but to within a few years. Thus, also, the typology of the pottery and objects which were found with them acquired a new significance since they could from now onwards serve as exact dating criteria when matched elsewhere. Since ceramic groups, well known from Alishar and elsewhere, were represented side by side with familiar north Syrian types, some fixed points could at last be established in contemporary chronology.

These Turkish enterprises at Karatepe and Kültepe have been landmarks in the post-war period. There has been much other work of the same sort, either in the form of minor soundings seeking the solution of some specific problem, or of major attempts on sites of primary importance, which are still in progress or suspended for purposes of publication. Some of them will be referred to in another context while discussing the conclusions which their results have helped to make practicable; but others cannot here be allowed to pass without special mention.

There were, for instance, the Anglo-Turkish excavations of Old Smyrna which were directed by J. Cook and E. Akurgal between 1949 and 1952, in the little olive-shaded mound called Bayrakli, once an island in the Bay of Izmir. Here the first Greek colonists had founded a city on the site of a Bronze-Age village, and a first temple was built when Greek architecture was still in the formative stage about which we know so little. The excavations brought to the Izmir Museum a rich assortment of archaic Greek pottery, ivories, and other antiquities, in addition to a useful collection of second millennium and earlier material. There were the excavations of the French Institute at the 'Midas City' site called Yazilikaya, among the Phrygian monuments. Once again at the Phrygian city of Gordium, in 1949 work was resumed on a large scale by the University Museum of Pennsylvania. There have been interesting soundings made in outlying parts of the peninsula, in an attempt to estimate the extent and possible origins of the Copper Age culture; Özgüç's excavations, for instance, at Dündartepe south of Samsun and those of Koşay at Karaz, where a new aspect of the Copper Age seemed to recall finds in the Caucasus region. An Anglo-Turkish sounding by S. Lloyd and N. Gökçe at Polatli on the plateau itself produced a clearly stratified series of pottery types covering the greater part of the second and third millennia (see also p. 92). Some sites, long abandoned, became the scene of renewed activity. The deeper levels at Sakjegözü were once more examined and something was added to Garstang's earlier conclusions. C. Schaeffer continued the work of Delaporte at Arslantepe, and in 1952 Bittel reopened his own excavations at Boghazköy. The wheel thus returns full circle to the Hittite 'homeland', and the time has come for an attempt to knit together the conclusions provisionally to be drawn from the results of so much and such varied research.

CHAPTER 4

Progressive Interpretation

BEFORE going on to review in detail the successive archaeological phases revealed by this saga of exploration, it seems
desirable to summarize the conclusions which it has made
possible in a rather simple or even narrative form. It may
thereby be possible to construct some sort of chronological
framework, upon which in the reader's mind the content of
the subsequent chapters may without undue difficulty be
arranged.

But a prelude to such a narrative must be a brief reference to
Palaeolithic finds in Anatolia; a subject upon which we have
so far hardly touched.

THE OLD STONE AGE

From the year 1884, when J. E. Gautier found a hand-axe of
Chellean (now called Abbevillean) type at Birejik on the
Euphrates, almost until the outbreak of the second World War,
Old Stone Age research in Turkey continued on haphazard
and unsystematic lines. Any maps which in those days existed,
indicating the distribution of Palaeolithic finds in Anatolia,
showed as a result a misleading concentration in districts most
often visited for one reason or another, by archaeological and
other explorers. The district of Carchemish was one; that of
Malatya another, and after the foundation of the Republic, the
environs of the modern capital. All this was greatly changed
after the opening in 1936 of an Anthropological Institute in
Ankara University, under the direction of Ş. A. Kansu. From
that time onwards, the researches of Turkish anthropologists
began to cover a much wider area. Some hundreds of caves or
open sites were investigated and more than a score of them
tested by excavation. The results up to 1947 have been summarized by M. R. Sauter in the following schedule of Palaeolithic periods and their representation by actual finds:

Palaeolithic	Lower.	Chellean	Uzaghil? (Ankara). Pendik? (Gulf of Izmit).
		Clactonian	Dülük? (Gaziantep area).
		Acheulean	Ludumlu? Birejik (Carchemish area).
	Middle.	Levalloiso-Mousterian	Adiyaman (Ankara area). Tuz Gölü? Ludumlu?
	Upper.	Aurignacian	Adiyaman. Perhaps some flints from Ankara area.
		Solutrian	Unknown. Probably absent.
		Magdalenian	Idem.

It may accordingly be concluded that human habitation in Anatolia goes back to the very beginning of the Palaeolithic period.

It will be seen that Adiyaman, on the upper Euphrates near Malatya, gains extra significance from the evidence which it shows of continuous occupation during a succession of periods. It has also been considered important as establishing the first link between the Syro-Palestinian province on the one hand, and on the other occurrences in Kurdistan and the Caucasus area. For the rest, it must be remembered that the evidence consists for the most part of isolated groups of surface-finds and unstratified deposits. Material in a more revealing setting is at present in the process of discovery by K. Kökten in a cave called Karain near Antalya, where the following cultures are found in successive stratification: Acheulean, Micoquian, Mousterian, and Aurignacian. Kökten has also discovered traces of some fossil vertebrate animals, notably the cave bear (*Ursus spelaeus*), and cave lion (*Felis leo spelaeus*). Among other remains from the same cave, M. Şenyürek has identified the tooth of a Neanderthal child.

NEOLITHIC

The changes in human behaviour which marked the beginning of the New Stone Age were of such a radical character that they are sometimes collectively described as the 'Neolithic Revolution'. The beginnings of systematic agriculture combined with the domestication of animals were alone sufficient to alter its whole pattern and to make the first serious demands upon man's technological ingenuity. Fortunately for the archaeologist, some products of the latter took a durable as well as tangible form, and their survival to-day provides typological criteria by which remains of the period can be identified. First among them are the movable clay vessels which soon became almost the most indispensable accessory of domestic life; their shaping and decoration served to stimulate the earliest embryonic interest in formal design. As might be expected from the terminology of the period, new kinds of stone implements had also to be contrived to meet new demands, and in Asia Minor the most common survivals among these are the flint blades which served as knives or teeth for wooden sickles, and simple points used for piercing leather.

The use of the name Asia Minor in this connexion, in preference to Anatolia, brings one back to the fact that the greater part of modern Turkey, and especially the region more correctly described as Anatolia, shows no sign whatever of habitation during the Neolithic period. Stone implements conforming to Neolithic types have been found only in the immediate vicinity of the Salt Lake on the central plateau, and these are considered to have been brought there by traders in search of salt. If this were so, they seem likely to have come a long way; for the nearest known settlements such as Mersin and Sakjagözü are three hundred miles further south beyond the mountains. The scene of the Neolithic Revolution seems in fact to have been an area limited to the north by the range of Taurus and the fringes of the Syrian plain. One explanation of this which is sometimes offered is that here was the natural habitat of the cereals upon whose cultivation the new agricultural economy depended. But wheat and barley are developments of natural grasses, which are known at that time to have grown equally well for instance in the Caucasus and the Crimea, and only a subsequent change of climate could explain their absence in Anatolia. Climatic conditions at which we can only guess, including perhaps the extreme cold of the Anatolian winter, must indeed by accepted as the most reasonable explanation of the geographic barrier, behind which Neolithic man seems so arbitrarily to have confined himself.

The sources of information about the Neolithic phase in the Middle East are not of course limited to excavations within the frontiers of Turkey. At Hassuna for instance in northern Iraq, the transition from a state of nomadic food-gathering to a settled village community, organized for the purpose of agriculture, could be followed stage by stage with remarkable clarity and pictured in considerable detail. More recently at Jericho in Palestine some surprisingly advanced accessories of such a community have been found, including a protective outer wall and sophisticated building methods pre-dating the invention of pottery: a pre-pottery settlement at Jarmo in Iraqi Kurdistan seems likely to represent an even earlier stage of development. But Garstang's Turkish excavations have served a special purpose in emphasizing the peaceful continuity of the Neolithic régime once it was established, and in identifying the characteristics which distinguished it from the succeeding Chalcolithic phase. It was represented at Mersin by eight metres of occupational débris, deposited during the same number of successive building levels, and though here as at Sakjegözü only a small area was excavated, the two sites together produced sufficient pottery, flint implements, and other small objects to create a useful skeleton of contemporary typology.

CHALCOLITHIC

The beginnings of the Chalcolithic period are also recognizable archaeologically by a number of conspicuous and far-reaching innovations; but their effect was to enrich and amplify an already existing way of life, rather than to create any revolutionary change. It was destined to last an immensely long time (perhaps throughout the greater part of the fifth and fourth millennia B.C.) and retrospectively it represents not a single phase, but a complex of early stages in the evolution of civilization as we know it to-day. By the time the peak of its accomplishment was reached, man was to be found (though not, that we know of, in Anatolia), living in walled cities with

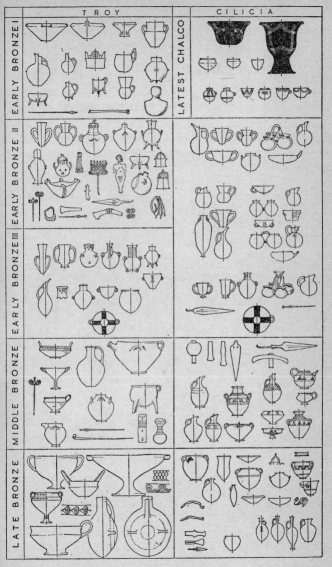

Figures 2, 3, and 4 (pp. 55, 56, and 57). Diagram of archaeological periods, with characteristic pottery and objects.

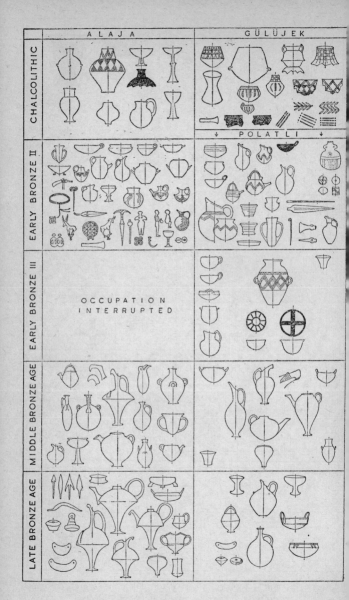

	ALAJA	GÜLÜJEK
CHALCOLITHIC		
		↓ POLATLI ↓
EARLY BRONZE II		
EARLY BRONZE III	OCCUPATION INTERRUPTED	
MIDDLE BRONZE AGE		
LATE BRONZE AGE		

56

ALISHAR	KUMTEPE AND FIKIRTEPE	
	UNPUBLISHED	2900-2600
	AHLATLIBEL	2600-2300
	LOUVRE CAPPADOCIAN	2300-1900
	KÜLTEPE	1900-1600
OCCUPATION INTERRUPTED	KUSURA AND BOĞAZKÖY	1600-1200

57

well-designed temples and palaces, codifying his own laws and shaping his life to their requirements. In Mesopotamia at least, he had already mastered the art of writing and could leave to posterity the first undisputed records of his own thoughts and acts.* The Neolithic stage, which after all corresponded to that of the most primitive savages to be found in the world to-day, was by then long forgotten.

The archaeological fabric of the Chalcolithic period was studied in great detail in the two decades following the first World War during a succession of excavating enterprises, mostly in the territory of modern Iraq. A village of adobe houses which succeeded the Neolithic huts at Hassuna; another of the Halafian phase with circular *tholoi* at Arpa-chiyah; the first monumental architecture of the 'Ubaidian phase at Tepe Gawra and Eridu; ceramic changes suggesting an infusion of new blood, first observed in the prehistoric settlement at Uruk, and evidence at half a dozen sites of the tremendous cultural advancement which followed all these, marked stages in the panorama of evolution which was gradually revealed. When the now-familiar criteria of these various phases were later found, first in north Syria and then at Tarsus and Mersin beyond the Turkish frontier, they were of interest as testifying to the westward and northward extension of the great Chalcolithic province; but of equal importance were the sharply differentiated local cultures which existed alongside of them. These were mixed in their later stage with intrusive elements from quite other parts of the world, whose equivocal dating could now be linked to the more reliable chronology of Mesopotamia. In this way the antiquity of prehistoric finds for instance from sites as remote as the lower reaches of the Danube became calculable. Though all the while, in the nearer foreground, Anatolia still remained a *terra incognita*, of whose very existence the Chalcolithic people seem only to have become aware during the very last years of their existence.

* For the brilliant 'Proto-historic' period in Mesopotamia must be regarded as the chronological equivalent of 'Late Chalcolithic' at Turkish sites like Mersin.

At Mersin, Garstang had been able to divide his Chalco-lithic remains into three sub-periods, which he distinguished as 'Early', 'Middle' and 'Late', and it was with the third of these that the earliest Anatolian settlements, when they did eventually appear, seemed to be associated in time, if not by any more tangible link. It was therefore necessary to assume that up to the end of the 'Middle' period (which corresponded to the 'Ubaidian phase in Mesopotamia) something approxi-mating to the old Neolithic 'barrier' still existed, and that beyond it Anatolia remained unpopulated.

Exploration and surface reconnaissances have now made it possible to define the lines of the 'barrier' with much greater precision. In fact, on a map showing the southern frontier of Turkey, it seems to correspond with surprising accuracy to the contour line at which the southern slopes of the moun-tains reached or exceeded a height of 2000 feet. The 'barrier' therefore, though oriented approximately east and west, follows an irregular line with deep indentations where, for instance, the valleys of the Tigris and Euphrates penetrate far into the highlands, and a notable extension northwards into the Cilician Plain.

FIRST SETTLEMENTS ON THE PLATEAU

This, then, was the situation at the time when Anatolian archaeology in the strictest sense may be said to have had its beginnings. For at some period in the closing centuries of the fourth millennium, the lands to the north of the old 'barrier' were at last discovered to be a possible habitat for an agri-tural people, and the first farming settlements appeared both on the plateau itself and in the Aegean province to the west. Our next subject of speculation must therefore be the direc-tion from which the first settlers arrived and the location of their previous home. To these questions, unfortunately, we shall find only the most inconclusive answers.

The material remains so far discovered of these earliest Anatolians are still extremely scanty and inadequate. They are derived from excavations at hardly a dozen sites, most of which were mere stratigraphical soundings, and from comparable surface finds made elsewhere. But it can at least be said that they cover a wide geographical area, from the Troad in the west to the banks of the Araxes on the Persian frontier. At first they were a mere series of isolated discoveries. Each site or group of neighbouring sites produced a distinctive repertoire of pottery types and other domestic accessories, assignable only by stratigraphical evidence to the Chalcolithic period. At Alishar, for instance, von der Osten associated an assemblage of material in his deepest deposits with a period pre-dating the Copper Age. Amongst an interesting group of sites examined by Özgüç, near Samsun, Dündartepe produced a clear picture of a Chalcolithic village, and its neighbours supplementary material of the same sort. At Büyük Gülüjek near Alaja, Koşay lit upon a prehistoric village whose remains were characterized by an abundance of most distinctively shaped and ornamented pottery, bearing no resemblance to the ubiquitous Copper-Age material. Immediately afterwards he was most gratifyingly enabled to authenticate its chronological precedence by similar discoveries in a sounding beneath the famous tombs at Alaja itself. At Troy, Blegen had tentatively dated the earliest settlement to the beginning of the Aegean Bronze Age and the third millennium B.C. But circumstantial evidence again enabled him to attribute finds from the nearby sounding at Kumtepe to a still earlier date. Upon the subsequent analysis and comparison of such isolated groups of material, our knowledge of the origin, character and distribution of the Chalcolithic settlers has till now depended.

Those who have had the opportunity to study the whole assembly of archaeological data, have tended to single out and emphasize the significance of certain individual features. These are usually of so distinctive a character that their appearance in different geographical settings, however widely sepparated, could not reasonably be attributed to coincidence. They may accordingly, like the finger-prints of a criminal, be used with confidence as marks of identification, and from them we may establish the movements or whereabouts of the people responsible for their invention. One such feature is a dish on a tall pedestal with a grey or black burnished finish, which has come to be familiarly known as a 'fruit stand'. Such fruit stands were conspicuous among the pottery of the Chalcolithic levels at Alishar. They have since been found at Alaja and other sites on the plateau, where one would expect a uniform culture; but they are also unmistakably recognizable among the finds made during the Turco-American sounding at Kumtepe, five hundred miles away in the Troad. This has been considered to rule out the theory, previously sometimes put forward, that the plateau and the Aegean province were separately colonized by peoples of different extraction, and developed independently from then onwards. On such fine threads as this must archaeological speculation in this case stand.

But perhaps the most distinguished as well as the most distinctive of all the plateau Chalcolithic finds to date are Koşay's finely-shaped vessels from Büyük Gülüjek with their elaborate incised ornament. Here is a whole corpus of shapes and patterns by which the first inhabitants of Alaja, and any cultural relatives which they may have possessed in other countries, should from now onwards be recognizable. Indeed, such connexions have already been suspected by Childe and others, with lands beyond the Aegean and northwards to the Danube. If these can eventually be authenticated, the first clue is provided to the direction of the migratory movement which led to the first population of Anatolia. Pottery recently found by Bittel at a site called Fikirtepe on the Asiatic shores of the Bosphorus, in its resemblance to that from Gülüjek, seems already to support such an inference and can be taken to mark the line of approach.

One curious but incontrovertible fact about these earliest finds in Anatolia is that they bear no relation whatsoever to contemporary developments beyond the old 'Neolithic barrier' in the south. One may therefore dismiss once and for all the possibility that the plateau was eventually populated merely by a northward expansion of the people who had for so long been confined within those limits. In fact, the first perceptible connexions between those people and their new neighbours in Anatolia date from the time of the first settlement at Troy.

EARLY BRONZE

It is to the beginnings of the Anatolian Copper Age that we must now turn our attention, and the reader will once more be reminded of the repercussions in archaeological circles resulting from the adoption of this name. In neighbouring countries such as Syria, Cyprus, and the islands of the Aegean the term 'Early Bronze Age' is used to cover the greater part of the third millennium B.C., and excavators in the peripheral districts of Turkey, such as Hatay, Cilicia, and the extreme western provinces, whose pre-history is judged primarily in terms of their foreign relations, could hardly be expected to welcome any deviation from this tradition. Here therefore a difficulty again arises, since the periods covered by the two terms do not exactly coincide. The Early Bronze Age of Aegean chronology is taken to include the first settlement at Troy, whereas the beginning of the Anatolian Copper Age corresponds to the foundation of the second settlement. It is partly for this reason that it has been decided here to retain the term Copper Age, when referring to Anatolia proper. It should be added that its acceptance is indeed made easier by the consistency and long duration of the culture by which it is represented on the Plateau; by the circumscribed and distinctive character which sets it apart from parallel developments elsewhere.*

We have already described the loose network of Chalcolithic settlements, and suggested that their diverse origin and circumstances may be reflected in the disparity of their material remains. At a period which cannot yet be precisely defined, in the early centuries of the third millennium B.C., these groupings seem finally to have become fused and consolidated into a new ethnological entity, whose character bore little resemblance to any one of the elements of which it was composed. A permissible parallel is perhaps the third and fourth generation of Americans to-day, the memory of whose diverse extraction has been subordinated to the reality of a collective individuality deliberately cultivated. In any case, there can have been little to interfere with their peaceful

* See diagram p. xx.

development, for they are to be found over a period of seven or eight centuries, in every hamlet or market town from the Sakarya to the Euphrates and from the Black Sea to the ranges of Taurus which form the southern lip of the plateau, living in the same sort of houses, using the same implements and preferring the same pottery shapes. The circumstances and equipment of their rural life are already well known from the score or so of such settlements which have been excavated, and at most of them it has been possible to detect only a single point at which the even tenor of their existence was interrupted by some migratory disturbance, strong enough to effect minor changes in their traditional craftsmanship and technology. Yet the overall character of their life remained the same till well after the end of the third millennium and its sameness in these rural communities was emphasized by an almost total absence of progress. In fact, if the evidence which they provide were the only standard by which the Copper Age could be judged, any comparison of its standards and development with those in the countries of the Fertile Crescent (for instance the contemporary Old Kingdom in Egypt), during this formative period, would be most unflattering.

In Mesopotamia some years ago, while excavating the Sumerian city of Eshnunna, the writer took part in clearing a group of private houses dating from the period of the early dynasties. Their appointments gave an impression of extreme austerity, as might have been expected from the social conditions which prevailed at the time. And archaeologically they stimulated one's curiosity as to the opinion that would have been held of the Sumerians if the impression obtained from this excavation were not supplemented by that of the tombs and temples which have made their reputation.

So in Anatolia, the Turkish Historical Society's chance discovery of the tombs at Alaja Hüyük changed, almost in a night, our whole conception of the Copper Age, and brought its cultural pretensions into a true focus beside those of neighbouring civilizations. Some details are given in another chapter concerning the magnitude of this discovery,* the

* See p. 96 ff.

contents of the burials and the implication of moral and technological advancement in a section of contemporary Anatolian society. It will be sufficient here to recall the tantalizing impression created by this isolated glimpse of taste and pageantry in the lives of a vanished people, and its promise of further surprises when eventually they are more fully illuminated.

We must next consider collateral developments during the Copper Age in the peripheral areas outside Anatolia proper, to which we have already had reason to refer. The most immediately interesting is perhaps the Aegean province, which seems to a large extent to have separated itself culturally from the Plateau at about the time that the first settlement at Troy was founded. Since Blegen would place this event soon after the beginning of the third millennium, we are, as has already been said, compelled to think of 'Troy I' as contemporary with the latest Chalcolithic settlements in the east, and to align the beginning of the Copper Age with that of his second settlement. In truth, few archaeological links between the two areas at this early period have yet been established to make an effective cross-check possible; but links between Troy I and the Aegean are plentiful and sufficiently conclusive to make Blegen's estimate acceptable.

At Troy, therefore, it is the second to the fifth settlements which represent the Copper Age and it is they which serve as the main criteria of the period for the whole Aegean province. Here again the evidence which we have to go upon consists on the one hand of rather humdrum remains, pointing to a modest agricultural economy, and on the other hand of isolated finds of great richness suggesting a more elevated standard of living amongst the upper social classes. The latter, of course, are represented by the treasures of gold and silver ornaments found by Schliemann in his second 'city'. It is interesting also that at Troy, as at Alaja, these major riches date from a period which terminated in some great cataclysm, and was followed in both cases by notable changes in the habits and tastes of the local inhabitants. At Troy, the second settlement ended in a conflagration, sufficiently great to leave a deep deposit of burnt débris and ash over the whole inhabited area. At Alaja the city had been similarly destroyed by fire soon after the last interment was made in the famous tombs. There is even reason to think that the two incidents may have coincided in time, and a tendency to attribute them to a date near the end of the twenty-fourth century B.C.

But these facts having once been noticed, parallels between the Aegean and Plateau civilizations during the Copper Age are virtually exhausted. In their metallurgy, indeed, there are types of implement and minor ornamental features common to both. But they are hardly more than sufficient to suggest the parallel stages reached in the development of a particular craft throughout the Middle East while in the realm of pottery it is only an occasional shape of great individuality, such as the two-handled goblet called *depas amphikypellon*, which can be used as a criterion for purposes of cross-dating between the two areas. For the rest, it is their discrepancy rather than their interrelation which can be most conveniently studied at sites like Kusura and Demirci Hüyük, which occupy debatable positions, subject to the influence of both cultures.

The other important peripheral area to which we must refer is Cilicia. As the Aegean province is oriented towards the islands and Europe beyond, so the destiny of Cilicia has often been shaped by its accessibility from Syria and the south. In the final stages of the Chalcolithic period, at sites like Mersin and Tarsus, there were scanty traces of contact with the new arrivals at Troy; and during the centuries of the Copper Age which followed, the signs are plentiful of a lively trade with the Plateau, presumably by way of the Taurus passes. But side by side with the material evidence of this affiliation are indications of the obvious influence of contemporary taste in Syria and even Palestine.

From Cilicia it would be logical to pass on eastwards to the river valleys and the piedmont country south of the old Neolithic 'barrier'; thence to the highlands east of the Euphrates and eventually to the Black Sea coast in the north. Unfortunately, none of these areas has yet been properly studied and anything said about their history in the Copper Age would be for the most part idle speculation. True, there is the solitary instance of a site called Karaz near Erzurum, where in a recognizably Copper Age setting, Koşay has recently discovered a new pottery having parallels in the Caucasus, and much is being made of its resemblance to the exotic and controversial products of Khirbet Kerak in Palestine.* But such isolated discoveries seem in a sense to emphasize the inadequacy of our knowledge, and serve only as pointers to new lines of investigation. For the rest, the northern, eastern, and south-eastern neighbours of our Anatolians remain at present an enigma, comparable to that of the Mediterranean coast west of Cilicia, which negative evidence has shown to have been virtually uninhabited at this time.

Thus, in a few paragraphs, the main outlines of what we know about the Anatolian Copper Age can be given. In deference to the small group of research workers by whom it has been rescued from total oblivion, the prospect which it offers of augmentation in the future must be accepted as compensation for its present inadequacy. In about 2300 B.C. its characteristics were greatly changed by the intrusion of a people with a taste for exotic painted pottery, and the termination of this 'Cappadocian' aftermath in about 1900 B.C. brings to an end the prehistoric period in Anatolian archaeology. From now onwards one may watch the mists lifting from the dim impersonal landscape of 'cultures' and 'village horizons,' which archaeology has created, and see some corners of it at least transformed by the illumination of contemporary description.

MIDDLE BRONZE AGE

Of the written records from which history is compiled, the first to be conclusively associated with Anatolia are the Kültepe tablets. Their evidence is supplemented by traditions related or re-copied 500 years later by the scribes of the Hittite Empire, and the two sources together help create a

* Cf. W. Lamb in *Anatolian Studies*, Vol. IV.

picture of the country in the early centuries of the second millennium, which, if not as detailed as one could wish, can at least be composed around such familiar concepts as rival dynasties of princes and city states. Philologists, too, from linguistic data in the texts, can enumerate the ethnological elements present in the population. They can identify among them those seeming to be indigenous, and estimate the probable source or sequence of migrations which account for the remainder. It should be the archaeologist's duty, not to distort his own conclusions to fit the hypothesis thus provided, but to submit the two classes of evidence to a process of mutual adjustment. Unfortunately, owing to the high degree of specialization which is common to both classes of research, few scholars' with the possible exception of Bittel, have so far proved themselves qualified to fulfil this task effectively. As a result, among the material remains of the early second millennium which one sees in museums or illustrated in excavation reports, some, which have been well classified, and the implications of their distribution carefully studied, continue to have an independent life of their own, unconnected with the picture of contemporary events and peoples envisaged by the texts.

An example of this is the elaborately painted pottery known as 'Cappadocian', which we have already mentioned as intruding on the Copper Age culture at the end of the third millennium. In a country with an unbroken tradition of plain and burnished ware, whose rare experiment in decoration had till now been almost completely limited to simple lines of white paint on a dark ground, the sudden appearance of these gay colours on a light clay must have been revolutionary, and can only have resulted from the admixture of a new element in the population. Sooner or later a tangible connexion must surely be found between this phenomenon and some major historical event, such as the arrival of the Indo-Europeans, who mingled with the indigenous people to produce the original Hittite stock. At the time of the Assyrian colony at Kültepe in whose records Indo-European names are already mentioned, this temporary ceramic fashion had already passed the peak of its popularity and was giving way to a fine new burnished˙style, more characteristic of local taste. This was to set the standard for designs in clay during the remainder of the Bronze Age, and its beginnings at Kültepe have led some scholars to describe the period as 'archaeologically though not politically Hittite'.

To the archaeological setting in which the Kültepe tablets were found, we have already had reason to refer, and we shall return to its details in another context.* It creates an interesting record of the environment in which these foreign traders found themselves living and it may even be taken to present a fair picture of domestic life in the kind of world which can dimly be discerned behind the more practical preoccupations of their writings. But we have not yet reached a period where the remains of civic and military architecture or the major accessories of religious ritual allow the pictorial background against which historical events took place to be authentically reconstructed. No public buildings of any sort are yet known, and no evidence, comparable for instance to that of the Copper Age tombs, of the appointments associated with the life of a ruling caste have yet come to light. With the exception of scanty architectural remains at Alaja, this situation persists for the four centuries which follow and throughout the period of the Old Hittite Kingdom, which is historically so comparatively well documented in the texts, archaeology can supply little of the material background against which events took place. As excavations, for instance by K. Bittel at Boghazköy, continue, there is no reason to suppose that this situation will long remain unchanged. Already important finds of the pre-Empire period are being made, and it is by no means impossible that through them the earliest foundation of buildings already excavated may eventually be more conclusively dated to the Old Kingdom. But for the moment we have to content ourselves with little besides the elegant monochrome pottery of Period II at Alishar and its counterpart in the local museum at Alaja Hüyük.

Nor are finds dated to the first half of the second millennium

* See Chap. 7.

in the outlying provinces of much help, except in defining limits for the distribution of the Cappadocian and Alishar II classes of pottery. Beyond these limits, Troy, for instance, continues in a world of its own, and the people of the sixth settlement are to be found still trading with the Aegean and developing their own craftsmanship on individual lines. Cilicia, on the other hand, has become an extension of the Plateau enclave; a centre of commercial exchange, where its wares are found side by side with those of North Syria and more exotic imports from the island of Cyprus. The eastern highlands and the Black Sea coast continue to be an unknown quantity.

The period of the Old Kingdom, which we have been discussing, is usually dated between 1600 and 1400 B.C. The following two centuries account for the Hittite Empire. Here at last we are on safer ground archaeologically, for the surviving architecture and sculptured monuments are alone sufficient to enhance the reality of textual evidence.

Indeed, up to the present time only two major Hittite cities on the Plateau itself have been excavated. But the rich finds at Hattusas, combined with the contemporary sculptured monuments which are scattered so widely over Anatolia, make as vivid a background to an imperial saga as the palaces of Nimrud or the Minoan Labyrinth. For here is the military architecture of a fortified city, more than five miles in circumference, with its ramparts and monumental gateways; temples with pretentious appointments; administrative buildings, interesting in themselves, quite apart from their precious content of official archives; houses and graves of the common people, and, perhaps most important of all, the sculptured symbolism of a traditional faith, with indications of the ceremonial through which it was expressed. The Hittite state and society during the Empire, its life and economy, laws, institutions, military organization and even a part of its literature, have been reconstructed in the most surprising detail from the contents of the tablets found in the storehouses at Büyükkale. Indeed collectively they are a product of the setting in which they were created and the environment which formed the Hittite character, both of which can be apprehended only in terms of their physical remains at Bogazköy.

So finally in the fourteenth and thirteenth centuries B.C., the two branches of antiquarian research can collaborate in recreating the complicated structure of an Anatolian imperial state and the history of its people. Some information can even be extracted regarding its political dependencies and relations with its remoter neighbours, so that the first tentative study of geography becomes practicable. One sees the Hittite 'homeland' within the Halys 'bend,' extended to include the whole of Cappadocia. Its control usually extends eastwards to an 'Upper Land' in Pontus and south-westwards to a 'Lower Land' corresponding approximately to Lycaonia. Cilicia is Kizzuwatna, a Hittite dependency from which campaigns against Aleppo and even Egypt are conducted, and to the west of it Arzawa extends inland across Phrygia, a province still imperfectly defined and less often in subjection.

In the south-east a new development has been on foot for some centuries past. A people called Hurri have moved westwards from Van and Zagros* to occupy the uppermost reaches of the Tigris, and, as an offshoot from the Hurrian stem, the young kingdom of Mitanni is established on the northern confines of Mesopotamia. North of the 'homeland', the Black Sea coast is in the hands of the Kaska tribes whose relations with the Empire, like those of Mitanni, are seldom friendly. Only in the remote west, the Aegean province (Assuwa) seems to have remained beyond the effective reach of Hittite authority.

At Troy this period comprised and ended with the Homeric, and the destruction of the contemporary settlement (VIIA) by fire in about 1190 B.C. is generally correlated with the fall of the city celebrated in the Iliad. There are debatable references to Troy and Trojans in Hittite texts, but no other connexion between the two peoples is known. Finds in the seventh settlement are once more enriched by importations from the islands and the Greek Mainland, as might be expected from

* Cf. I. Gelb, *Hurrians and Subarians*, p. 70, for the origin of the Hurrians.

the fact that the command of the sea is known to have been in Mycenaean hands during the fourteenth and thirteenth centuries. Similarly at other sites on the Aegean coast, such as Miletus, and on the Mediterranean littoral as far as Cilicia, both at Mersin and Tarsus Mycenaean material now occurs. The contrasting relationship, however, between Kizzuwatna and Hattusas is emphasized by the fact that at Mersin Mycenaean pottery is found in association with a typical Hittite fortress of the Empire period. Clues such as this have served to confirm the Hittite Kings' own accounts of their foreign relations.

IRON AGE

The fall of Troy seems likely to have been no more than an incident in the far-reaching upheaval which drove the Hittites out of central Anatolia; an eastward thrust of peoples from Thrace and Macedonia which ended after some centuries of confusion in the establishment of the Phrygians as rulers of Asia Minor. With written texts no longer available, the stages by which Hittite power thereafter receded from the Plateau are not accurately known, but it is certain that a stand was made for some centuries by cities such as Malatya (Arslantepe) and Tyana (Bor). Proof of this are the plentiful finds dating from the twelfth to tenth centuries, both at these sites and at others south of Taurus such as Sinjerli and Carchemish. Their eventual downfall began in the eighth century with the Cimmerian invasion from the north, which, recoiling from the Assyrian frontiers, turned westwards to seek easier prey. It was completed after the fall of Nineveh by the Medes, between whom and the Lydians Anatolia was for a short period divided.

But we are anticipating and should return for a moment to the establishment of the Phrygians in Asia Minor.

The best evidence for their early appearance south of the Hellespont is the familiar reference to them in Homer as neighbours of the Trojans at the time of the events described in the Iliad.* Nor is the theory of their origin in Thrace dependent solely on the testimony of Herodotus and other

* *Iliad* III, 184.

Greek writers; for centuries later the same tribal divisions, and even names of localities, are to be found still in use on either side of the straits.* Their new home was even occasionally referred to as Asiatic Thrace. But to assign a date to the time when the impetus of their migration carried them to the eastern fringes of the Plateau and left them to assume the mantle of authority over all Anatolia relinquished by the Hittites is less easy. For the event with which we are concerned is just beyond the horizon of Greek history. To the Greek colonists so recently settled on the Asiatic coast of the Aegean, developments in the interior were a closed book, and their traditions on the subject, if any, were not of the sort to be recorded by their later chroniclers. The Assyrian annals on the other hand have something to contribute. The armies, first of Tiglath Pileser I in the twelfth century, and then of Sargon II in the eighth, were in contact in Taurus with a people called Muski, who have tended to be identified with the Phrygians.† The only archaeological evidence is provided by Phrygian inscriptions in southern Cappadocia and north of Hattusas in the old Hittite 'homeland', dating from the middle of the ninth century B.C. These at least create a *terminus ante quem* for the disappearance of the Hittites from the Plateau.

The resemblance of the Phrygian language to American at first sight appears to support Herodotus' theory that these people were an offshoot of the same stock. The alphabetic script in which it is written is an eastern form of archaic Greek, closely related to Phoenician. But the relationship is not yet fully understood, and little has been learnt from the very few inscriptions which have survived. They are mostly to be found in the province which the newcomers early adopted as their own 'homeland', astride the valley and sources of the Sangarius river (Sakarya). Here, clustered around the fabulous Midas City is the group of extraordinary rock-cut monuments, by which Phrygian art is best known. These and the ruins of Gordium, at the easternmost bend of the same

* Cf. Perrot and Chipiez, *History of Art in Phrygia*, p. 2.
† This equation is by no means certain. Cf. O. R. Gurney, *The Hittites*, p. 39.

river, lend some substance to the legendary dynasty of kings, called always either Midas or Gordios, one of whom eventually appears in history, as a result of his contacts with Sargon II in 709 B.C. Another group of such monuments is to be found in Mount Sipylus, north of Smyrna. This was an early settlement which the Greeks associated with the name of Tantalus, and with a period when Phrygian fleets sailed in Aegean waters. Combined with their occasional description of Sinope on the Black Sea coast as a 'Phrygian city', this would suggest the extension of Phrygian power at some time both to the western and to the northern seaboard.

The Cimmerian invasions at the end of the eighth century would appear to have been the first step in the downfall of the Phrygian power. This was an incursion of peoples from Southern Europe by way of the Caucasus, the effects of which were felt even by the Assyrians and as far afield as the Urartian kingdom centred on Lake Van. Meeting and combining with a similar wave from the direction of the Bosphorus, they overwhelmed the cities of Anatolia, and tradition tells how the current King Midas was driven to commit suicide by the unconventional expedient of drinking bull's blood. The tide seems to have receded almost as fast as it came, but it had greatly weakened the Phrygian kingdom, whose access to the sea was also now obstructed by the increasing power of the Greek colonies. By the second half of the seventh century it submitted to the dominion of Lydia, a new state which had grown up within its sometime frontiers.*

The story of the Lydian kings in their capital at Sardis, the extension of their frontiers to the Halys, their relations with the Greeks of Ionia, alternating between violent conflict and profitable collaboration, their tolerance or adoption of Phrygian culture and their eventual destruction by the Achaemenian Persians, are subjects well documented historically. The archaeology of the period is too closely linked with the beginnings of the classical régime in Asia Minor to fall within the scope of the present work.

* The survival of Phrygian culture in Lydian times is discussed in Chapter 11.

CHAPTER 5

First Phase : The Earliest Settlements

A GOOD deal has already been said about the Neolithic settlements dating probably from the fifth millennium B.C., along the northern and western fringes of the 'fertile crescent', and about the limits of their extension into Anatolia. It has also, perhaps, already been sufficiently emphasized that they are separated in time from the beginnings of the Anatolian Copper and Bronze Ages by the long-protracted panorama of the Mesopotamian Chalcolithic, whose successive phases are associated with the names of Hassuna, Sâmarra, Tell Halaf, 'Ubaid, Uruk, and Jemdet Nasr: an epoch, in fact, whose minimum length has never been estimated at less than a thousand years, and often at a much higher figure. Finally it has been concluded that the earliest settlements, both on the Anatolian Plateau and in the Aegean province, must be correlated chronologically with the tail-end of this epoch, and considered as a kind of 'Indian summer', perhaps even postdating its termination in lands further to the south. It will therefore be understood that the term Neolithic as sometimes applied in the past to these last-mentioned settlements by scholars more familiar with Aegean chronology is open to misinterpretation and should on the whole be avoided.

Let us then first attend to the true Neolithic remains, the presence of which within the area covered by this survey is due to occasional northward extension of a cultural province lying for the most part beyond its limits. We shall find ourselves primarily concerned with the results of excavations at two sites, Sakjegözü and Mersin, and a little supplementary evidence from other sources in the areas which they dominate. Unhappily these two mounds share with others in Syria and Mesopotamia, where Neolithic remains have been found, the disadvantage of long and continuous occupation in subsequent ages. The traces of their earliest occupations are accordingly buried beneath many metres of later débris, and could only be explored by the unsatisfactory method of deep trenching. Yet this system of vertical 'sounding' has at least served to establish their chronological position unequivocally and to give some idea both of their duration and of the sucessive stages in their development. From this point of view, by far the most revealing excavation has been that at Mersin, where the first recognizably Neolithic remains appeared as much as 10 metres above the datum level at the base of the mound, and the last, at a point some distance beneath the latter, where seepage water made further penetration impracticable.

MERSIN*

The settlement at Mersin was on the left bank of a fast-flowing stream, less than a mile from its mouth, and seems likely to have marked a ford where it was crossed by a road of some importance, running eastwards along the coast, and afterwards perhaps inland by way of the Calycadnus valley. From the earliest period of which traces have been found there appear to have been houses with walls built of loose round stones, and floors at successive occupation levels were usually marked by deep layers of ashes scattered from domestic hearths. Finds inside the houses consisted for the most part of pottery and implements of obsidian and chert. Garstang divided the eight recognizable building levels into sub-phases described as 'early' and 'late' Neolithic, and during the first of these the pottery was all monochrome. An important proportion of it was black, grey or brown burnished ware, mostly of rather simple bowl shapes, such as was already familiar from Sakjegözü and other sites south of the Turkish frontier. Such decoration as it bore consisted of incised marks beneath the rim, which, at their first appearance suggested the imprint of a thumb-nail, but afterwards developed into a kind of continuous 'rocker' pattern which could have been made with a round-ended shell. There were also occasional sherds

* J. Garstang's *Prehistoric Mersin* is the one-volume final publication of this excavation.

of red-faced ware, due more probably to irregular firing than to any deliberate intention on the part of the potter.

The Neolithic flint industry at Mersin was really the most interesting feature of the settlement, rising, as it seemed, to a peak of accomplishment about the middle of the period and thereafter slightly deteriorating. The most commonly used material was the black volcanic glass of which there is a likely source just north of the Taurus mountains. The shapes included arrow-heads, lance-heads, daggers, points, and sickle-blades, though the latter were more often of chert. In Anatolia to-day the threshing of corn is normally accomplished by driving over it wooden sledges into whose flat bottoms are set rows of such blades, napped by the peasants themselves from brown chert; and Garstang suggests that in Neolithic times they may have already been used for this purpose. Of the obsidian weapons, the lance-heads and daggers were parti-cularly impressive, the former usually having a tang and both being trimmed by pressure-flaking until they were approxi-mately triangular in section, with a very sharp point at one end. Apart from the chipped implements, there were also examples of the polished greenstone celts, which are generally considered characteristic of the period.

In the later Neolithic levels the pottery showed some inno-vations, including, most significantly, the first clumsy attempts at decorating vessels with coloured paint. This seemed to coincide, as it well might, with the first appearance of a system of firing resulting in a light-coloured finish. The designs seem to have started with a simple line of red paint around the rim of the vessel, but this tended to be so clumsily applied that drops of the wet liquid ran down in irregular trickles, sug-gesting in their turn further decorative possibilities. Curiously enough, a class of pottery found at Sakjegözü and considered most typical of the period seems not to have been represented at Mersin. This was a group of flat-bottomed bowls with almost straight, outward-sloping sides, black slipped and highly burnished. The decoration, which consisted of neatly-drawn cross-hatched bands or triangles, was applied in the form of fine incised lines filled with a white substance to

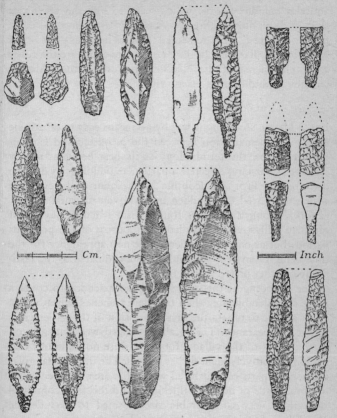

Figure 5. Neolithic obsidian weapons from Mersin

emphasize them. At Mersin this form of ornament did indeed
appear in the earliest phase of the subsequent Chalcolithic
period, but it was applied to more clumsily made vessels of a
different shape; nothing there quite resembled these thin,
almost metallic black bowls which were such a feature of the
Sakjegözü sounding. Apart from pottery and flints, neither
sounding produced any small objects or other features of
great interest, beyond the simple piercing implements of bone

and clay spindle whorls, which seem to link the sewing of skins and spinning of thread to the very beginnings of village life. For the rest, it has remained for sites in other parts of the Middle East, like Jericho in Palestine, to illustrate the fuller accomplishments of the Neolithic period, in the realm of technology and even of plastic art.

CHALCOLITHIC

In the Mersin sounding it was by no means easy to determine the line of demarcation between the Neolithic and Chalcolithic cultures, the terminology at its best being extremely arbitrary. Garstang selected a particular building level to be described as 'Proto-Chalcolithic', on account of the evidence which it showed of a sudden improvement in rural organization. Among the objects found, a small tanged javelin of obsidian still strongly recalled the industry of the previous period: but as negative evidence, the non-appearance for the time being of any copper could be subordinated to the testimony of other progressive tendencies.

The sounding at this stage had been extended to cover a more considerable area than the mere trenches beneath, and one was able to obtain the first impression of the settlement's physical appearance. The locality revealed was evidently on the outskirts of the village, for there were no buildings that could be positively identified as houses. The three rectangular enclosures, parts of which fell within the area, were enclosed by stone walls of no great thickness; and this fact, combined with their very considerable size, seemed to exclude the possibility of their having been roofed. By the excavators they were accordingly identified rather as 'sheep-folds'. To increase the resemblance to a farmyard the spaces between these 'folds' were thickly crowded with the stone foundations of circular structures, identified as grain bins or 'silos', obviously used to store winter supplies and perhaps the seed grain for the coming spring. On their stone bases these bins were constructed of clay to an approximately conical shape and, judging by analogies in later times, the grain was poured in at the top and then perhaps withdrawn through a trapdoor near the base. Some individual grains recovered from one such bin were brought back to England for examination, but germinated with such facility that their presence in a Neolithic setting had eventually to be attributed to the burrowing of field mice.

Another indication at this time of increasing technical experience took the form of a notable improvement in building method. The outer angles of one wall were even strengthened with bonded quoin-stones, pounded into an approximately prismatic shape. The fact that it remained standing in places to a height of nearly two metres testified to the efficacy of the device. Early in the Chalcolithic levels which followed, houses were found with stone walls of this type, supporting an upper structure of mud brick, and the inner faces of rooms uniformly plastered over brick and stone alike. This technique in domestic architecture was to remain unchanged for at least two millennia, throughout the whole Anatolian area, the only improvement being the addition, in districts where timber was available, of wooden ties in the thickness of the brickwork.

At Mersin the Chalcolithic period was represented by about eight metres of stratified débris in which no less than twelve building levels were recognizable. Their disentanglement and elucidation was from every point of view a fascinating experience. For here once more, in a somewhat alien guise, was the composite picture created by half a dozen separate excavations in Mesopotamia, this time in uninterrupted sequence and with interesting regional peculiarities. First came a long period of peaceful existence, with signs only of minor changes and improvements in the pattern of agri-cultural life. The smelting of copper was now generally practised, and its first products appeared in the excavation in the form of simple pins with their heads curled over into an open 'eye', then of small chisels and axes. The all-important flint industry of the Neolithic period had correspondingly declined into a craft of subsidiary importance and indifferent proficiency. Ornamental spindle whorls and loom weights testified to the increasing demand for woven materials.

During these 'early' and 'middle' phases of the Chalcolithic period, the village was completely rebuilt as many as seven times, and though this seems to have been effected without noticeably interrupting the life of the community, it is possible that these occasions in some cases corresponded with the introduction of new elements into the population of Cilicia. Waves of migration at this time seem to have succeeded one another with considerable frequency, and it is curious that, among the physical remains of the village at Mersin, they should be reflected in nothing less trivial than fashions in the shaping and decoration of pottery. Here, however, we are on reasonably sure ground from a chronological point of view, for the ethnological vicissitudes which affected the early population of northern Mesopotamia seem to have had corresponding repercussions in Cilicia.

The earliest appearance of painted pottery at Mersin foreshadowed an increasing preference for light-coloured wares, which could be decorated in this way, and in the first phases of the Chalcolithic period the fashion was already in the ascendant. But the patterns and technique were those of Hassuna, 500 miles away on its upland above the Tigris, and for a period of many generations the potters of the two villages were to work figuratively hand in hand. Starting with what, at the Mesopotamian site, is called the 'archaic' technique – chevrons and other designs in matt red paint on a burnished surface or shiny paint on a dull finish – they developed in time a 'standard' form of decoration, in which the most common element is a closely cross-hatched band of ornament around the rim of the vessel, and the paint matt upon a matt surface. Then, at both sites, came what Garstang has called the Halafian impact; the adoption of an entirely new style of ware and ornament of the type first found by the German excavator M. von Oppenheim at Tell Halaf on the Turco-Syrian frontier, but best and most fully revealed by M. E. L. Mallowan at Arpachiyah near Nineveh. This is an attractive kind of pottery, finely made and finished with a half polish, which gives it a 'soapy' feeling in the hand. Paint of two different colours is used in its advanced form, and a repertoire of patterns, sometimes arranged centrifugally on the inside of an open dish, which it would be impossible here to describe or enumerate. During this period at Mersin locally peculiar features among the pottery are difficult to isolate; but in its final stages there already begins to appear a large, gourd-shaped jar with ornament in groups of parallel lines, which was to become the symbol *par excellence* of Mersin painted pottery at the height of its Chalcolithic development, as represented by the now-famous Level Sixteen.

PREHISTORIC FORTRESS

For it was in this level and at this juncture in the history of the Cilician site that the evidence was found of something entirely epoch-making having occurred. From a peaceful agricultural village, unprotected save by its now considerable elevation above the level of the plain, the place was suddenly changed into a carefully planned and constructed military fortress, with quarters for a considerable garrison. Gone were the stock-folds and granaries of the farming community and the unplanned tangle of peasants' cottages. In their place Garstang's excavation revealed a segment of an enclosure surrounded by a polygonal fortress-wall with a fortified gateway, and within, a range of uniform 'quarters' for the defenders. Also falling within the area examined was part of a more commodious building, perhaps the residence of a garrison commander. The evidence thus suddenly provided of highly organized military activity at so early a period was hardly less surprising than the discovery a few years earlier at Tepe Gawra, a contemporary site in North Iraq, of a sacred precinct containing three elaborately planned temples. To the concept of organized religion is thus added that of communal defence and the outcome in both cases is the birth of formal architecture.

It was clear from the beginning that the little fortress at Mersin had been destroyed by fire, perhaps deliberately after a successful assault. The buildings were filled with ashes and the charred remains of their timber roofs, beneath which, as is often the case when the occupants have left in a hurry, their furniture, weapons, or other possessions and the general

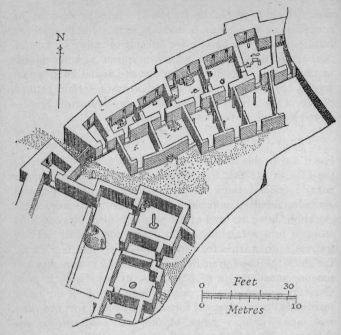

Figure 6. The prehistoric fortress at Mersin

mise en scène of garrison life remained substantially as it had been before their departure on that ill-fated day, some time in the first half of the fourth millennium B.C.

The fortress-wall was of mud-brick, about a metre and a half thick, standing upon a high stone base. There were shallow offsets where it changed direction and irregular shaped towers with gate-chambers protecting the entrance on either side. An amusing feature directly inside the gateway was a well-worn 'mounting-stone', such as one would find at the entrance to a medieval English castle. The 'barrack rooms' which were ranged against the inside of the wall each consisted of a standard unit; a living-room and enclosed courtyard, divided from its neighbours by a party-wall. Each room was provided with two slit-windows, commanding a view (and possibly an 'area of fire') over the slope of the mound outside, placed at a low level near the floor, for the convenience of a people who relaxed in a squatting position. The furniture of a typical room consisted of a hearth in the centre, a hand grindstone of which the lower element was built into the floor, some pottery vessels of various sizes, and, in one corner a large bin, constructed of sticks and clay, into which grain or flour could be poured from above and drawn off into a jar through a hole in the bottom. The yard outside each room had post-holes in the floor, suggesting that it too had on some occasion been covered in. In every case one corner was occupied by a pile of unused sling ammunition; pellets of baked clay about the size and shape of a hen's egg, which suggested that a prolonged defence of the fortress had on this occasion been anticipated.

The part of the 'commanders' residence' which could be examined, consisted of a range of three much larger rooms, approached by passing through a vestibule into an open court which contained a huge domed baking oven. These rooms also had been destroyed by fire, and crushed beneath their fallen roofs were a number of pottery vessels of all sizes in a reasonably good state of preservation. They represented for the most part types of painted ware, including the 'gourd-shaped' vessels which in this and the immediately succeeding levels are peculiar to this site.

In terms of Mesopotamian chronology the little fortress at Mersin represented the transition from the Tell Halaf to the Al 'Ubaid period.* Indeed, among its ruins were found the first fragments of pottery ornamented with the freely-drawn 'swags' and 'meanders' which one associates with that phase. But side by side with these and in far more common use were local products like those found in the 'commander's residence'. The 'gourd-shaped' vessels were particularly common. They had two loop-handles at the shoulder and were decorated with dark paint on a burnished cream slip. There were two sorts of design: one being groups of straight or wavy

* In *Antiquity*, No. 109, M. E. L. Mallowan proposes a somewhat later date.

parallel lines applied with a 'multiple brush' (rather like the battery of pens which every schoolboy at some time endeavours to use for his 'lines'), and the other, panels or chevrons of parallel lines, painted separately. There were also small bowls, similarly decorated, with two tag-like upright handles on the rim, and others with a design of white-filled incisions on a black finish like Neolithic ware. Both these and other more eccentric forms of ornament presently to appear, such as the tri-chrome pots in which burnishing is restricted to certain parts of the pattern, would be more worth describing in detail if their origin or foreign relations were known. Unfortunately this is not the case, and for the moment they can only be regarded as locally peculiar or otherwise enigmatic.

The ruins of the Level Sixteen fortress seem to have been most effectively razed after the fire which destroyed it. Yet the attempt to render the settlement defensible was not abandoned. At least twice during the 'late' Chalcolithic period new enclosure walls were built, and a large square tower of mud-brick rose to protect the entrance. But the character of these later fortifications was less easy to determine on account of the chance circumstance that the area covered by the excavation was at this level honeycombed with circular grain pits of a later period. This phenomenon had the additional disadvantage of imperilling the reliability of stratigraphic evidence, and was partly responsible for the fact that the contents of the last and in a sense most vital Chalcolithic strata were a shade less well-defined than those below. Their importance of course consisted in the fact that now for the first time evidence appeared of connexions with the new settlers in the Aegean province and Anatolia proper.

Among the remains of these final Chalcolithic occupations at Mersin only the pottery could serve any useful purpose. Sandwiched between rather decadent survivals of the 'Ubaid ware were some features suggesting the so-called Jemdet-Nasr phase in Mesopotamia, which marked the transition from pre-history to the dynastic régime in the first centuries of the third millennium. But so closely associated with these that they could only be separated by a rather arbitrary subdivision of the final occupation, were shapes till then associated with the first settlement at Troy, and, perhaps most significant of all, a group of impressive vessels, some of them of the 'chalice' type, in burnished black clay, decorated over the burnish with lines of matt white paint. This pottery was already known at Troy and half a dozen sites in Anatolia, where it was considered to be essentially the product of a people committed by usage to a black or dark red pottery with a shiny finish. At Mersin where the shiny wares of the Neolithic period were long forgotten it looked distinctly exotic.

FIRST ANATOLIAN SETTLEMENTS

Now, therefore, we must once more face the whole vexed problem of the first Chalcolithic settlements in Anatolia and their comparative chronology: but first it may be well to examine in greater detail the earliest foundation of a city at Troy, to which these finds at Mersin have now suddenly drawn our attention.

TROY I*

Traces of the first occupation of the Hissarlik mound had already been revealed at an early stage in Schliemann's excavations by the great 'north trench' which he cut across the summit. But to-day, hardly more is known than that it was founded upon the natural rock and took the form of a tiny fortified enclosure less than 50 metres across at its widest point. What remained of the enclosure wall was of stone, about $2\frac{1}{2}$ metres thick, with a scarped face on the outside. By analogy with later structures this is now taken to have been the substructure of a wall of sun-dried brick, perhaps strengthened with wooden beams. Just sufficient had survived to suggest that it had projecting towers; and one of these, which was located directly beneath a gateway of later times, may have guarded the entrance. The irregular angle at which this structure is set is a slightly reminiscent of the Chalcolithic fortress at Mersin, which chronologically must be considered

* Published in detail by Blegen. See Bibliography (2).

the only precedent by which it can be judged. The only other significant architectural finds associated with the first settlement were made by the American expedition. These were the stone foundations of houses – rectangular buildings with the two longer sides prolonged at one end to form a porch. In them it was immediately possible to recognize the *megaron* – a standard domestic unit, favoured by Early Bronze Age builders on the distant mainland of Greece, and accordingly considered until quite recently to be characteristic of that area. Its evolution was even ingeniously traced through a succession of geometrical adjustments from a circular shepherd's hut.* To-day, however, the impression is rapidly gaining ground that it may equally well have had an Anatolian origin.

Another group of identical or closely affiliated people appear simultaneously to have settled beyond the narrow straits which separate the coast of Asia Minor from Lesbos (Mitylene); and the excavations of W. Lamb at Thermi on the north-east coast of that island have effectively supplemented the information about them provided by the deepest levels of the Trojan mound. Miss Lamb described them as : 'a peaceful, pastoral community, living in well-built stone houses of a considerable size without any fortification' – till finally a threat from overseas made elaborate defences necessary. She says: 'They possessed the usual animals, goats, pigs, small dogs, and probably oxen; they supplemented their stores by hunting and fishing; they probably tilled the soil, growing grain for bread to bake in their ovens, though no trace of corn has been found. Milk and meat are the most obvious items in their bill of fare. . . . Their handicrafts display varying stages of ability; as metalworkers they were primitive, as stone-workers degenerate, as potters enterprising and artistic, as spinners and weavers adequate to their needs. In short, their development was in no way abnormal.' One might in fact go further and say that there was little beyond their ignorance of money and explosives to distinguish them from the Aegean

* Cf. W. B. Dinsmoor, *Architecture of Ancient Greece*, p. 5 ff. A megaron has recently been discovered at Kültepe in a Late Bronze Age setting.

peasants, say of Lord Byron's time. The reader will therefore be hardly surprised to learn that archaeologically their most revealing legacy is pottery.

'Troy I' potters had no knowledge of the revolving wheel, and fired their vessels to the darkest colour possible, some-times pure black. Like the Neolithic wares which have been described earlier in this chapter, they usually also polished them with a pebble or bone to give a shiny finish. One distinc-tive shape, which afterwards became characteristic of Anato-lian ceramics throughout the whole of the third millennium, was a rather globular jug with its vertical neck cut away to form an upward-pointing spout and a single loop-handle between the nape and shoulder. These had round or flattened bottoms, but there were also open vases supported on deep ring bases or even projecting feet. Perhaps most charac-teristic of all – an absolute criterion in fact of the period, even when found beyond the limits of the Troad – are bowls with a sudden thickening and carination just below the rim. In general, the Trojan potters seem to have preferred pierced 'lugs' to handles, and in the case of these carinated bowls, they take the form of two ornamental excrescences laid horizon-tally along the rim. Another typical bowl had a flat, bevelled surface inside the rim, ornamented with a variety of simple incised designs, or occasionally elementary human features. Little more need be said, save that white-filled incisions and the white-painted designs we have observed at Mersin appear both in this setting and the contemporary one at Thermi.

At both sites copper-workers made needles or pins and simple knife-blades; stone-workers shaped hammer-axes out of greenstone or even jade. As for the burial practices of the period, they are illustrated in extra-mural cemeteries, disco-vered at sites like Yortan and Babaköy in the vicinity of Troy, which also yielded a great deal of supplementary pottery. The skeletons were almost invariably enclosed in *pithoi* – large earthenware vessels laid on their sides, with their mouths oriented towards the east. But burial beneath house floors, a favourite Anatolian custom, was not uncommon even in the west.

Blegen's analysis, both of his own finds and those from Schliemann's 'first city', showed parallels with the Early Helladic and Early Cycladic settlements in the Aegean, which led him to equate 'Troy I' with the first phase of the Early Bronze Age in those parts, and to date it approximately between 3000 and 2600 B.C. But, since he also attributes the latter date to the beginning of what we must call the Copper Age on the Plateau, the Anatolian Chalcolithic settlements which we are about to discuss, and which directly preceded the Copper Age, must also be attributed to that same period.

We are therefore again faced with the terminological anomaly of a late Chalcolithic period on the Plateau corresponding to an early phase of what is already called 'Early Bronze Age' in the west; a situation from which there at present seems to be no escape, though it greatly confuses the discussion of finds intermediate between the two areas.* Setting aside, then, for the moment sites in the west such as Kumtepe near Troy and Fikirtepe on the Bosphorus, which have produced material demonstrably earlier than Troy I, let us now turn to the Chalcolithic settlements on the Plateau.

ALISHAR 'O'†

First, then, there is the evidence of the deepest levels reached by von der Osten at Alishar Hüyük, and it should be said at once that it would not be possible here to go into details of the controversy which still persists as to their dating. It must suffice first to mention once more the so-called 'fruit-stands', large bowls supported on footed stems. Clumsily proportioned when they first appear, they become more elegant as the potter's skill or taste increases. They are made of dark grey or black clay with a polished slip, and some later examples have the extra refinement of horizontal fluting in the stem. With them are jars running to very large sizes in the same ware, and in the earlier stages, much smaller vessels decorated with incised ornament. Secondly it should perhaps be recorded that

* See diagram p. xx.
  Published by von der Osten. See Bibliography (1).

Bittel has detected in the material from this source an 'early' and 'late' period, both of them Chalcolithic, and suggests that the transition from the first stage to the second takes place a little earlier than the foundation of the first settlement at Troy. The 'early' period would thus be placed in the final centuries of the fourth millennium.

GÜLÜJEK*

Koşay's interesting little settlement at Büyük Gülüjek, near Alaja in the Halys 'bend', had little in common with Alishar. On the surface there was an occupation dating from Phrygian times, and then a deep deposit of sterile clay. Patiently removing this, Koşay found 'a homogeneous culture filling about two and a half metres but showing three architectural subdivisions'. There were bone, flint and obsidian implements, bored axes of stone and two of copper, obviously made by accomplished smiths, all lying among ruins of the usual mud-brick house-walls on stone foundations, such as one would find at any period anywhere else in Anatolia. But the pottery was most distinctive; handmade vessels in dark brown burnished clay, with a tremendous variety of ingenious incised ornament. There are 'bold groups of deep indentations, sometimes bordered by incision, or finely drawn linear patterns ... lines with punctures at the ends, like stitches in leatherwork, or at either side like leaves'. Again the vessels run to very large sizes, and there are curious low-waisted jars with two handles at the neck, the latter being adorned on top with extraordinary modelled excrescences sometimes in the shape of animals. Generally speaking there is little here to remind one of Alishar, and had it not been that many of its features were afterwards found in the deepest levels at neighbouring Alaja, Gülüjek might even have been hard to place chronologically. As it is, Koşay is satisfied that it represents a stage immediately preceding the beginning of the Copper Age, and that the transition from one to the other created no interruption in the life of the Alaja settlement.

* To be published by Koşay.

DUNDARTEPE*

One more group of sites in Anatolia must be mentioned. These were discovered by Özgüç, in a district near Samsun on the Black Sea coast, which, like so many others, at that time remained *terra incognita* from a prehistoric point of view. At Dündartepe, the most conspicuous site, the Chalcolithic pottery combined features both of Alishar and of Gülüjek, though the famous 'fruit-stands' were missing. Here for a change were rectangular houses built of 'wattle-and-daub', as one might perhaps have expected in an afforested area.

Apart, then, from surface finds, which have begun to give the first evidence of distribution, the greater part of our knowledge concerning the Chalcolithic settlements on the Plateau is thus accounted for. It only remains once more to emphasize the significance, first of Bittel's discovery at Fikirtepe† on the Bosphorus of a village using pottery like that of Gülüjek, and secondly, the occurrence at Kumtepe near Troy of 'fruit-stands' identical with those used at Alishar. The comparative dating of all these settlements in relation to Troy I, as far as it is at present known, can be represented in a simple diagram (p. xx).

The occurrence of the 'white-on-black' pottery (which also appears at Gülüjek) in or after the absolutely final phase of the Chalcolithic period at Mersin, once more draws attention to the tardiness with which Anatolia was apparently populated, in comparison with lands further south. At the same time, one must always bear in mind the minimum of pre-historic research which has so far taken place in this area. A recent mound survey in south-western Turkey has, for instance recorded sites where the monochrome pottery, and even a few painted sherds, are most intriguingly similar to those from the early levels at Mersin. Until these and other archaeological 'pointers' have been adequately investigated it would perhaps be unwise to invest the negative evidence with too much significance.

* Discussed by W. Lamb in *Iraq*. See Bibliography.

† The writer is indebted to Dr H. Çambel for allowing him to see the material from this site in Istanbul University.

CHAPTER 6

Second Phase : The Copper Age

IN a previous chapter we have already visualized the Copper Age as a prolonged and formative phase in the evolution of Anatolian culture. During six or seven centuries of tranquil development, the Plateau at last came to resemble an enclave of simply equipped communities at a more or less similar stage of agricultural development. It may well be shown by discoveries in the future to have been no less politically united than the Hittite kingdom which it remotely anticipated. In the absence of any written records referring to the period, our ability to characterize it even in these general terms implies a tribute to the patient efforts of a small group of excavators in our own generation. Yet the glimpses which their individual discoveries have afforded us are mere tantalizing vignettes, like 'stills' from a film, which must eventually be co-ordinated into a coherent document. To fill the many gaps in that picture is a task for the future.

One becomes particularly conscious of this situation if any attempt is made to visualize for instance the architecture of the Copper Age. For no traces of any public building belonging to the period have yet been found in Anatolia proper and our knowledge even of military defences is limited to formless scraps of enclosure-wall encountered at Alishar and elsewhere. In fact the settlements so far examined have mostly been of the village or market-town variety, where formal planning has generally to be sacrificed to exigencies of space; and little has consequently been learnt till now even about fashions in domestic architecture. It is accordingly hardly surprising that, after taking note of exceptional discoveries such as the Alaja tombs, archaeology has been compelled to fall back on the typology of small finds, and above all on that 'indestructible relic of bygone activity', the pottery vessels. Any attempt, therefore, which may be made here to summarize our conclusions to date concerning the chronological and regional sub-divisions of the Copper-Age discoveries, is liable to involve us in a tangle of 'wares', shapes and ceramic techniques, and their attribution to stratigraphical phases at a score of sites, whose very numbering has frequently been amended in deference to the outcome of professional controversy. For the present purpose a solution which has occurred to the writer is to outline the results of a small sounding made by him in collaboration with a Turkish colleague, N. Gökçe, as recently as 1949 at a Plateau site where the evidence of occupation during the Copper Age proved most fortunately to have been both continuous and characteristic, successively incorporating, as it appears now to have done, many of the most significant features of comparable discoveries made elsewhere in Anatolia.

POLATLI*

Unlike most sites on the Plateau, Polatli Hüyük showed no traces of occupation during the Chalcolithic period. The earliest settlers, who built their houses on clean gravel beside a spring of water, used rather primitive pottery and implements, but these showed no traces of the distinctive features characteristic of, say, Büyük Güllüjek or the deepest levels at Alaja and Alishar. By the time the village had been twice re-built on its earlier ruins, the well-known criteria of the Copper Age were everywhere apparent, and continued to be so during thirteen successive building levels, which represented two-fifths of the mound's total height of 25 metres. The sixteen occupation levels, by which these were succeeded, dated from the Kültepe and Hittite periods.

One of the first facts which became evident during the Polatli excavations was that the Copper Age could be divided into two distinct sub-phases, and that the earlier phase had ended in the complete destruction of the village by fire. Apart from the actual trenches, where the effects of this disaster could be studied in detail, a dark red line of burnt débris could be traced all round the unexcavated flanks of the mound. Here

* Published in *Anatolian Studies*. See Bibliography.

then at once was an event in the history of the place which one might attempt to correlate with the Copper Age chronology of other excavated sites, and when a detailed examination was later made, particularly of discrepancies in the pottery before and after the disaster, the parallelism became most convincing.

A temporary interruption in the continuity of the local culture, followed by some typological innovations, could be detected at half a dozen other plateau sites, like Karaoğlan in the west at Kusura and in the north and east at places as far afield as Dündartepe near Samsun and Karaz in the Erzurum area; furthermore in several of them the transition was marked by some obvious disaster. At two sites, Ahlatlibel and Alaja, the later sub-phase seemed to be entirely missing and in the case of the second of these it was easy to assume, as indeed the excavators themselves had already done, that, after the confla-gration which occurred at a period immediately subsequent to that of the famous tombs, the site remained unoccupied almost until Hittite times. From this one inferred that the tombs should be dated to Polatli's earlier sub-phase, and this was most gratifyingly confirmed by the discovery in Polatli's early Copper Age levels of a small copper jug and a shaft-hole hammer axe, both exactly comparable to metal objects from the Alaja tomb treasure.

Pottery. The pottery too seemed admirably to fit the picture of successive ceramic fashions at other sites. The final occupa-tion levels of the earlier phase were the richest, and these were characterized by a profusion of small bowls and jugs, orna-mented with shallow fluting or corrugations, and beautifully finished with a burnished or polished red slip. Occasional examples with a polished black finish reminded one that the contemporary pottery of Ahlatlibel near Ankara, where a black slip was generally preferred to a red one, could only have reflected a local fashion. Most of the pottery just described was hand-made. In fact one of the first fragmentary vessels to show traces of the potter's wheel proved, after piecing together, to be a fine example of the elegant two-handled goblet called *depas amphikypellon*, associated in everyone's

minds at that time with Schliemann's 'second settlement' at
Troy in the Aegean province. At Polatli it appeared with other
features of Troy II at a level directly preceding the destructive
fire; so that there was an immediate temptation to connect this
disaster with that which destroyed the Trojan citadel about
the same time. Typological parallels between the 'Treasure of
Priam', found buried beneath the burnt débris of the latter,
and the Alaja tombs, whose interments preceded a similar
disaster, had in fact already given rise to some speculation on
these lines, and even provided material for Schaeffer's study
of the areas affected by earthquakes.

'*White-on-Black.*' Pottery in the first Copper Age phase at
Polatli was almost universally monochrome black or red in
colouring, with the black giving way to red and brown in the
later levels. An interesting exception to this rule is the ware
ornamented with lines of white paint over the burnished surface. These vessels are really extraordinarily similar to those
discovered in a Chalcolithic setting at Mersin and elsewhere,
which we have already described; only now the ornament is
applied to some of the most characteristically Copper Age
shapes, and is used on red-slipped vessels as well as black. It
makes a simultaneous occurrence at sites in the Ankara area,
notably at Karaoğlan, and in the west establishes a link with
the Aegean province, where examples have been found at
almost every site excavated. A recent mound survey of South-
western Turkey has shown that its centre of distribution
appears to have been in Pisidia, where it perhaps represents
the most common form of decoration at this period. If, as has
been suggested, its earlier appearance in the Chalcolithic
period implies a relationship with lands north of the Aegean,
one must take it that this connexion was now renewed after a
lapse of several centuries. The technique itself is highly
unpractical, owing to the ease with which the paint can be
removed by rubbing, and it would hardly have been used
except by a people committed by convention to dark pottery
with shiny surfaces. Fragments of pottery ornamented in dark
paint on a light clay are indeed so rare in the Copper Age

generally as to appear exotic, when found at Polatli, Alishar and elsewhere.

'Cappadocian' and 'Red-Cross.' The beginning of the secondary phase was characterized by the disappearance of almost all the distinctive classes of pottery mentioned above. In their place came a number of innovations which included a much more general use of the potter's wheel. In its final levels the first sherds of painted 'Cappadocian' ware were beginning to appear and examples of the curious bowl with a red cross painted across the centre, which here, as at virtually every site which has been excavated from the Aegean to the Euphrates, heralds the end of the Copper Age and indicates a date sometimes in the twentieth century B.C. This 'secondary phase' of the Copper Age (Phase II at Polatli) in fact had so little in common with its predecessor that we have more recently come to think of it as transitional: in the revised terminology now proposed (Diagram p. xx), it is accordingly designated as 'Early Bronze III'.

Architecture. The sounding at Polatli revealed no more and no less than other sites in connexion with domestic architecture. Parts of several substantial houses were cleared, whose walls were of sun-dried brick on a stone foundation about a metre high. In one case there were traces in the thickness of the brickwork of wooden beam reinforcements. These might well be expected, even at this early age, since they represent an age-old technical tradition, reflected in the 'half-timber' houses of modern Anatolia. We shall presently describe in detail its employment in large-scale contemporary buildings at Troy.

Burials. Burial customs were also illustrated at Polatli, plain shaft-graves in the earliest levels; urn-burials in those directly preceding the end of the first phase; and a cist-tomb lined and sealed with thin slabs of limestone, in which the skeleton lay in a contracted position facing southwards. The copper jug,*

* See p. 93.

matching gold vessels in the Alaja tombs came from a similar grave. The burial in the stone-lined cist had an interesting sequel. It was located in an empty space between two houses, and in the building level immediately above that to which it belonged a little circular building of the *tholos* type had been constructed directly above it, and its rectangular porch was found to be full of small offerings. Circular buildings of this sort had already been noted at certain sites such as Etiyokuşu in the Ankara area, and the new discovery suggested that they might have had the function of funerary chapels, built to mark the traditional location of a grave, a practice till now unknown at this period.

THE ALAJA TOMBS*

The mention of burial customs brings us logically to the important subject of the Alaja tombs. Some indication has already been given of the unique position which they occupy in the records of Anatolian archaeology, and it needs hardly a glance at the aggregate of their contents, skilfully restored and displayed in the Ankara Museum, to convince one of the artistic accomplishment which enhances their intrinsic value. In this context, therefore, they merit rather prolonged attention.

One has first to imagine a group of interments, small in number (the Turkish expedition could discover no more than thirteen) and crowded together in an area hardly 30 metres square, but dating from a succession of occupation levels, which must have represented at least several generations. The fact that, in addition, several tombs contained the bodies both of a man and a woman and that both were accompanied by rich funerary gifts, some of them of an obviously secular nature, has encouraged their finder to think of them collectively as a 'royal cemetery'. If this be correct, its conspicuous position near the centre of the city in a situation presumably surrounded by buildings must have been considered a deterrent to tomb robbers.

The average tomb consisted of a rectangular pit measuring

* Published by Koşay. See Bibliography (12).

4·00 × 8·00 × 0·75 metres deep, with a line of stones laid around its base. In one corner of this the body was placed, lying on its side in a contracted position, with its face, as may accordingly have been the common practice in the Copper Age, turned approximately to the south. If it was a man he was accompanied by his weapons and if a woman by her ornaments and toilet requisites. On the side towards which the body faced there was laid a variety of objects which seemed to have a religious significance, such as 'solar' discs and figurines. Also in the neighbourhood of the body lay domestic vessels and utensils, and, usually at about the centre of the pit, various metal images of bulls or stags. After these objects had been deposited in their correct places the shaft was covered in with a ceiling of wooden beams and these in turn were sealed with clay and loose earth. At this point a second row of stones was placed to mark the position of the tomb, and beside them were laid in pairs the heads and hoofs of beasts which had been sacrificed as part of the funeral ritual. A litter of other bones, perhaps belonging to the same animals, directly above the tomb sometimes suggested that the ritual had ended in a feast. In at least one case the bones of a favourite dog lay among those of the animals sacrificed.

To give some further details of a typical example: in the tomb distinguished by the excavators as 'H', the occupant had clearly been fully dressed and wore a variety of ornaments, including a gold filigree diadem with a tassel of gold ribbons, double bracelets, ankle rings, a row of small double violin shaped figures and a quantity of pins and fastenings, all of gold. Laid in front of his face was a grotesque trio of female figurines in copper, two golden bowls in a metal container and another full of small gems, a number of finely fluted jugs and other gold vessels, one of them inlaid with fragments of jade* and a metal comb. Elsewhere in the tomb were vessels of silver, a copper 'feeding-bowl', a copper 'solar disc' of the open 'grille' type with a sort of buckle by which it could be suspended, some gold and silver bands which had evidently served to strengthen a wooden chest, and finally the copper

* Cf. Koşay, p. 157.

'terminal' figure of a steer, bound and inlaid with electrum, which is now considered one of the masterpieces of Copper Age metalwork. (Plate 5)

Some individual items from other tombs also deserve special mention. Among the weapons is a dagger with a blade of iron (a metal far more valuable than gold at this time) and a gold handle in the form of a crescent, which has been compared to a similar weapon found in the 'Royal Tombs' at Ur. Another copper dagger, of a type which has parallels in Cyprus during the Early Bronze Age, has a ribbed blade with two small eye-holes and a tang bent at right angles. There is also a spherical stone macehead and battle-axe, both with handles sheathed in gold. Among the vessels there are the beautiful gold chalices with their stems delicately fluted and the strange metal cauldron with its ornament of snakes in relief. Notable minor objects are the copper figurines with breasts and, for some reason, boots of gold, large simple belt-buckles of gold, pins with double-spiral heads and a great variety of beads and pendants, mostly of precious metal.

The 'standards' have become too familiar from illustrations to need describing in detail. The basis of one type is a trellised metal disc with various excrescences and pendants: the other is a simple figure of an animal, usually a ruminant stag, or ox, with its legs drawn together to fit the narrow base, attachable to a carrying staff. Sometimes both elements are used, the beast and disc being decoratively combined. The prevalent impression that such objects formed the terminals of standards carried in procession was strengthened by the presence in their vicinity of fluted gold handles, perhaps belonging to the staffs upon which they were mounted or the supports of a canopy. The radial excrescences on one disc have been partly responsible for their identification as sun symbols, and horn-shaped protuberances on another have even been associated with the crescent moon.* Little can be said about the animal symbol-

* More recently it has been suggested that the discs were fixed upright on the shaft of a chariot and that upon these 'horns' the reins rested. Apart from practical considerations, the occurrence of the 'horns' only on a minor proportion of the discs makes this less probable. (Cf. Plates 4 and 5)

ism, save that the species to which special significance seems to be attributed, such as the stag and panther, suggest the mentality of a mountain people.

The figurines and 'idols' generally have been compared by H. Z. Koşay to the 'teraphim' household gods of the Old Testament. Almost without exception they have female attributes grotesquely accentuated and, from the conventionalized figurines, which include the little 'fiddle-shaped' ornaments, cut out of sheet gold and linked together in pairs by their hips and hands, to the much larger and more freely modelled images with their gold boots, they should perhaps be thought of as symbols of the 'mother-goddess', the age-old fertility cult of the east, whose central figure survived in the person of Phrygian Cybele and the Roman Magna Mater.

From the Alaja tomb finds much is clearly to be learnt about the technological advancement of the Copper Age, particularly in the realm of metalwork. As Koşay emphasizes, contemporary craftsmen had long passed the apprentice stage. They were proficient both in smelting and hammering and could make a rigid joint by soldering precious metals. Relief-ornament could be obtained by a *repoussé* process and sheet metal manipulated for sheathing or inlay. Gold could be drawn into wire or polished with fine sand. It would even appear that for welding, say gold and silver together, an alloy was introduced to reduce the fusion point of the two metals. Iron, which is known from documents of later times to have been at some periods at least ten times as valuable as gold, now appears almost simultaneously, both here and in Mesopotamia, for the first time in the history of metallurgy. (Almost the next example of a knife with an iron blade is from the tomb of Tutankhamen, which may be dated about a thousand years later.)

Dating the Tombs. When the Alaja graves were first found and their date still uncertain, there was a tendency to compare them with the tombs of the early Sumerian dynasties at Ur, and the similarity of certain objects found in both settings resulted in a suggestion that the Anatolian culture might be an

offshot of the Mesopotamian. But this theory has since been
discarded owing to the discrepancy in time and the notable
absence at Alaja of so many primary characteristics of Sumerian craftsmanship. Since then, a most determined effort has
been made to find typological parallels in other settings. Here
some success has been met with, for instance, among the
Trojan 'treasures', where the battle-axe, double-spiral ornament and various forms of ear-rings and pierced pins are also
represented, and in the case of distinctive types like the
'Cypriot dagger'. Koşay in fact finds some indication that
Central Anatolia was a technological 'distribution centre'.
Indeed, if availability of raw material may be expected to give
some measure of its capacity for this function, an abundance
of copper and some silver has always been plentiful there, and
even gold could be obtained locally in small quantities by
'washing'.

Yet finally to summarize both Koşay's own conclusions
and those of other scholars, who have studied the implications of this rich material, in regard to the status and origin of
the Copper Age culture which they represent, would be to do
no more than emphasize the enigma which till now it seems
to present. Landsberger, for example, draws attention to the
fact that its material culture in vernacular form, as illustrated
for instance by ceramic practice, survives into the subsequent
Hittite period with only minor changes and innovations. Its
aristocratic, or as one might say, 'mandarin' manifestation,
however, as represented by the appointments of the Alaja
tombs, ends with the period, and its most distinctive characteristics never again appear. He infers from this the mere
substitution of one ruling caste for another, with little effect
upon the body of the nation. This seems convincing, but
leaves the origin of the earlier rulers of Alaja in doubt. Koşay
prefers on the whole to visualize an eclectic culture composed
both of indigenous and extraneous elements.

As a postscript to this subject it should be added that a
chance find in 1950, in a somewhat equivocal setting at a site
near Amasya, has produced a fluted jug and chalices of gold,
together with a quantity of silver and copper objects, identical

with those in the Alaja tombs. It may no longer, therefore, be possible to think of the city of Alaja as culturally unique or of its culture as narrowly localized.

WESTERN PROVINCES

We must now leave the Copper Age folk on the Plateau and turn to examine the parallel development of peoples in the Aegean province to the west. Here at last we may start by seriously considering the subject of architecture, for at Troy there are some traces of military fortifications and even of public buildings. They belong, of course, to the second settlement, excavated by Schliemann and Dörpfeld, which they imagined at the time to be the remains of the Homeric city. After their much greater antiquity had come to be understood, they were re-examined by the American excavators: but in view of the large proportion of the citadel covered by the original excavations, this later investigation could not be expected to add much to the original picture. Dörpfeld had detected three main building periods during the lifetime of the second settlement, and among the eight sub-periods into which Blegen afterwards divided it, these correspond to the 'phases' called IIa and IIc. Owing to the unique position which they occupy in architectural history, the construction dating from both periods merit a rather detailed description.

TROY II

The citadel, as it appeared at the beginning of the second settlement (IIA), was still by any standard extremely small – hardly more than 100 yards in diameter at its widest point; and it is a little difficult now to see how the early excavators were able to reconcile its modest appointments with Homer's grandiose descriptions of the city and its palaces.* Dörpfeld himself had already come to assume the existence of a much larger enclosure for which the citadel on its central hill provided a nucleus, though he had been unable to discover any archaeological evidence in support. In fact, even at the early period in the third millennium, to which the second settlement

* E.g. *Iliad* VI, 242.

is now attributed, it can hardly be taken to represent anything more pretentious than the fortress of some local chieftain.

The Fortress (IIA). It took the form of an irregular polygon, with small square towers at the angles, and could be approached, as far as is known, only through a single gateway on the south side. The wall itself was about 12 feet thick and built of sun-dried bricks equivalent in size to two of the kiln-baked English variety laid side by side. At intervals of about three courses, it was reinforced with wooden beams about 12 inches square, laid longitudinally in the thickness of the brickwork and occasionally strengthened with cross-braces, whose ends appeared in the face of the wall. Only the charred remains of these beams survived in the chases through which they had passed, and the surrounding brickwork was much discoloured and hardened by fire. Dörpfeld therefore at first assumed that their purpose had been for baking the brickwork *in situ* after the construction of the wall. It was some time before he realized that the traces of burning were due to a general conflagration.

It should here be mentioned that the description of the wall construction just given (IIA) applies actually to its remains when reconstructed to a new alignment in the third sub-phase of Troy II. On that occasion (IIc) the whole brick upper structure of the earlier wall was apparently removed, and all that remained was the stone sub-structure upon which it had stood. This consisted of a rubble core faced with large stones of irregular size, scarped at an angle of 45 degrees on the outside. By a fortunate circumstance the remains of the main gateway on the south side of the enclosure were also reasonably well-preserved, so that its plan and some details of its construction could be recovered. It proved to have been a remarkable structure for which it is hard to find a parallel in military architecture of so early a period. It took the form of a colossal tower about 18 metres square projecting from the citadel wall, through the centre of which the entry passed like a tunnel, sloping upwards to reach the higher level inside the enclosure. Having passed beneath the wall itself, but still not attained the required height, the ramp was prolonged, presumably in the form of an open cutting, and ended in a flight of steps opposite the entrance to the principal building within the citadel. Jambs at the southern entrance to the tunnel suggest that here the actual door was situated: the interior walls were of stone, strengthened at intervals of 2 metres by vertical wooden posts, which must also have supported the beams of a flat ceiling.

Buildings in the Citadel. In the interior of the citadel virtually all the original buildings seem to have been levelled at the beginning of the third sub-phase (IIc), preparatory to a new layout and general reconstruction (see Figure 7). A large section of the enclosure wall on the south side, as already mentioned, was rebuilt to new alignment, enclosing the ruins of the old southern gateway; its tunnel was now blocked and its towers demolished. To take its place two new gateways appeared, the more imposing of which faced south-east and the other south-west. Both of them, in common with a small inner portico which we shall presently mention, conform to a uniform plan, which must therefore be accepted as a contemporary architectural convention. In the large examples two gates face one another across a square chamber, whose side walls are prolonged at either end to form porticoes on the pattern of a *megaron*. In its simplest form the plan is H-shaped with a single door in the centre. Whether, like the megaron itself, this type of propylon was covered with a gabled roof or was prolonged upwards to form a tower, there can be at present no means of knowing.

A fairly clear impression of the general layout inside the citadel can now be obtained, partly as a result of the additions to and clarification of the plan, resulting from Blegen's secondary investigation (see Figure 7). The central feature is a building of the *megaron* type in its simplest possible form; square porch with a single doorway leading into a larger rectangular compartment having no more conspicuous feature than a central hearth. Beside it and only separated by enough space to allow for drainage, is a narrower building of the same sort, but

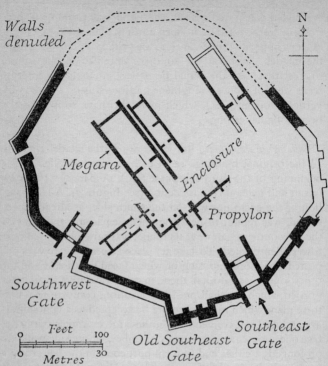

Figure 7. The Troy II citadel: second rebuilding

with two intercommunicating inner compartments. It has always been assumed that these two buildings together constituted the 'palace' itself, the larger one being for men and the smaller for women. If this assumption is correct, as it may well be, one's surprise at the elementary simplicity of the building is only modified by the realization of its impressive size (the larger *megaron* is over 33 feet wide and the length of the building more than three times as much). At a time when in Mesopotamia the Akkadian Kings or the Governors of Lagash were building their great complex residences, and the Pharaohs of the Old Kingdom their fine temples, these barn-like structures, with their rustic origin still so very evident, can only bring to mind the tribal austerities of the Aegean world in the third millennium.

As for structural details, like the outer enclosure, these *megara* had a stone sub-structure 8 feet deep, covered with stone slabs, upon which rested a wall of sun-dried brick 4 feet 9 inches thick. At every fourth course horizontal beams were laid along either face of the wall, tied together at intervals by cross-pieces. The ends of the projecting *antae* on either side of the porch were faced with six contiguous square posts standing on a stone base. These 'parastades', which occur also as terminations to the *antae* in the various gateways, have parallels in the later architecture of Greece, where, however, they occupy a more obviously practical position on the inner face of the antae, and support the main beam carrying entablature and pediment. Uncertainty as to the function of these Trojan examples makes the elevation of the porticoes problematical.

The approach to the palace unit was through the south-east gateway which was set approximately on the main axis of the larger *megaron*. But before reaching it one had to pass by way of a minor portico through a second wall enclosing an inner precinct. The southern corner of this precinct has been excavated by Blegen and gives at last a more comprehensible idea of the architectural setting in which the *megara* stood. Its wall has deep buttresses projecting at intervals of about 6 metres, and between these the Americans found the stone bases of wooden columns. It is therefore at least legitimate to think of the precinct as surrounded by a shady colonnade, in which one could have awaited one's turn to visit the palace. For the rest, buildings between the precinct and the outer enclosure wall, with the exception of two further *megara*, are fragmentary and appear to us without obvious meaning.

It will be remembered that, after the destruction of the second settlement by fire Troy fell upon less prosperous times, and it is thought that during the third, fourth and fifth period of its history, which account for the remainder of the Early Bronze Age, the citadel hill was occupied by a mere market town. From the point of view, therefore, of architecture at this time, little can be added to the testimony of the buildings described above.

The 'Treasures'. After the buildings, the next most important evidence of third-millennium culture at Troy was the metal objects discovered in the ruins of the second settlement. The main source of these were the various caches or hoards of valuable objects found by Schliemann among the ashes of the conflagration which destroyed the settlement in its final phase (IIG).

There were nine of these hoards in all, and the most important contained a very large collection of weapons, implements, ornaments and vessels of gold and silver, which came to be known as the 'Treasure of Priam'. In recent times so much controversy has arisen as to the number of the sub-phase, or even of the settlement to which these objects should rightly be attributed, that it may be interesting here to quote Schliemann's own account of their discovery, if only to emphasize how little conducive to accurate observation were the circumstances under which the find was made. He says: 'While following up the circuit wall and bringing more and more of it to light, I struck, at a point slightly north-west of the gate, on a large copper object of the most remarkable form, which attracted my attention all the more as I thought I saw gold glimmering behind it. On the top was a layer of reddish and brown calcined ruins from 4 to 5 feet thick as hard as stone, and above this again the wall of fortification (5 feet broad and 20 feet high) which must have been erected soon after the destruction of Troy. In order to secure the treasure from my workmen and save it for archaeology it was necessary to lose no time; so, although it was not yet the hour for breakfast, I immediately had the *paidos* (interval for rest) called, and while the men were eating and resting, I cut out the treasure with a large knife. This involved risk as the fortification wall, beneath which I had to dig, threatened every moment to fall on my head. And indeed I should not have succeeded in getting possession of the treasure without the help of my wife, who stood at my side ready to pack the things I cut out in her shawl and to carry them away. As I found all these articles together, packed into one another in the form of a rectangular mass, it seems certain that they were placed inside a wooden chest.'

This account, combined with supplementary evidence discovered by Blegen himself, has nevertheless enabled him confidently to attribute the major treasure, as well as the majority of the smaller hoards to the period immediately preceding the fire which put an end to the second settlement.* In the careful steel engravings which Schliemann published, and afterwards in the Völkerkunde Museum in Berlin, the aggregate of their contents made an impressive showing.

Yet it could not help being observed that the forms of the metal objects were on the whole primitive and the workmanship very rude. The personal ornaments in particular are merely cut out of gold sheeting or built up with coils of wire. The two most conspicuous groups compose elaborate diadems, one of which is seen as worn by Mrs Schliemann in a well-known portrait (Plate 3). It adorns the forehead with a fringe of little gold chains ending in small leaf- or flower-shaped pendants and longer tassels hang down at the sides. Both diadems, together with the sets of multiple necklaces and ear-rings with which they were worn, had been packed into a large silver jar; one of a dozen such vessels which were included in the hoard, and whose shapes were in some cases already made familiar by the contemporary pottery.

Particularly conspicuous were two silver jars with cup-shaped covers over their mouths and tubular lugs attached to the shoulder, through which a cord could be passed, while perhaps the most attractive shape of all was a 'sauce-boat' in gold with loop handles on either side and at either end the 'channel-spout' so much favoured by local potters. There were

* The opinion that Priam's Treasure was stratigraphically associated with the third city (Troy III) and not with the second is maintained by a leading French archaeologist, C. F. Schaeffer, in his book, *Stratigraphie comparée et chronologie de l'Asie occidentale*, p. 200 ff., and his conclusion has been accepted by R. Dussaud, *Prélydiens, Hittites et Achéens*, 1953, p. 80 ff, but this view is not held by Blegen and does not at present command general assent.

also spear- and arrow-heads, knife-blades, chisels, and other implements in bronze. Among objects of other materials were a grotesque and interesting female figurine of lead, with a swastika engraved on the pubic triangle, fiddle-shaped idols, conspicuously beautiful shaft-hole hammer-axes of semi-precious stone, and a little crudely carved ivory.

Among the items of jewellery found separately, some more elaborate bracelets and hair ornaments originally attributed to this level have since come to be considered as belonging rather to the Mycenaen period.

Other small objects of copper, bone, or terracotta were found in abundance; but their importance being largely for dating purposes, and their stratification usually inconclusive, their significance has been superseded by the small finds so meticulously catalogued by the American expedition. Many of the simpler features of everyday life, such as ornamental spindle whorls and terracotta brush handles, to take two random examples, at this time favoured forms which were common to the whole of Anatolia, and, indeed, to several neighbouring countries.

Pottery. The pottery of Troy II is closely linked with that of the three subsequent settlements, and ceramically at least there is no obstacle to thinking of the four combined phases as a single epoch. There are certain innovations after the end of the second settlement which may possibly correspond to the break in the continuity of the Copper Age, noted on the Plateau; and later in the fifth phase, the end of the third millennium and of the epoch concerned is heralded by the appearance of the now familiar 'red-crossed bowls' and the first tall-spouted pots of the Anatolian type.* For the rest, the pottery in general is on the whole unlike anything we have so far encountered. True, it is almost unrelievedly monochrome and the colouring black or red with a tendency to burnishing or polish. But the shapes for the most part have a strong individual

---

* For this reason, in the new system of terminology (diagram p. xx) Troy III, IV and V are equated with Polatli II and designated 'Early Bronze III'. (Cf. p. 64.)

Diagrammatic view of the excavations at Mersin

(a) and (b) Gold jewellery from Schliemann's 'Treasure of Priam'

Mrs Schliemann wearing the Trojan jewellery

Copper-age 'standards' from the tombs at Alaja

4

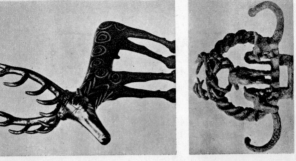

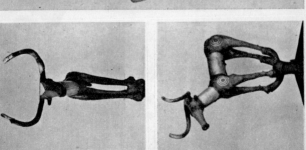

Objects in gold, silver, and copper from the tombs at Alaja

5

(a) Kültepe. A house in the Assyrian merchants' quarter

(b) Clay hearth and pottery in the *karum*

Business documents of the Assyrian merchants at Kültepe bearing the
impression of cylinder seals in several distinctive styles

Red burnished pottery
from Kültepe

8

Four painted vessels from the *karum* at Kültepe (Middle Bronze Age)

9

Two theriomorphic figures in painted clay from the *karum* at Kültepe

Stamp-seal and lead figurine from Kültepe,
both characteristically Anatolian

11

(a) Portal sculptures of the Hittite period at Alaja
(Late Bronze Age)

(b) Portal sculptures of the Hittite Empire period at Boghazköy
(Late Bronze Age)

(a) The 'Young God' embracing the figure of the King

(b) The 'Dagger God'

(c) The famous 'Warrior' sculpture from a city-gate at Boghazköy, now in the Ankara Museum

(a) and (b) are rock sculptures in the Yazilikaya shrine at Boghazköy

(a) Rock sculptures in the Yazilikaya shrine at Boghazköy.
A line of running warriors in the inner sanctuary

(b) Rock sculptures and Hittite masonry at Gavurkalesi near Ankara

Colossal statue of Hittite king from the palace gate at Malatya.
Eighth century B.C. Now in the Ankara Museum

(b) A Syro-Hittite relief from Carchemish, now in the Ankara Museum

(a) Statue of a god mounted on twin lions from Carchemish . . . The base only is now in the Ankara Museum

16

Two Syro-Hittite reliefs from Carchemish (not originally adjoining)

17

Entrance to the Syro-Hittite palace at Sakjegözü

(b) Figure of the King in a Sakjegözü relief

(a) The sphinx column-base from the palace at Sakjegözü

19

(a) Double-lion column-base from a portal at Tell Taynat. Syro-Hittite

(b) Ornamental column-base from Tell Taynat

The eighth century rock-relief at Ivriz in Taurus

Karatepe. A group of sculptures *in situ*, showing portal lions and inscribed slabs alternating with reliefs

Karatepe. Two slabs from the Upper Gate, composing the 'Banqueting-scene.' The smaller slab represents the 'Assyrian' style; the larger the 'Anatolian Hittite'

(a) to (c) Reliefs from Karatepe, including part of a hunting scene

24

An Urartian bronze cauldron and tripod from Altıntepe

(b) Loose turret of an Urartian model building

(a) Part of a bronze model of a building from Urartu

(a) Urartian bronze shield incised with lions and bulls

(b) Nude figure of a goddess or votary. A Vannic ivory

29

Two examples of Phrygian polychrome painted pottery

Two architectural terra-cottas of the Phrygian period:
(a) Centaur; (b) Warriors

31

The 'Midas Monument' in Phrygia

character which tends to make them easily recognizable when found in an extraneous setting in some other part of the country.

Perhaps the most distinctive feature of all are the so-called 'face urns' – round-bottomed jars with rudimentary human features modelled in relief on the neck, pellets to mark the breasts and navel, and sometimes projecting lugs like vestigial arms. Schliemann depicts one comic example, shaped like an almost spherical human figure with modelled arms carrying a small amphora and a tiny bowl balanced on its head. When there are no whimsical additions of this sort three or more legs are sometimes applied for the jar to stand on. Two gracefully looped handles are also a favourite device, and on this theme a distinctive variation is the elegant beaker with handles springing from its narrow base, which Schliemann associated with the *depas amphikypellon* mentioned by Homer, and whose appearance on the Plateau we have already noted.

Dating. The multiplicity of distinctive objects and wealth of ceramic material recovered from the remains of these four settlements (Troy II–V) as a result of Schliemann, Dörpfeld and Blegen's successive efforts, makes a formidable assemblage of archaeological material. It might in fact have been supposed that its detailed comparison with the results of many similar excavations in contingent areas such as Anatolia and the islands of the Aegean would by now at least have made practicable the establishment of some fairly precise system of dating. Unfortunately this is far from being the case. In Blegen's final summary of conclusions as to external relations and chronology, more than a little sense of frustration is evident. His primary complaints are, first, the prevailing doubt as to the exact provenance of almost all the objects in the Schliemann collection, secondly, the obstinate conservatism of the local craftsmen, which resulted in the elements most useful for external comparison remaining virtually unchanged throughout the entire period, and thirdly of the still unreliable chronology of the foreign material available for such comparison. He treats with some reserve the attempts of other scholars to overcome these limitations, and shows how the first of them impairs the reliability for dating purposes of almost all the key pieces, for instance among Schliemann's metal objects. As an example of the second circumstance he cites the case of the *depas* vessel, through whose occurrence in settings as remote as Central Anatolia on the one hand and Bulgaria on the other, Bittel had hoped to find parallels in those regions for the culture of Troy II, and points out that examples of the *depas* have now been found among material from the third, fourth and even fifth settlements. Generally speaking, he is himself hardly prepared to do more than loosely equate the four settlements in question with successive phases of the Early Bronze Age in the Aegean, eschewing all temptation to the hazard of more exact dating. The approximate initial dates to be inferred for each of the four settlements would accordingly be as follows: Troy II – 2600 B.C., Troy III – 2300 B.C., Troy IV – 2200 B.C., Troy V – 2050 B.C. He places the end of the Early Bronze Age at 1900 B.C.

CILICIA

In order to complete the picture of the Anatolian Copper Age, it is only necessary to add some reference to the few indications available of its development in Cilicia.

At Mersin the period from the end of the Chalcolithic Age to the beginning of the second millennium is poorly represented, and its remains less clearly stratified than the material from levels above and below. In compensation for this deficiency the American expedition at Tarsus was able to study at least the ceramic developments during these centuries in some detail. The reader, therefore, who is less surfeited with pottery-shapes than one imagines the workers at this site must have eventually become, may observe that the types are preponderantly those of the second to fifth settlements at Troy; multiple jars, footed bowls, and the ubiquitous *depas amphikypellon*. There is, however, an admixture of jugs with sharply rising spouts and other features more characteristic of the Plateau; and in the final stages the 'red-cross' bowl appears with its usual punctuality, side by side with the first examples of a Syrian ware, painted in dark colours on a light ground, which is the local substitute for the Cappadocian.

All this tells one what might well have already been anticipated, namely, that since trade routes both from the Aegean and the Plateau pass through Cilicia to Syria, the pottery fashions of both areas were there represented, with a slight preponderance of the former, perhaps on account of supplementary communications by sea.

CHAPTER 7

Kültepe : The First Documents

IN our effort to trace and account for the sequence of developments in the lives of the earliest Anatolians, we have hitherto found ourselves in a situation comparable to that of a criminologist who must rely in his investigations upon the examination of circumstantial evidence. Just as he is aware that his painstaking study of the many trivial details upon which such evidence depends may at any moment be subordinated in importance to the testimony of a reliable eye-witness, so in the sphere of our present study we ourselves have been conscious from the first of the limitations inherent in the system of archaeological reasoning and of the disabilities to which we are subjected by the absence of contemporary records. When, therefore, we are in fact faced with such records for the first time, the revelation is sensational. A respite is momentarily granted from the tedium of typology and stratigraphy, and the whole paraphernalia of archaeological deduction can temporarily be relegated to a subsidiary status. The entire horizon of our interest is for the moment dominated by the new 'eye-witness account' – the personal testimony of contemporary individuals – and it becomes understandable if their claims to our attention take precedence over the material evidence of the circumstances in which they lived. It is as though, seated in a theatre, we had for long been compelled to contemplate a darkened and empty stage. The scene, indeed, was set, and certain properties could be discerned and recognized as hinting at the nature of the play. But the players themselves were absent. Now, suddenly they are there: the stage is lit and the voiceless prologue at an end. They reveal themselves in speech and the fabric of the play emerges from the pattern of their exits and entrances.

So in Anatolia, during the first quarter of the second millennium our interests are confined almost exclusively to the lives and behaviour of an orderly community of Assyrian merchants living in a circumscribed cantonment on the outskirts of the Cappadocian city called Kanesh. The reason for their voluntary exile and the complicated conventions by which their lives and their relations with the indigenous people were controlled, emerge from their own written documents in the form of casual allusions or references, having a significance to posterity of which the writers themselves can have had little conception. For these tablets which the Kültepe excavations have produced in such vast numbers are not historical or political documents, nor are they concerned for instance with literary and religious traditions. They are the prosaic records of commercial dealings and the laconic correspondence of business firms or individual merchants. In the letters, for instance, even the courtesies of addresss usual to Mesopotamian correspondence are dispensed with, or employed only for the obvious purpose of flattery, when a favour is to be asked. Such, then, is their character; and the task of reconstructing from them a picture of Anatolian life in the nineteenth century B.C. has been by no means an easy one. (A perhaps comparable problem would be a reconstruction of China in the first decades of the present century, based solely on the proceedings of the Shanghai Chamber of Commerce.) Yet it has been tackled with some success and the results, at least in so far as the colony itself is concerned, present an intensely interesting spectacle.

DATING

First then, as to the date of the tablets: evidence for the period which they cover has been found, not in the actual content of the texts, but among the personal seals used to impress signatures upon them. To explain this we must pause for a moment to note the appearance of the tablets themselves. We find, of course, the usual cushion-shaped clay pads, in this case rather square in proportion and with a maximum dimension of about 3 inches. The cuneiform writing is impressed upon them with a stylus while the clay is still wet and they are then hardened by baking in a kiln. Also, the

Kültepe tablets being business documents, they are almost invariably enclosed in an outer envelope of clay. Upon this, in the case of a letter, the address is written, or if the document records an agreement, a summary of its terms is repeated and signed by the parties concerned. The seals used for this purpose can be either the cylindrical variety, which is rolled laterally leaving a repetitive impression, or the simple stamp seal more familiar in modern times. It is the former type which in at least one case has provided all-important chronological evidence. This was a seal of the Mesopotamian king, Ibi-Sin, last ruler of the Third Dynasty of Ur, in approximately 1960 B.C. There was evidence to show that it had been acquired and re-used by some less exalted individual, which could hardly have happened in the king's lifetime. The seal can therefore do no more than establish a *terminus post quem* at least a generation after his death. A *terminus ante quem* is provided by the mention on one tablet of Puzur Assur, son of Sargon I of Assyria, giving a date a little after 1800 B.C. T. Özgüç is accordingly at present inclined to equate the lifetime of the colony with the nineteenth century B.C.

As for the origin and nationality of the traders, from the first appearance of the tablets, and before even the provenance from which they derived had been authenticated, the matter was hardly in doubt. The language in which they were written was Akkadian, the old commercial language of Mesopotamia, in a form identifiable as Old Assyrian. The names of Assyrian gods such as Assur, Ishtar and Adad were frequently mentioned, and the Assyrian capital on the Tigris was familiarly referred to simply as 'the City'. From Assur, then, they had come and in Cappadocia they were established at a place where many trade routes converged from the Taurus passes and all parts of Anatolia. So let us finally turn to the organization of their lives and their commercial activities.

To select a text at random from among the tablets is like opening a new volume by some familiar author of our own time. A few sentences are sufficient to evoke the atmosphere in which his characters live and to revive one's interest in them. A Kanesh merchant, for instance, called Pushukin, has a letter from Assur-imitti, his business contact at home. 'I have received your instructions and the day the import of your tablet was made known to me, I provided your agents with three minas of silver for the purchase of lead. Now, if you are still my brother, let me have my money by courier. . . .' At once one is beside him in the upper room of his Anatolian home, as the envelope is broken from the letter and he smiles at the urgency of the request for payment, seeing perhaps in his mind the face of his correspondent and feeling once more the heat of the Mesopotamian sun. But always uppermost in his mind must have been the *karum*, the organization which made such transactions possible by regulating the life of the community in which he and his fellow-merchants lived and assuring their status in an alien land.

THE KARUM

Primarily then, the *karum* was a sort of Chamber of Commerce controlling the mechanism of trade between Assyria and the cities of Anatolia. It was responsible for the dispatch of caravans and their safe conduct, the payment of dues and a simple system of credit by note of hand to minimize the risk of actual money transfers. But it also had the secondary function of a tribunal for the fixing of prices and the settlement of disputes. It could arrange for the deposit of securities against a loan or consider a creditor's claims against a debtor's capacity to pay. In authority was an annually appointed eponym or *limmu*, whose name, in the Assyrian manner, would afterwards provide a designation for the year in which he held office: there was also a further sub-division of the year by appointments depending on a formula not yet properly understood, evidently based in some way upon multiples of five (*hamustu*, according to some scholars a pentacontad of fifty days, to others a fifth of a month, i.e. six days). Between eighty and a hundred of the *limmu* who held office during the existence of the colony are already accounted for in the texts and their names known (though not their sequence). 'Judges' and 'elders' are also both mentioned as arbitrating in disputes.

GEOGRAPHICAL EVIDENCE

Kanesh was not apparently the only *karum* in the Anatolian area, but it appears to have been the most important: a sort of distribution centre upon which the others were dependent. Of the latter, Burushatum is the most often mentioned, but there are also Hahhum, Hurama, Nahria, Turhumit, Ursu, and Wahsusana, none of which, unfortunately, has so far been conclusively identified with an ancient site. There are also eight names of *wabartum*, trading stations subsidiary to the actual *karum*, whose location is equally uncertain. In fact, the whole subject of Anatolian geography at this period is still so vexed by uncertainties that, though many of these places survive into the days of the Hittite Empire, their equation with modern place-names has hardly yet begun to carry conviction.

This indeed applies in equal measure to places in Anatolia with which the *karum* traded, and only the road used by their caravans in making the direct journey from and to 'the City' can yet be followed with any certainty. True, among the tablets there is no detailed itinerary available, even for this most important of all routes. But there are notes of expenses incurred by travellers during certain stages of the journey, and much is to be learnt by piecing these together. Goetze,* who has studied the problem, benefited much from the comparison of Babylonian itineraries covering approximately the same route, particularly one from Mari on the Euphrates, across whose territory the Kanesh caravans must have passed. With their route before leaving the frontiers of Assyria we are less concerned, but it appears to have brought them by Sinjar to the river Khabur (Habura) and then westwards along the fringes of the desert to Harrân (Harranum). The 'Royal Road' of later times is then recognizable, leading by way of Sürüj (Zalpa) to a crossing of the Euphrates near Birejik (Dadania?), but the Kanesh caravans thereafter diverge northwards by Gaziantep to the Sinjerli valley (Simala) and through the pass northward of Maraş to Elbistan (Hahhum) and Cappadocia.

* A. Goetze in *Journal of Cuneiform Studies*, VII, 51 ff and 64 ff.

THE CARAVANS

References to the actual means of transport show that the goods were almost invariably carried on the backs of donkeys, to which, for some reason, the epithet 'black' is usually applied. Wheeled vehicles are not mentioned and their use may indeed have been rendered impracticable by the nature of the roads. Yet a curious feature of these documents, recording the innumerable journeys of such donkey caravans over a period of several generations, is the apparently high standard of security which was somehow maintained upon the roads. Lawlessness can hardly have been unknown, and indeed there is a chance reference in one text to the plundering by thieves of a temple; but no single record has yet come to hand of a caravan being robbed.

Since the colony seems to have functioned as an authorized component of the Assyrian state economy, official messengers played an important role in maintaining communication between capital and colony – between the great merchants of Assur and their agents in Kanesh. The passage of these individuals from place to place seems also to have been without hazard and there is no recorded case of a messenger's failure to arrive. The whole system of communication in fact seems to have worked with the greatest regularity, as is shown indeed by the recurrence of such phrases as ' ...by earliest messenger' or ' ... by return of post'.

In the task of assuring so high a standard of dispatch and delivery an important part may have been played by individuals with the function of 'transport factors' whose names are often mentioned. It was they who accepted personal responsibility for the safety of a consignment of goods, from its acceptance until delivery at its destination. For this service they were apparently highly paid, as they might well be, and were allowed to present separate expense accounts, for instance for fodder, donkey-boys' wages, and the payment of tolls, either legitimate or otherwise, of which evidence could be produced.

COMMERCE

The actual character of the goods exchanged between Anatolia and Mesopotamia seems to have varied little from year to year. The primary exports from Assyria were lead and woven materials. The value of the former in proportion to that of silver (by which the standard of prices was set) varied from 1 : 6 to 1 : 17 according to the quality. Cloths and fabrics were of the widest possible variety and there were famous tissues called by exotic names, which to-day can only tantalize us. The wide range of qualities can be inferred from the fact that their prices varied from one to sixty half-shekels per unit. (The unit itself is unfortunately still undefined, though it is known to have been related in some way to the normal load of a donkey.) Among the goods dispatched in return from Anatolia, copper features as by far the most important commodity. The names of the localities from which it is derived, Haburata, Tismuma, and Washania, are recorded and the ratio of its value to silver again suggests qualities varying from 1 : 46 to 1 : 80. Silver was used not for trade but as currency, and in making payment it was weighed out or passed in packages sealed by the *karum*. The rate of gold to silver was normally 8 : 1, and an even more valuable metal, which is thought probably to have been iron, had five times the value of gold and forty times that of silver. Other costly minerals have been tentatively identified as carnelian and amber. It should be added that payment in precious metals against the delivery of goods was by no means always the rule. Simple barter was common practice and travelling merchants would often exchange their wares *en route* for the produce of the countries through which they were passing.

ANATOLIAN NEIGHBOURS

We must now once more recall the proximity of the Assyrian colony to a large and presumably powerful Anatolian city, and consider the relations of the colonists with the indigenous population. Unfortunately the character of the local administration is hardly brought into focus by the scanty references in the texts. There is a ruler called *ruba'um*, 'lord', and in one case his female counterpart is mentioned (*rubatum*). There is also a single reference to a 'Lord-of-lords' (*ruba'um rabi'u*) whose city, Burushatum, one may imagine to have been temporarily in the ascendant. But direct dealings between the colonists and these princes is infrequent. They are in fact confined to rare cases of a prince intervening to protect one of his subjects, for example when he is in danger of being reduced to servitude on account of his debts. For the rest, the colonists' dealings seem to be with the 'palace' (i.e. the organ of administration) and to be of an entirely routine character. All merchandise, for instance, on arrival at the *karum*, had first to 'enter' and 'leave' the 'palace'; that is, to be subjected to local control. A tax (*nishatum*) was then levied on certain commodities such as cloth, and the 'palace' had the first option to purchase. Once 'cleared', the goods were free to be disposed of as the Assyrians wished.

The Assyrians of Kanesh seem freely to have intermarried with the Anatolians among whom they lived and generally to have been on the most friendly terms with them. Much is to be learnt from the many personal names mentioned in the tablets, amongst which recognizable Indo-Europeans are already to be found side by side with Hattic families. In addition, it is perhaps worth listing the names which are included of cities with Anatolian rulers: Burushatum, Kanes, Nenassa, Sirmia, Timelkia, Tuhpia, Wahsusana, and Washania.

THE EXCAVATIONS

The direct evidence of the texts has thus been summarized. We have listened to the personal testimony of the characters in our play and can now turn our attention to the *mise-en-scène* against which their appearance was made. In a word, we may now examine the archaeological setting in which the tablets were found. This brings us 20 kilometres out of modern Kayseri on the newly metalled road leading to Sivas, and across the fields to the village of Karahüyük. Already, as we leave the road, the great mound beside the village makes an impressive silhouette, and piles of rubble can be distinguished where the early excavators sought in vain for the source of

the famous tablets. But the site of the *karum* is not yet visible:
it lies concealed by lines of willows beneath the flat meadows
at the base of the mound. It is easy to imagine the elation
which Hrozny must have felt when he at last learned this
secret of local topography and could make his first sounding
in the authentic remains of the Assyrian colony.

As these words are written, work on the *karum* is still in
progress under the direction of T. and N. Özgüç.* Their
excavations have occasionally overlapped those of Hrozny,
and in such cases, evidence in the vertical side of the new
cutting recalls the now obsolete practice adopted by him, of
'dumping' back earth into the cavities already excavated. By
contrast, the Turkish excavations are a model of orderliness.
The principal occupation level in Assyrian times is now some
metres beneath the surface of the fields; so that one is looking
from above on to the roads and houses of the settlement. The
principal furniture of the rooms: storage jars, ovens and
hearths have been left in place, and outside in the street, the
paving stones are worn into ruts by the continual passage of
cart-wheels. Were it not for the fact that the upper structure
of the houses has fallen and their walls are discoloured by the
great fire which destroyed them, one would think that the
inhabitants had only recently departed.

THE HOUSES

The tablets were found in the houses, which evidently
served both as residence and place of business. In the case of
individual merchants like Laqipum and Adad-Sululi, whose
homes were discovered during the first season of the Turkish
excavations, their entire archives could be recovered from a
single building. It was in fact the circumstance of the place
having been destroyed by fire which made this possible. What
must have been a shattering disaster for the colonists themselves has proved a great benefit to posterity. For owing to
the hasty departure of the occupants, the contents of the
houses had to be abandoned and they remain to this day
substantially as they left them. Only the more fragile articles

* For Özgüç's publications, see Bibliography (13).

in the ground-floor rooms have been crushed by the collapse of the roof or upper storey, and the tablets and other objects which had fallen with the latter are conveniently separated from those below by a layer of burnt débris. It has accordingly proved possible to reconstruct both the houses themselves and the arrangement of their contents in some detail.

They are built according to the age-old Anatolian tradition, on a foundation of uncut stone, the upper structure consisting of sun-dried brick, straightened with wooden beams. In this case the timber reinforcement is not inserted at random, but consists of a sound framework, in which horizontal elements laid directly upon the stone sub-structure are effectively tied by pairs of vertical posts to wall-plates above, and upon these the ceiling or roof beams rest. The length of the bricks matches the thickness of the walls and their inner and outer faces are both carefully plastered. The plans are simple but convenient, incorporating almost invariably an open court, either centrally placed, with the rooms surrounding it, or reached from the street by a corridor, off which the rooms open. There is evidence of two storeys, and certain rooms in both seem to have been open to the court on one side, as is the practice to-day in many parts of Anatolia.

It seems likely that the upper floor was the scene both of the merchants' business activities and the family's leisure, the rooms below having the character of domestic offices, work-rooms, and stores. Here everything was arranged in the most orderly manner. When the process of removing the débris was complete and the whole apparatus of the household could be seen tidily disposed about the rooms, each object in its appropriate place, it was the evidence of craftsmanship and good taste which first struck one. Apart from the ordinary earthen-ware vessels (many of which were of the 'Cappadocian' variety, painted with intricate designs and contrasting pleasantly with the warm, burnished surfaces of the 'Hittite' vessels), there were examples of skilful modelling based on animal forms – theriomorphic vessels resembling mythical animals, cups in the shape of bulls' or lions' heads, and in one case shaped and painted to resemble a snail. The Kültepe potters' appreciation of such modelled forms was everywhere apparent, and even the more practical vessels were often unexpectedly embellished with small clay beasts or birds. The very shapes of the 'Hittite' vases seemed to lend themselves to a more fanciful treatment here than elsewhere, and tended to be furnished with multiple handles, often of more than one shape. (Plates 8 and 9)

Particularly in rooms serving as kitchens, there were other immovable appointments whose function could easily be understood. An interesting feature was a terracotta hearth, shaped like a horse-shoe and terminating above in three vertical supports on which a large cooking vessel could rest. Near this would be a small *mangal* or brazier for charcoal and a large, domed baking oven of the normal Near-Eastern type. Even bigger examples of such ovens, usually placed in the courtyards, had been used for baking and hardening the tablets. Water-coolers and large storage jars completed the picture. (Plate 6)

BURIALS

Another curious but archaeologically productive feature of these houses was the graves. Here at Kanesh as, for instance in the almost contemporary dwelling-houses dating from the time of the patriarch Abraham at Ur, there had evidently been a feeling that, when a member of the family died, his body need not be entirely separated from the comfortable intimacy of his home. The burials would consequently be made beneath the floors of the house. At Kültepe they were either enclosed in a terra-cotta coffin or in a 'cist', lined and sealed with slabs of stone. In both cases the deceased was generously provided with funeral gifts, and many of the more valuable finds made by the excavators were derived from this source. The list includes – 'Pots and pans made of bronze, silver, gold and lead, and precious stones, scales, weapons, small animal statues and decorative objects'. Among the last-named was 'a small lead statue of a Hittite god, in a short decorated dress, wide belt, beard, sharp-pointed head-dress, and with a mace in his hand'.

The Tablets

The tablets had for the most part been stored in the rooms at ground-floor level; but many had also fallen from the floor above, and these can perhaps be taken to have been the documents actually in use at the time. Those not found lying on the floor had been arranged upon wooden shelves or stored in large earthenware vessels, often as many as fifty to a jar. Among them were various forms of label or sealing, evidently retained for reference. Another, somewhat enigmatic find, usually made in the vicinity of the tablets, was a pottery ornament shaped and painted to represent a high boot with an up-turned and pointed toe, in the traditional Anatolian manner. These have been (perhaps too readily) explained by the excavators as 'libation vessels'.*

Seal Impressions (Plate 7)

One of the most revealing aspects of the tablets is the impressions which they bear of the merchants' seals. Some 800 different impressions have already been collected, and when eventually they have all been carefully studied and compared, the information to be derived from them should be of the greatest importance. The stamp seal had by this time been long obsolete in Mesopotamia, so that the examples which occur here are all of the Hittite type (clumsy predecessors of the signet, carried on a fob in the eighteenth century A.D.) and bear Anatolian designs. But the cylinder seals show the widest variety. Most of the foreign seals are straightforward examples of various Mesopotamian styles, carved in the land from which the colonists had come. But there is also a number of purely Anatolian designs and a wide and interesting range of 'modified' designs, in which the Assyrian or Babylonian formulae are adapted to the requirements of local taste and symbolism.

* M. E. L. Mallowan in *Iraq* IX, Part 2, pp. 99–100 has an interesting note on the purpose of these model shoes. It appears that in Mesopotamia and elsewhere they were used in certain circumstances as token payments to validate business transactions. He quotes E. A. Speiser, who thus interprets *Amos* 8 : 6 as referring to the exploitation of the poor by legal casuistry.

In Mesopotamia itself, the little frieze-reliefs which these seals imprinted, had begun in Sumerian times to resemble loosely arranged pictures, in which mythical episodes were represented and the gaps filled with religious and other symbols. The consequent effect of overcrowding was corrected in the Akkadian period, when the heraldic groups were isolated and their fine drawing seen to better effect; but in the period with which we are dealing at Kültepe the conventionalizing process had been carried a stage further, and the field is occupied by processions of tall stylized figures, only occasionally interrupted by an inscription. The most common subjects depicted are the presentation of a worshipper to a seated deity, or the combats with beasts of the mythical heroes, Gilgamesh and Enkidu. The Anatolian seal cutters of Kanesh show a tendency to favour the earlier Sumerian style, and to crowd their design with isolated motives. So in their hands the Assyrian convention is also modified to satisfy propensity for space-filling. Their insertions and additions are in themselves often interesting, since among them exclusively Anatolian concepts are often recognizable. Religious figures, such as the naked Ishtar, contemporarily absent from the Mesopotamian repertoire, are here to be seen side by side with the bull symbol of the Anatolian Storm God, and some of the vessels and other objects of ritual character which accompany them can be recognized among the actual finds made in the Kanesh houses. Such details as these, combined with the rare mention in the texts of local deities (Haramatum, Hikisa, Kubabat, Ana, Nipas) are the only evidence available as to the character of the pre-Hittite Anatolian religion.

CHARACTER OF THE COLONISTS

In a sense, the most striking thing about the Kanesh colonists is the extent to which they appear to have adapted their lives to the society in which they found themselves, without impairing their political allegiance to Assur. Apart from the identity of the language in which they wrote and the religious implications of the pictures on their seals, there is little to be found among their personal effects which testifies to their origin. A Babylonian 'duck-weight' or an imported Assyrian trinket have an alien appearance among their other belongings, which are confined entirely to the products of local markets. Their houses are built in a technique adapted by centuries of experience to the requirements of the Anatolian climate. They have adopted, perhaps from their Anatolian wives, the domestic practices of the Plateau and they respect the Anatolian gods. Even their methods of interring the dead are adapted to their peculiar environment. It was perhaps this capacity for political self-effacement which enabled the colony to continue its peaceful function apparently without interference over a period of six or eight generations.

LEVELS

Before leaving Kültepe we must record some purely archaeological deductions made by the Özgüç's from their finds. Even in this comparatively ephemeral settlement it was necessary to observe the stratigraphy, since the successive stages in its existence were marked by four distinct building levels. Two of the periods thus defined, corresponding to Levels Ib and II, had ended in the total destruction of the settlement by fire, and it is from them that the tablets are almost exclusively derived. There has been some question whether the Assyrian colony were not already in existence in Level III; but Levels IV and Ia seem respectively to have preceded and succeeded it in time.

POTTERY (Plates 8 and 9)

The slight changes in the pottery from level to level also have some significance. This is the era of painted ornament, unique in the Bronze Age history of Anatolia, and the technique of decoration in black and red on a light ground is everywhere to be seen on vessels and ornaments. But it can be noted that the pure style known as 'Alishar III' hardly survives the arrival of the colonists, and that during the lifetime of the *karum* it is replaced by a rather different local variant, which has long been called 'Cappadocian' painted ware. Present beside this elegantly decorated pottery are the plain burnished products now known as 'Hittite' (Alishar II). What these lack in ornament they make up for in subtle beauty of outline. They represent the climax of a ceramic theme which has been seen developing on less pretentious lines in the Copper Age and is to appear again indifferently reflected in the inferior pottery of the Hittite Empire. Another site at which they were found in great quantities was Alaja, and they are perhaps seen to best advantage in the attractive little local museum now erected on the site of the excavations, where each show-case seems to contain a more lovely combination of shapes. The patina of the red-burnished vessels contrasts unexpectedly with an occasional example of the rich golden slip, an invention peculiar to this period. Özgüç himself has noticed how this pottery is merely a superior development of that used during the Copper Age, and how its decadence may be witnessed in the products of the imperial period. This evidence of technological continuity may be taken to support Landsberger's contention to which we have already referred, that the vernacular culture of the Plateau persisted throughout the whole Bronze Age, unaffected by the substitution of one ruling caste for another.

CHAPTER 8

Hittite Archaeology

THE emphasis which the opening paragraph of the previous chapter laid upon the significance of written records may in some degree have prepared the reader for the situation to be encountered in the two centuries which followed the disappearance of the Assyrian colonists from Kanesh. For there is a period upon which excavations have so far proved capable of throwing little light, but which, thanks to the historical records of a later age can be reconstructed in terms of political events and peopled with individuals whose names and characters are known to us. These are in fact the days of the Old Hittite Kingdom, during which a dynasty of fourteen kings consolidated its power and authority in central Anatolia. In the absence, then, of any considerable archaeological legacy, there is at this point some pretext for examining the historical aspect of the ethnological synthesis upon which the creation of the Hittite nation depended.

To begin with, then, the westerly migration in the late third millennium of a people belonging to the linguistic group known as Indo-European, was a movement of the kind which must have taken place in several stages and occupied some centuries. On reaching the Black Sea and Mediterranean, one can imagine the fan-shape created by its various extensions, on the one hand towards Europe and on the other into the countries of western Asia. One would accordingly expect to find that – 'the Celts for instance reached Gaul later than the Italiots reached Italy or the Hellenes Greece, and, above all, much later than their kinsman who migrated to the area between Asia Minor and India, and who had merely to march directly south'.* Anatolia is, in fact, merely the first centre in which the effects of the migration are historically authenticated, as proved by the appearance of Indo-European names in the Kültepe tablets.

* R. Weill, *Phoenicia and Western Asia*, p. 85 (London, 1940).

When Assyriologists came to decipher the Bogazköy archives, they were considerably surprised to find, not one language but several. Easily identified, though incomprehensible, was the language (Hatti-li) of the indigenous, Early Bronze Age inhabitants of Anatolia, whose name, Hatti, had hitherto served as a label for their country. Obviously superimposed upon this were a variety of Indo-European languages which included Luvian, Palaic, Nesite, and a fourth associated with hieroglyphic writing. It accordingly became clear that, in the state of which these documents represented the official archives, they were dealing with a people of composite extraction, whose name 'Hittite' suggested a heredity which only a part of them could in fact be said to share.

The next question which arose was as to how long the great fortress city at Boghazköy had been their capital and the focal point of their national life. Its name, Hattusas, had already been recognized in the Kültepe inscriptions, where it was included in the list of cities to which Assyrian commercial communities were attached. The next clue was again provided by these same documents, preserved among which, by a piece of good fortune, were three tablets mentioning the names of a local prince called Pitkhana and his son Anittas.* For it is from these half-legendary individuals that Hittite royalty of later times claimed its descent. Their home was the city of Kussura, and a famous text from the Boghazköy archives gives the story of how they fought with and defeated a federation of other cities including Hattusas, which they not only destroyed but declared accursed. This does not appear seriously to have interfered with its prosperity, for, when Hittite history once more comes into focus, during the middle of the sixteenth century B.C., a king called Labarnas II, now in the authentic line of Hittite royal descent, has selected it as his capital in place of Kussura, and changed his name to Hattusilis.

From this time onwards Hattusas remained the administrative centre, if not the official residence of the Hittite kings, and is recognizable in the annals of their reigns as the strategic

* According to B. Hrozny Anittas is mentioned in the Kültepe texts.

centre from which the military and political expansion of the kingdom was contrived. Through the medium of the Assyrian *karum*, the Hittites must long ago have come to understand the superior wealth and attainments of the people occupying the riverain country beyond their mountains in the south, and from the first it was in this direction that their political ambitions were oriented. A first stage in their realization was marked by the conquest of Aleppo by Mursilis I, and this was followed soon afterwards by the meteoric and entirely surprising campaign in which (as is confirmed by the Mesopotamian annals) he reached and momentarily subdued the king, Samsu-ditana of the Amorite dynasty reigning in Babylon. One has only to imagine the feelings of this precocious adventurer from an almost unknown kingdom in the remote uplands of Anatolia, on finding himself temporarily master in so great a centre of world civilization, to realize that such a conquest could hardly have had more significance than a successful raid, and indeed, in the reign of his successor, Hantilis, we find the Hittite kingdom not only confined once more within its old limits, but threatened from the east by a people called the Hurrians, who are now mentioned for the first time. These threats seem in the end to have been repulsed, and King Telepinus, whose death is taken to mark the end of the Old Kingdom, defined and fortified its frontiers, which, in the south now extended no further than the Taurus mountains.

With this intrusion into the realm of written history we are approaching ground which has been most adequately and interestingly covered in a companion volume to this work.* In the story of the Hittites, we have now in fact reached the 'imperial' period, during which they evolved and perfected the pattern of social and political life there described, and one must pause to consider what amplification of the subject can be expected from an archaeological, as opposed to a philological and historical approach. We have had reason to refer elsewhere to the comparative poverty in workmanship and materials of such remains as have survived to bear witness to

* O. R. Gurney, *The Hittites*, Pelican Books.

the Hittite 'way of life', and have suggested that it argues a
certain austerity in their national character. Naturally this
reflection must be taken to refer primarily to the ordinary
appointments of domestic living, for in the realm of monumental architecture and public ornaments the effect, at least of
parsimony, is absent and the deficiency, if any, is to be attributed to a certain excess of ingenious virility. This, and
for that matter, practically any other aspect of Hittite art
or technology can best be studied at Boghazköy, the site of
Hattusas itself, where by far the most conspicuous material
remains of the period of the Hittite Empire have been found
gathered together.

BOGHAZKÖY

The ruins at Boghazköy have frequently been described.
Between the accounts of early travellers, like Texier in the last
century, and the meticulous records which Bittel and his
colleagues have contributed in recent years,* there is literature
to suit all tastes, and one hesitates in appending yet another
contribution, which at best can only help to stimulate interest
in the lay reader. Yet to do so with this object in view, has
to-day the point which would have been lacking in the past,
that the place can now comparatively easily be visited. For
this purpose, at the beginning of the present decade, one
travelled by road to Alaja Hüyük and from there rode somewhat precariously in a farm-cart over the twelve miles of
mountain track which separated it from Boghazköy. To-day
there is a metalled road from Ankara to Sungurlu and a mere
five hours of motoring bring one from the Turkish to the
Hittite capital.

One approaches the site from the north-west along the
contours of a wide and fertile valley which tapers gradually to
a point where the hills on either side converge. Here the
village which has given its name to the site lies at the con-
fluence of two torrents and the junction of the rocky gorges
from which they discharge into the plain. Isolated on either
side by the precipitous flanks of these gorges is an abruptly

* See Bibliography (10).

rising spur of the hills, broken into irregular formations by outcrops of rock and commanding a fine view of the valley over the flat roofs of the village and its counterpoint of Lombardy poplars. This was the setting chosen for the city of Hattusas, and the outline of its site is marked by the remnants of a fortress wall seven kilometres long which originally enclosed it.

The older part of the town, which incorporates the remains of the third millennium settlement, is a mere 350 metres long. It occupies the gentler slopes of the hill directly above the village, and terminates at the south-east end in the high, flat-topped rock called Büyükkale, which had the function of a citadel, having its own system of fortification. This is the city which Hattusilis I made his capital in about 1500 B.C. and its walls are attributed to Hantilis I. In the centre of it are the ruins of 'Temple I', by far the largest building which has yet been excavated. In the imperial period, with so sudden an increase in the wealth and authority of the Hittite court, the size of the old city became inadequate and a vast extension was created. Perhaps in the time of Suppiluliumas a tremendous crescent of new fortifications was flung up over the hillside to the south, leaving the old enclosure just above the modern village and returning to it beneath Büyükkale. In this area four more temples have been excavated, and several isolated rocks are crowned by remnants of masonry suggesting major buildings: elsewhere excavations have revealed the character of the actual dwelling-houses.

The Fortifications. The first thing which strikes the visitor about Hattusas is its immense size compared with most other Bronze Age cities, for it takes the greater part of a morning or afternoon to make the complete circuit of the walls at a comfortable pace: the enclosed area must be well over 300 acres. Next, one is impressed by the formidable strength of the fortifications, particularly the southern enclosure wall of the extended city, and imagines the Herculean task which their construction must have presented, in the fourteenth century B.C. A huge rampart of earth, of which the outer slope is sometimes

(a) Plan of gate

(b) Reconstruction of a gate, inner side

(c) Reconstruction of a gate, outer side
Figure 8. Boghazköy

faced with a *glacis* of dressed stones, raises the foundations to a consistent level. Above this is the main wall, built in the form of a double shell, with rubble-filled chambers between and punctuated by projecting towers. In the more vulnerable sectors there is a lower 'apron' wall, also with towers, and this would have had to be breached before the main wall could be approached.

The Gates. In the southern enclosure wall there are five gateways, three of which have been given names ('Warrior, 'Lion' and 'Sphinx-Gate') suggested by the relief sculptures with which they are ornamented. They have a uniform plan – square flanking towers, each divided internally into four or six compartments, and between them an inner and outer portal, the former flush with the wall on the town side and the latter set in some distance from the outer faces of the towers. The appearance of the portals themselves, with their suggestion of an elliptical archway, contrived by corbelling over two gigantic monoliths, are too familiar to need describing. It is upon these monolith door jambs that the sculptured figures are carved in relief, the animals facing towards the open country. The famous 'warrior', who turned in profile towards the archway on the left-hand jamb of an inner portal, has now been removed to the Ankara Museum. (Plate 13c)

The character of the masonry is also best to be seen in these gateways. The heavy blocks of which it is composed are not laid in regular courses, but vary greatly in size and are often polygonal in shape. They are skilfully fitted together without mortar and, though heavily 'rusticated', their joints are adjusted with precision to the prescribed plane of the wall face. It has always been assumed that, starting from a point some-what above the portals, both walls and towers had an upper structure of mud-brick, reinforced with timber beams, of which nothing now remains. (Plate 12b)

The 'Sphinx-Gate' is located in the southernmost curve of the enclosure wall. Here, as one approaches from the lower slopes of the hill, two long stone stairways lead obliquely upwards to gate towers in the 'apron' wall, and so the gateway itself. Here also is to be seen one of the most curious features of the whole fortification system. For deep down, below even the rampart on which the wall stands, a postern or sally-port is created by a long tunnel, carefully lined with stone and vaulted by rudimentary corbelling. There are smaller posterns in the wall separating the old city from the new, but none requiring a tunnel of such remarkable length. To-day even its purpose is obscure.* The sculptures on either side of the gate itself are crude sphinxes in the Egyptian manner; reminiscent, perhaps, of examples seen by the Hittites during their campaigns in Syria. The most interesting fact about them is that, unlike the figures ornamenting the 'Lion Gate', which are confined to the outer face of the monolithic door jambs, they extend laterally into the reveal of the doorway, like the Assyrian portal colossi of much later times. They in fact represent the earliest known example of an architectural device, which was to become a commonplace in the first millennium.

Temples. Four buildings in the extended town have been identified by the excavators as temples. Their plans have much in common with each other, but little with other religious buildings of the ancient east. Admittedly, like most Babylonian temples, they are grouped around an open court, but the porticoes and cloisters giving on to it are a peculiar feature, more reminiscent of a Minoan palace than of anything in Mesopotamia or Egypt. The main sanctuary, too, in which the emplacement for a cult-statue is in every case recognizable, is distinguished from those, for instance, of Babylonia by an indirect approach through a series of vestibules. Its position in the plan is usually contrived so that the end of the chamber, where the statue stood, projects beyond the adjoining parts of the building. In this way lateral lighting could be obtained to supplement that provided by windows in the rear of the image. For here again is an architectural characteristic peculiar to these buildings: their rooms obtain light from windows in the external façade in addition to that penetrating from the

* Similar tunnels have been observed by Koşay at Alaja.

courtyard. Apart from the actual sanctuaries the shape, size, and disposal of the remaining chambers is seen to be dictated by conventions of which we are to-day unhappily ignorant.

These minor temples are on the whole poorly preserved, but some details of their construction, and even of their original appearance, can be conjectured after studying the remains of Temple I, their more imposing counterpart in the old city, which they must have closely resembled. In this case the temple itself, a building of enormous proportions (64.00 × 42.00 metres), stands isolated by stone-paved streets in the centre of a labyrinthine complex of intercommunicating store-houses and repositories. Their purpose is indicated by the serried ranks of huge earthenware storage jars or *pithoi*, with which, in a manner again reminiscent of a Cretan palace, many of the longer galleries are filled. Another such gallery contained the cuneiform tablets which constituted the temple library.

The plan of the temple itself once more shows a rectangular courtyard approached through a formal system of vestibules and provided with a colonnade on the side facing the entrance. But beyond this colonnade, the sanctuary and subsidiary chambers connected with it form a detached group, asymmetrically annexed to the main rectangle of the building. To emphasize this impression of segregation its walls are built of granite, whereas those of the main building are of limestone. Granite was also used for a small isolated structure in the corner of the courtyard nearest to the sanctuary which has been explained as the base of an altar or statue. Here again there are windows in the external façades of the building, and the height to which the walls remain standing has made it possible to see that these were not the small, grilled openings high up in the walls, to which one has become accustomed elsewhere, but dignified features of the façade, starting in some cases only a few feet above the ground, and empanelled between vertical pilasters. Above all, enough has survived of this building to impress one with the colossal scale and proportions of the masonry. The stones of which these lower parts of the walls are composed are often as much as two metres in length and the courses a metre deep. The thresholds of doors are flat mono-

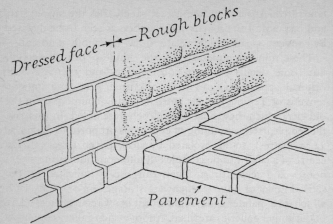

Figure 9. Base of temple walls before and after final dressing

liths, and one would imagine that their lintels had the same character. Even the pavements are composed of colossal slabs of limestone, and where they meet the base of the walls a most curious effect is produced by the procedure which the masons must have adopted. The method of construction seems to have been to lay the courses one upon the other almost at random, and only after the pavement had also been laid, to dress them back to a uniform wall face (see Sketch). This created a recession in the lowest course at pavement level, which at first appears quite inexplicable.

The Alaja Temple.* Temples like that just described were apparently not peculiar to Bogazköy. Inside the famous Sphinx Gate at Alaja and about 25 metres from it, Koşay excavated the remains of a large and pretentious building, constructed in very much the same style, which he has since pronounced to have been dedicated to a non-secular purpose. Actually, since the walls were for the most part denuded to below the ground-floor level, very few doorways could be reliably located, and consequently in the plan, the function

* H. Z. Koşay, *Les fouilles d'Alaca Höyük*, Ankara, 1951, pp. 111 ff.

and interrelation of the various rooms and courtyards cannot exactly be ascertained. Nevertheless there were several interesting features. The building stood in a temenos, approached through its own double gateway, and in its façade facing the central piazza there was an open loggia, supported by columns, which must have stood upon square stone bases: in the rear wall of the loggia there was a stone pilaster corresponding to each column. Another important discovery made by the excavators was that similar colonnades existed in an earlier version of the same building, dating probably from the time of the Old Hittite Kingdom. (See Fig. 1.)

Other Buildings. At Boghazköy as at Alaja, secular architecture is less well represented than religious. There are remains of small fortresses at Yenikale, for example, and Sarikale, but little clue to their appearance. There are also secular buildings within the area of the citadel, Büyükkale, but the most conspicuous of these are two simple ranges of long, rectangular store chambers in one of which the famous archives were discovered. The only other building of any considerable size was denuded to its foundations and even a part of these had disappeared. Nevertheless enough survived to provide the subject of a considerable controversy. This was concerned with the so-called 'bît-hilani', an architectural element with which we shall find ourselves in contact in dealing with palaces of the Syro-Hittite period in the first millennium. In the eighth century it was referred to and even copied by the Assyrian kings who regarded it as characteristically 'Hittite' and the excavators of Boghazköy hoped to have recognized its prototype in this building of the imperial period at Büyükkale. But the *bît-hilani* has more recently been categorized by H. Frankfort as a purely Syrian invention, whose existence at this time and place could hardly be substantiated without more conclusive evidence.* 'The ruined building found at Boghazköy,' he says, 'presents an oblong room surrounded by a row of smaller rectangular rooms – the commonest plan for

* Cf. *Iraq* XIV, Part 2, p. 127. This subject is discussed at greater length on p. 163 ff, below.

houses throughout the Near East at most periods. The mere juxtaposition on one plate of the extant remains and the restoration in the guise of a *bît-hilani* shows the artificiality of the reconstruction.'

The German excavators have on the whole been most concerned at Büyükkale with the stratification of the citadel remains. They have ingeniously disentangled the fortification walls and occupation levels of successive periods, penetrating eventually into the third-millennium settlement beneath. Also, in the buildings of imperial times, they have recovered a collection of small objects upon which our knowledge of contemporary craftsmanship largely depends. In a category of its own is an assemblage of stamped *bullae*, usually impressed with a royal or other name in hieroglyphs, and serving for this reason to supplement the evidence of the cuneiform texts.

Graves. Important discoveries are also at present being made in other parts of the site.

Outside the city, in the neighbourhood of the rock called Büyükkaya, which faces Büyükkale across the eastern gorge, Bittel has located what appears to be the main necropolis area of Hittite times. Two-thirds of the graves are of the sort in which the body has been cremated and the ashes are contained in earthenware urns, a practice which is thus shown in Anatolia to date back at least as far as the middle of the second millennium. There are no funerary gifts of any great value, but much evidence of animals, particularly horses and oxen, having been sacrificed to accompany the dead, as was done in the Royal Tombs at Alaja. Some of these burials are in open cemeteries, but wherever there is a substantial outcrop of live rock, such caves or recesses as it may offer are crowded with graves. It is as though, in the Hittite mind, the rock itself were invested with some power of protection or other virtue by a chthonic deity.

Yazilikaya

Any speculation of this sort on the subject of Hittite religious beliefs leads, like the path which winds upwards across the necropolis area, to the famous sanctuary called Yazılıkaya in a fold of the hills, two miles east of the city. Here, at a height of 600 feet above the roofs of the modern village, a spring of water must once have created the setting for a sacred grove. Above it, the 'jaws of a limestone cliff open on to a gentle slope', and within is a system of galleries, open to the sky, the vertical rock-faces around them ornamented at eye-level with processions of deities and other participants in religious ceremonial, all sculptured in relief. The impression it gives would be comparable to that created by the sculptured walls of an Egyptian tomb, were it not for the exaggerated significance which the norm of Anatolian reticence gives to so remarkable an utterance. If its message is alone insufficient to stimulate the imagination, the atmosphere of the shrine itself must appeal to any visitor with ordinary sensibility. About his ears as he approaches are the small sounds of the Turkish countryside: the whine of distant cart-wheels or the barking of dogs. But as he passes into the shadow of the rock the silence becomes complete. Short turf and flowers make the pavement of this primitive cathedral, and the open sky its vault: small twisted shrubs bloom in the crevices of its walls, and a variety of rock plants to delight an alpine gardener. Only the exuberance of the creepers has been restrained and a briar clipped to prevent it from obscuring the sculptures. For such small courtesies and the maintenance of the place in its unspoilt simplicity are the only tributes which can to-day be paid to the kings and priests who worshipped there.

More than sixty divine and human figures appear in the reliefs, and they are accompanied here and there by hieroglyphic emblems, conveniently relating them to the historical texts in the citadel archives. The purpose of the sculptures and their iconography has been a subject of continual debate since the days of the earliest visitors, whose impulse was to interpret them in terms of Mesopotamian, Cretan, or even Greek mythology. Indeed the most recent commentators have tended to recognize in them a congregation of purely Hittite deities with their attendants and attributes – the Sun Goddess

Arinna; the Storm God standing upon his mountain genii and accompanied by his sacred bulls, Seri and Hurri; a 'Young God', who embraces the image of the king, and a 'Dagger-God', whose body tapers into the blade of a great poignard, thrust into the rock. They have interpreted the grouping and the lines of running figures with their purposeful movement, as re-enacting pictorially a central mystery of the Hittite faith or the ritual by which it was symbolized. The names of the principal gods could even be recognized in the pattern of hieroglyphs carved before their faces, and a human figure identified as the Hittite king, Tudhaliyas IV. (Plate 13)

But in the realm of antiquarian scholarship, nothing for long remains static, and the brightest figures in the pageant of antiquity created by historians in the lay mind may suddenly require re-modelling. So in recent years the science of Hittitology has made sudden progress. The meaning of the hieroglyphs is better understood: philologists working in other fields have learnt facts about the movements and relationships of peoples, which archaeological evidence alone could never have disclosed. In 1952 E. Laroche published an article,* from which it is finally to be concluded that Yazılıkaya, at least in so far as the subject of its sculptures is concerned, is not Hittite. Up till that time it had naturally been assumed that the gods and goddesses depicted in the reliefs represented the constituent members of the old Hattic pantheon, and the interpretation of their hieroglyphic 'labels' had been accordingly prejudiced. Laroche based his re-examination of the problem on four forms of evidence: (1) the minute details now available of the sculptures themselves; (2) the correct reading of the several hieroglyphic names treated individually; (3) the inventories and descriptions now published of cult statues found elsewhere; and (4) an analysis of the Hattic pantheon into its constituent elements. This eventually enabled him to transcribe in cuneiform the names of more than twenty deities, many of which were immediately recognizable. The remarkable conclusion to be drawn from his list was that these are deities, not of the Hattic,

* See Bibliography, under 'Journal Articles'.

but of the *Hurrian* pantheon and that any ritual which may be represented is therefore presumably that of the Hurrian religion. Laroche was inclined to explain this unexpected circumstance by the existing historical evidence which suggests that the latter was introduced to the Hittite court by Puduhepa, the Hurrian wife of Hattusilis III, who after her husband's death became for a time co-regent with Tudhaliyas. He accordingly inferred that this happened in about 1250 B.C.

To return to the arrangement of galleries in the grotto, one comes first into the main shrine, which is a chamber more than 60 feet wide and 100 in depth. It is here that the whole pantheon of Hurrian deities is arrayed in order, and the focal point of the procession where the principal god and goddess confront each other occurs on an isolated rock, facing diagonally towards the centre of the chamber. At its base there is a flat shelf of stone which could perhaps have supported an altar or offering-table. On the right of this chamber there is a narrow cleft in the rock leading to the inner sanctuary, and one notices the grotesquely carved figures whose threaten-gestures guard its entrance. The sanctuary itself is a much narrower gallery, originally perhaps accessible from outside, though the alternative approach is now blocked with fallen stone. The scenes on its walls (King embraced by 'Young God', facing 'Dagger God' on the left; procession of running figures on the right) are oriented towards the inner end, and here the hieroglyph symbols of the king's name, isolated upon an empty wall face, suggest that there may have been a free-standing statue. (Plates 13a and b, 14a)

Excavations on the terrace in front of the grotto have revealed traces of a complex building, guarding the approach to the galleries. Only the foundations had survived, and among these there was evidence of rebuilding on several occasions: so the plan was by no means easy to disentangle. But the German architects have attempted a reconstruction, and in this one sees three distinct units. First, to the north-west there is a propylon with a wide flight of steps. This brings one, again by steps, to a temple building with a courtyard, somewhat similar to those in the town, but having its sanctuary replaced by a portico leading to the rock-chamber behind. Finally, there is another detached portico screening the blocked entrance to the inner gallery. If the reconstruction is correct, the appearance of these buildings against their background of rocks must have been most striking.

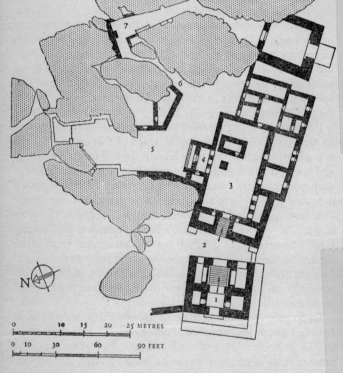

Figure 10. Plan of building excavation outside the shrine at Yazılıkaya.

The galleries at Yazılıkaya contain by far the largest known assemblage of sculpture dateable to the period of the Hittite Empire. Otherwise the site of Hattusas has little to offer in this respect, save for the figures decorating its three main gateways. Of these the famous 'warrior' figure at least with its armour and weapons is of considerable archaeological interest, but it is hard to see in any of these works evidence of much aesthetic sensibility on the part of the sculptor. The same may be said of the contemporary sculptures at the neighbouring site of Alaja; the Sphinx figures guarding the gate and reliefs from the gate chamber behind, which gives one the impression of craftsmen working in an unfamiliar medium. As for sculpture in the round, we are unhappily in no position to form an opinion, since small figurines only have survived. Of the larger metal statues, described with so much detail in the texts, we have been deprived by the avarice of succeeding generations and must content ourselves with their empty bases. (Plate 12a)

THE ROCK MONUMENTS

For a more interesting aspect of Hittite sculpture, we should perhaps turn to the quite numerous rock monuments which are scattered over the countryside. These fall into several categories. First there are those which, like Yazılıkaya itself, denote the existence in Hittite times of a religious sanctuary or shrine. Among these are, for instance, the sculptures at Eflatun Pinar, north of the Beyşehir Lake; the two sanctuaries at Karadagh and Kizildagh, near Karaman, and another on Mount Sipylos, above Manisa (Magnesia-ad-Sipylum). The second group are mere rock reliefs, and there has in the past been some doubt about their purpose, the earlier travellers having tended to see in them commemorative memorials like those on which Assyrian kings were wont to record their victories. We shall, however, presently suggest reasons for believing that they too have a purely religious purpose. There are two on rock faces at Fraktin and Sirkeli, respectively overlooking the Seyhan and Jeyhan rivers; one at Gavur (Giaour) Kalesi, near Ankara; an important one on the Karabel pass near Manisa and another at Hânyeri, on the Gezbel pass. Finally there are miscellaneous monuments, such as the altars with their troughs for libations, at Emir Gazi and Köylütülü Yayla, the stela at

Karahüyük near Elbistan and the great statue of a deity at
Fassiler.

The mention of two monuments so far afield as Manisa in
the remote Aegean province at once raises an interesting
problem. For though the arguments for attributing the whole
list to the period of the Hittite Empire are extremely convincing, the justification for calling them all 'Hittite' is much
more debatable. Before going into this question, however,
we should perhaps examine more closely the character and
purpose of the monuments themselves, allowing the subject
of their authorship spontaneously to present itself. As an
instance, then, of a sculpture upon which our improved
understanding of hieroglyphs has thrown some new light, we
may first take Karabel.

KARABEL*

From Kemalpaşa east of Izmir, a mountain track leads through
the Karabel Pass, which gives direct access from the Hermos
valley to the plain of the Cayster to the north. It is here that
the famous sculpture is carved on a conspicuous rock-face
60 feet above the road. Occupying a rectangular niche about
9 feet high, is a figure carved in relief, wearing a 'Hittite' kilt
and boots with a peaked and horned cap upon his head. He
carries a bow in his right hand and a staff or spear in his left,
while a sword hangs from his belt. In front of his face is an
inscription in hieroglyphs, which is unfortunately hard to decipher, owing to its being badly weathered. The title, however,
can at least be read of the individual who set up the monument,
and he describes himself as 'Great King'. Among the remaining groups of signs one authority has supposed that he could
recognize the name of Tudhaliyas IV, the Yazılıkaya king, and
suggested that the monument might be intended to commemorate his victory (alleged in the texts) over the kingdom of
Aššuwa, a name apparently associated in Hittite times with the
Aegean province. Others, however, reject this reading of the
king's name. They prefer to think of the relief as the work of

* Best picture in Bossert, *Alt-Anatolien*, Nos. 557-9.

a local Aššuwan ruler and to explain it as some sort of religious monument, for, as they point out, the figure represented both here and in a very similar relief at Gezbel, also set up above the road on an important pass, is that of a god, and that none of the inscriptions which accompany such reliefs make any mention of a victory. The belief has in fact eventually become prevalent that all such inscriptions and the acts depicted in the reliefs are of a religious character.

One or two other cases may be cited in support of this conclusion. There is, for instance, the interesting relief at Fraktin, in Cappadocia, overlooking the Kara Su, which is in fact an upper reach of the Cilician river Seyhan. Half a century ago Ramsay had already identified the place as the Dastarkon of Strabo, and taken note of it as an important Hittite shrine. He had even remarked how, in Christian times, its sanctity had been perpetuated by the local foundation of a bishopric. In this case, the subject of the relief is a fairly elaborate one, but the central group can be clearly identified by the hieroglyphs which are incorporated. The Hittite king, Hattusilis III and his Hurrian wife, Puduhepa, whom we have already mentioned in connexion with Yazılıkaya, are making offerings on an altar to a figure who may just possibly be a Kizzuwatnian god, Ais. In the similar relief, overlooking the Ceyhan River near Misis (Mopsuestia) in Cilicia itself, an earlier king, Muwatallis, son of Mursilis II, is again seen in an attitude of adoration: but in this case the figure of the god is missing and only the smoothed surface on which it was to have been carved can be distinguished. Returning to Mount Sipylos in the Aegean province, there is another famous monument of the shrine type among the rocks above Manisa.* This is the 30-foot female figure seated in a niche, from which she looks out over the fertile plain, watered by the Cayster River. But here again there is a much-weathered group of hieroglyphs, and the sign for a goddess can be distinguished, suggesting that the implication in some words of Pausanias that she was the great Asiatic 'Mother-Goddess' ought rather to be considered.

* Best picture in Bossert, *Alt-Anatolien*, Nos. 560–2.

EFLATUN*

Still in the same category is the shrine at Eflatun Pinar, some ten miles east of Beyşehir. Only, unlike the monuments with which we have been dealing till now, the ground upon which it is carved is not the natural rock, but a colossal 'altar', built up with blocks of masonry. The front of the structure bearing the relief overlooks a pool of water from which a stream flows westwards towards the lake. The composition of the sculpture is interesting. The central group consists of a god and goddess, both seated on thrones and surmounted by winged sun-discs, the god wearing a high peaked cap and the goddess a halo-shaped coiffure. On either side are groups of five genii with various attributes, two of which support the outstretched wings of an immense sun symbol by which the whole scene is surmounted. The Sun-God and Sun-Goddess should perhaps be taken to be Estan and Wurusemu of the old Hattic pantheon, but there is only the character of the masonry to justify the classification of the monument as 'Hittite'.

KARADAGH†

Next, there are two curious relics of imperial Hittite times in the district of Karaman. One of these is at the ultimate summit of the high mountain called Karadagh, on whose sides stand the ruined shells of the famous 'Thousand-and-one-Churches' (Binbirkilise). It can be identified as a cave sanctuary by a long hieroglyph inscription on the rock, but all other characteristics are obscured by the ruins of a monastery chapel which was built over it in about the ninth century A.D. This again has been cited by Ramsay as illustrating the respect shown by the early Christian Church for localities sanctified by pagan tradition. A sanctuary of a rather different type occupies a rocky spur called Kizildagh, projecting from the western flank of the same mountain. Here, in a position commanding a

* Best picture in Bossert, *Alt-Anatolien*, Nos. 526–7. Also cf. K. Bittel in *Bibliotheca Orientalis*, X (1953), p. 225, Plates 1, 2, and 3.

† See W. M. Ramsay, *Thousand and One Churches*, Figs. 371 a and b, 375, Plates V 9 and 10, VI 11 and 12.

magnificent view over the lake and marshes at the foot of the mountain, the rock has been carved into the shape of a huge, empty throne, and adorned with a relief representing a seated king and two hieroglyph inscriptions. Both here and at Karadagh the name of a 'Great King' is mentioned and he is described as 'Son of Mursilis'; but his name itself is only sufficiently legible to prove it unrelated to any known child of the Hittite king Mursilis II.

FASSILER*

One more important sculpture remains to be mentioned, though it stands in a class apart from those with which we have so far been dealing. It is a cult statue of monumental proportions – perhaps the only example surviving from imperial Hittite times – and it is to be seen lying prostrate on a hillside, above the village of Fassiler, ten miles east of Beyşehir. It is of local stone, and one must conclude that, having been quarried and carved somewhere in the neighbourhood, cirstances prevented it from being transported to its intended destination and that it was consequently abandoned and forgotten. The monument itself is really a stela upon which is carved, partly in relief and partly in the round, the figure of a god more than four metres high. Wearing a peaked and horned cap he stands with one arm raised above his shoulder and the other extended in front of him. Beneath his feet is a smaller figure, probably a mountain-genius, like those which appear in the central group at Yazılıkaya, and the base of the stela is supported on either side by a pair of lions, also carved partly in the round. It ends below in a tongued projection, obviously intended to fit a socketed pedestal. At a distance of about four miles there is a mound representing the remains of a substantial 'Hittite' settlement, and this has been proposed as the site of the temple for which the statue was originally destined.

The above brief account of the principal monuments generally considered to date from the time of the Hittite

* Best picture in Bossert, *Alt-Anatolien*, Nos. 565-6, 568-9.

Empire, will be seen to have produced much evidence pointing to their exclusively religious character. There remains, as
we have said, the question of their authorship. Some of them,
of course, like those at Fraktin and Sirkeli, are shown to be
authentically Hittite by the 'signature' of a king whose name
is familiar. But others, and particularly those which are
located in places remote from the Hittite 'home-land', deserve
further scrutiny, since they record names which are significantly absent from the Hittite king-lists, and could well refer
to the rulers of neighbouring states. The fact that, in such
cases, a 'Great King' is sometimes mentioned, may be taken
to imply that these rulers felt justified in thinking of themselves as equal if not superior to their rivals at Hattusas.

From our limited knowledge then, of contemporary
geography, we are perhaps justified in concluding that the
'Great King', mentioned for instance in the Karabel inscription, is a ruler of Aššuwa. Nor is there much reason to doubt
his justification in assuming so pretentious a title, when one
recollects the references to Aššuwa in the Hittite records.
Tudhaliyas, for instance, in a campaign against an Aššuwan
ruler called Piyama Lama, is said to have captured 10,000
prisoners and 600 chariots, a fact, which, even allowing for
a little understandable exaggeration, classes him as a formidable enemy. Again on the basis of geographical evidence, one
could suppose that the rulers mentioned on the monuments
on Karadagh and even the authors of the anonymous sculptures at Eflatun and Fassiler might be kings of the great state
called Arzawa. In the Hattusas archives one observes the
respect shown by the Hittites, at least for the military strength
of their Arzawan neighbours, and recognizes once more a
nation whose ruler might well describe himself as 'Great
King'. Through the medium, therefore, of the Anatolian rock
monuments we are introduced to a much wider subject;
namely the character and inter-relations of other powers with
whom the imperial Hittites found themselves in contact within
the geographical limits which have been prescribed for our
survey.

ANATOLIA IN HITTITE TIMES

Let us start then with the lands in the west, of which the remote 'Aegean province' is composed. Having once more returned to the use of this convenient term, it will first be desirable to consider its meaning more carefully. We must, for example, provisionally exclude from it the regions which afterwards came to be known as Caria and Lycia, on account of their exclusive character. Large parts of them were probably virtually uninhabited at this time. This will leave an area extending approximately from the river Meander in the south, to the Hellespont and Marmara in the north, and limited to the east by the debatable frontiers of Arzawa. If, thereafter an attempt is to be made to identify the whole of this province with the Aššuwa of the Hittite records, the question will at once arise as to its relationship with Troy.* For the fourteenth and thirteenth centuries with which we are dealing must be considered as bridging the short period of time during which the affairs of that city are so suddenly and brightly illuminated, if not by historical records, at least by literary tradition. Unfortunately where our immediate interest is concerned the tradition itself is surprisingly uninformative. For the Iliad throws no light at all on the status of Troy as an Anatolian city and little on the names and disposition of neighbouring peoples at this period. The implication of this negative evidence is of course that the Troad at least must be excluded from the Aššuwan state which we are trying to envisage. It is a curious fact, however, that the archaeological evidence, if it alone were to be considered, would point to a somewhat different conclusion. In most respects the keynote for the whole area we have been discussing is set by finds associated with the contemporary settlements at Troy (VI and VIIA). These we should now observe.

TROY VI AND VIIA

The period of Anatolian history, which lasts from the destruction of the Assyrian colony at Kültepe down to the end of the

---

* See also O. R. Gurney, *The Hittites*, p. 56, for the linguistic evidence on this problem.

Hittite Empire, corresponds at Troy to the settlements which are numbered VI and VIIA. Blegen dates the beginning of the sixth settlement to a little before 1725, and its final destruction by earthquake to 1275. The ninety or so years which followed would account for the lifetime of the Homeric city (VIIA) which rose upon its ruins. Unfortunately, for the present the final report on the American excavations stops short of Homeric Troy and we are left to assume that, both in architectural character and material culture generally, it closely resembled the previous settlement in its final stages.

The first fact which becomes clear in the early stages of the sixth settlement is that there has been a very considerable increase in the prosperity and importance of the city. After a period of deterioration into an undistinguished market town it has now returned to its old status as the seat of a ruler and centre of administration. This can be inferred from the remains on the fortress hill, in spite of the peculiar circumstances which have so regrettably reduced their extent and impaired the completeness of their testimony. To understand this it is necessary once more to recollect the nature of the citadel itself, as we have already seen it in the early second millennium, forming an emplacement for the Chalcolithic and Early Bronze Age settlements.

The Citadel. The top of the rock is not level, but slopes down from a precipitous edge on the north side to easier approaches on the south. It was natural therefore that the principal buildings – in this case presumably the palace of the ruler – should occupy the most elevated position to the north. This had evidently continued to be the case down to the Homeric age, with the result that when, in Hellenistic and again in Roman times, the summit was artificially levelled to provide a dignified platform for a temple and other buildings, it was the most important of the earlier remains which suffered. The ruins of ancient palaces were removed bodily and the highest part of the citadel once more denuded almost to the bare rock. In the case of the Late Bronze Age settlement, only one circumstance saved it from complete obliteration. As a result of the city's increasing importance, the area of the fortified enclosure had been considerably extended, with the result that, on the lower southern slope the peripheral defences and certain outlying, subsidiary buildings survived as an indication of the general lay-out.

How then should we picture the Troy of Hittite times, to which Priam's fortress must be assimilated? It is still an oval enclosure, and it now has a maximum dimension of about 200 metres. There is a main gateway, guarded by a tower, and at least three subsidiary ones, from which roads about three metres wide lead radially inwards towards a vanished centre of interest in the north-central area. The walls, like those of the Early Bronze Age settlements, are built on a stone sub-structure, raked at a sharp angle outside. They are five metres thick and have a shallow break in the face at regular intervals, where the angle changes. In the absence of projecting buttresses, this would have given vertical accentuation to their architectural appearance. By contemporary standards, however, the appearance of the fortress as a whole can hardly be considered to have been in any way remarkable. Surviving within the walls are half a dozen dwelling-houses, probably residences of retainers or dependents of the ruling family. They are simply planned but large rectangular buildings, and the considerable span (in one case over eight metres) between the walls is reduced by intermediate supports – wooden columns on stone bases or tapering piers of ashlar masonry. They doubtless had more than one storey and there is no regular feature of their plan which would justify their identification as *megara*. In fact, in Blegen's words, 'it may be wondered if a true megaron occurs at all in Troy VI'.

Innovations. In other fields the new inhabitants of Troy in the time of the sixth settlement were responsible for a number of drastic innovations. They had an almost universal preference for a grey pottery with a burnished surface of a type which has no antecedent in Asia Minor. It has, however, been familiar on the Greek mainland since the time of Schliemann, who christened it Minyan after the place where it was first found. Among the animal bones from earlier settlements, those of the horse had been conspicuously absent; but the makers of Minyan pottery seem also to have been horsemen. They cremated their dead like the Hittites, and buried them in cinerary urns, but their contacts seem to have been pre-eminently with the Aegean and the west. Not a sherd of Hittite pottery was found, and very few other indications of trade with the interior. Among their possessions the most elegant objects, such as carved ivory ornaments or swords with alabaster pommels, were clearly imported from Greece; yet it was not until the final years before the destruction of the settlement that Mycenaean pottery began to be imported in very large quantities.

Whether or not, during these years, Troy was identified or associated with a state known to the Hittites as Aššuwa, comprising the entire region afterwards called the 'Province of Asia', it can at least be said that there is nothing among the material remains to distinguish it from any other site in that area so far archaeologically investigated. Products of or similar to those of Troy VI have already been found from the Meander valley to the shore of Marmara.

MYCENAEAN RELATIONS

Troy is by no means the only site in the coastal provinces of Asia Minor where Mycenaean pottery has been found in use. In the Aegean area it comes from places like Miletus, Phokaia, and Kolophon; excavations at the last-named in 1922 even revealed a *tholos* tomb, robbed, it is true, in antiquity, but still containing some fragments of Mycenaean pottery. In Cilicia Mycenaean ware is plentiful, not only in the excavation at Tarsus, where it has been discovered by H. Goldman, but at many other sites which till now are only known by surface finds. In the majority of these cases no other explanation is needed than that commercial contacts between Greece and Asia Minor were already sufficiently well established for Greek commodities to appear in Anatolian markets. The unique exception is the case of Miletus, for here the German excavations of 1938 revealed quite a different situation. There was definite evidence of a fortified town, with pottery covering the whole Mycenaean period, and its discoverers were satisfied that, rather than an Asiatic city importing Mycenaean wares, this was indeed an actual Mycenaean settlement. They could even infer from it that Miletus was first founded by settlers from Crete.

On reflection this would appear to have been a significant fact. The settlement at Miletus can hardly have been unique, and, if one is already at this early period to imagine a multiplicity of such colonies on the west and south coasts, it is difficult not to conclude that the culture of the Asiatic states in the interior may to some extent have been influenced by them.

One must recollect at this point the existence in the Hittite records of a people called Ahhiyawâ; a thalassocracy at the time of the empire which had established a foothold on the mainland of Asia Minor and entered into relations, not always friendly, with the Hittite state. O. R. Gurney has shown in *The Hittites*, that there is a good case for identifying the Ahhiyawans with the Achaeans, and so with some subdivision of the politically disunited Mycenaean world. He suggests that the kings of Ahhiyawâ might be equated with the rulers, if not of Mycenae itself, of some minor Aegean kingdom.

The principal foreign contacts of the Hittites, however, determined by commercial or political expediency, were with countries east of the Mediterranean. One might now expect to find that, on the contrary, those of Aššuwa or Arzawa were with Crete and Mycenae through the medium of these Asiatic outposts of Greek civilization. Their character would in this case hardly have remained totally unaffected.

ARZAWA AND KIZZUWATNA

It is a curious situation that to-day we should be in a position to speculate only in such vague terms as these about the non-Hittite states of Anatolia. One contributory factor is the paucity of archaeological information. Here, for instance, in the case of Arzawa, is a nation which, at any moment, we are prepared to see revealed as a serious rival to the Hittites themselves in the cultural as well as the military field. Yet its material remains have till now been restricted to the results of half a dozen minor excavations at village sites, where the period of its greatness could be represented only by a dozen pottery vessels and a few bronze implements. The case of Kizzuwatna is hardly less deplorable. A seal found by the American expedition at Tarsus in 1935 and bearing in hiero-glyphs the name of Isputakhsus, a Kizzuwatnian king, pro-vided the first shred of tangible archaeological evidence to confirm the philological hypothesis that the Cilician plain was included in the territory of that state. No other has since been found, and upon this single object still rests the responsibility and justification for identifying certain anonymous products of Cilician excavations with historical Kizzuwatna.

The matter has indeed proved of some importance, since the archaeological harvest in this case has not been negligible. Contemporary occupation levels, for example, at Tarsus made it possible to assess the extent and direction of trade with foreign countries like Cyprus or Syria. At Mersin products characteristic of Hittite craftsmanship showed only slight local modification, and a fortress built at this period, guarding the northern approach to the coastal plain, had an unmistak-ably Hittite appearance. Such discoveries are significant as constituting the only material legacy of a state on whose support or subordination Hittite power so often and so greatly depended.

OTHER NEIGHBOURS

Laroche's curious discovery in connexion with the subject of the Yazılıkaya sculptures has already served to emphasize the intimacy and importance of the relationship between the ruling dynasty at Hattusas and its Hurrian neighbours. The Hurrians are a people who materialize historically early in the second millennium B.C., from a provenance corresponding to modern Kurdistan, and extend their territory westwards across northern Mesopotamia as far as the Euphrates. The king-dom of Mitanni, whose name begins to appear early in the fifteenth century, was ruled over by a powerful aristocracy, served by Hurrians and perhaps federated with independent Hurrian states. Its territory was the rich piedmont country between the two great Mesopotamian rivers, where desert meets the foothills of the Anatolian mountains. Its neighbours to the west of the Euphrates were small Syrian states, like Haleb (Aleppo) and Alalakh (Atchana). A great part of the Hittite records are concerned with the relations of Hattusas with these states, whose status during the intervals of peace, varied from enforced dependence to uneasy alliance. Archaeologically their history is moderately well documented, particularly in the case of Alalakh by Sir L. Woolley's brilliantly successful excavations at Atchana. The character of the Hurrians also was revealed in great detail by the American excavations at Nuzi, near Kirkuk in Iraq, where, in addition to an archive of tablets, the appointments of a small palace were found in a well-preserved condition. The material culture of Mitanni, which no doubt was largely similar to or even identical with the Hurrian, must however for its authentic revelation await the discovery and excavation of its capital Waššukkanni. In any case, none of these states may be legitimately considered to fall within the province covered by this book.

With the countries of the Black Sea coast, whose archaeology is at least as tenuous as that, for instance of Arzawa, the circle of Hittite connexions is completed. Their mere enumeration will have served to emphasize the monopoly of interest which Hattusas itself has succeeded in establishing, and by contrast, the obscurity in which so much of its political environment is still wrapped, owing to the unbalanced state of our present knowledge.

CHAPTER 9

The Syro-Hittite Period

THE political identity of the Hittite people was not, like the temporal power of their emperors, obliterated by the disaster which overwhelmed the empire. In a changed setting, Hittite culture survived, retaining even something of its individuality for a further five centuries. To this 'Indian summer' indeed we owe a greater heritage of monuments than that bequeathed by the empire itself, but in order to understand its character, one must first attempt to visualize the different social and geographic milieu in which its creators now lived.

In the archaeological scheme of chronology we have now passed the point of transition from the Bronze Age to the Iron Age. During the centuries which we are about to consider, it was the use of iron weapons on a large scale which made the Assyrian armies irresistible and so led them to conquests and political contacts far beyond the confines of their old Meso-potamian territory. Accordingly, in the absence of any other historical source, it is mainly from isolated references to the Hittites in the Assyrian records that one may reconstruct a bare outline of their history and guess at their varying fortunes.

In 1110 B.C., for instance, Tiglath Pileser I encounters a political federation based on Milid (Malatya), to which he refers as 'Great Hatti'. A few years later he is in contact with another principality of the same name at Carchemish on the Euphrates: so that one is led to assume that these two cities, which had already attained political maturity under the Empire and survived its downfall, had now come to serve as rallying centres for the dispersed remnants of its people. After this, new place-names begin to be mentioned, and the city states designated as Hittite increase in numbers. Tuwanuwa (Tyana) is understood to survive precariously on the fringe of the lost 'home-land' in Cappadocia; Marqasi (Marash) and Sam'al (Sinjerli) appear east of the Taurus: Til Barsip (Tell

Ahmar) on the Euphrates below Carchemish. Aleppo and other north Syrian cities have been part-Hittite since imperial times. By the end of the tenth century other states have been added and their constellated pattern begins to acquire definition. Their size is in some cases unpretentious, the state territory extending hardly beyond the suburbs of the city from which it takes its name. Yet their capacity for political unity appears negligible, and their only common aim a determined resistance to Assyrian domination.

It appears in fact that this sufficed to keep them in relative independence until the revival of Assyrian power under Adad-nirari II in about 900 B.C., when their position became more precarious. In 876 B.C. they were subjected by Assurnasir-pal, for some reason almost without resistance, and made to pay tribute, but during the half century which followed were almost continually in revolt, latterly in alliance with and under the leadership of the Urartian kings. The final downfall of their temporary federation was at the hands of Shalmaneser III, and in the two final decades of the eighth century they were one by one annexed by Sargon II and finally lost their independence.

What is known from the historic records serves at least to give some impression of the geographical circumstances in which the Hittites found themselves under the new régime: a constellation of cities or city states, spreadeagled across the Taurus ranges and extending southwards into Syria. But politically and socially the picture is by no means complete. It would be wrong, for instance, to think of this enclave as an exclusively Hittite realm, in the sense that the Anatolian 'home-land' had been in earlier times, or to imagine its complete monopolization by the Hittites after a mass migration from one to the other. There is indeed evidence to show that an important element of the Anatolian population moved southwards, but being unable or unwilling to displace the peoples whom they found in possession of the southern provinces, could only allow themselves to become gradually absorbed into an existing political fabric. Let us glance, then, at this fabric as it existed before their arrival.

In the final centuries of the second millennium, the Taurus and north Syrian states had a composite population comprising at least three distinct elements. Longest established of all were the Semitic communities; no longer Amorites, but Aramaeans; sometime nomads in the Syrian desert who had adapted themselves to life in settled communities. The next component was a Hurrian stratum, surviving from the days of Mitannian expansion beyond the Euphrates: an element whose influence now took a more cultural than political form. And finally, in those cities which had for long remained dependencies or protectorates of the Anatolian Empire, there were already true Hittite communities of considerable proportions. In some states, therefore, the new influx of Anatolians would tip the balance in favour of a Hittite political monopoly: in others the newcomers would remain a minority or contest the political authority of their Semitic rivals with a degree of success which varied from generation to generation. In fact, of the city states Carchemish seems from the first to have remained more uncompromisingly Hittite than the rest. Others like Sinjerli and Til Barsip passed through long periods of submission to Aramaean rulers. Tell Halaf, far to the east of the Euphrates was hardly subject to Hittite influence at all and developed an exclusively Semitic culture.

Now, therefore, the pattern of the Syro-Hittite world becomes more clearly visible; individual states, composed of diverse political elements, whose varying preponderance made federation precarious. From the culture which developed in such an environment one would expect neither consistency nor distinctive vitality, and indeed political and social conditions are everywhere reflected in the archaeological remains.

The Antiquities

It will be recollected from the summary of archaeological discoveries included in an earlier chapter, that our knowledge of Syro-Hittite culture results primarily from a series of major excavations which took place in Turkey and elsewhere for the most part during the early years of the present century. Foremost among those which fall within our present geographical sphere were the British excavations at Carchemish and those of the Germans at Sinjerli. Sakjegözü also made a major contribution, and in more recent years a new chapter has been added by the work of French archaeologists at Arslantepe (Malatya). In addition, there are individual monuments from Maraş, Gaziantep, Urfa and elsewhere, but these, unfortunately, in themselves constitute the only clue to the ancient cities from which they came. Accordingly, in a dissertation for example on the subject of Syro-Hittite architecture or sculpture, one would draw primarily upon the results of these excavations, but there would be supplementary sources outside this immediate province, in Syria and even Palestine, which for a complete picture should occasionally be taken into account.

SCULPTURE

What, then, is the nature of our heritage from Syro-Hittite times, and of what do the surviving antiquities consist? First and foremost there is a formidable collection of sculptures, mostly small stone slabs ornamented with figures in relief, which to-day are distributed fairly equally between British, German and Turkish museums. The slabs are 'orthostats' (a term merely denoting that they are intended to occupy an upright position) and their purpose, when arranged side by side in series, was to form a kind of 'dado' ornament at the base of the walls inside or outside public buildings. Archaeology has been familiar with this form of architectural ornament already for over a century; the Assyrian palaces revealed by the earliest Mesopotamian excavations were decorated with such slabs – more impressive indeed than their Hittite counterparts, since they stood usually to a height of three metres or more, and were carved with greater technical skill in a more suitable stone. But in Assyria there are no examples of such slabs which can be dated to a period earlier than the reign of Assur-nasir-pal, who made Nimrud his capital early in the ninth century; whereas in the Hittite world we have already seen a monumental gateway at Alaja ornamented in this way in the fourteenth. We must therefore conclude that both the orthostat reliefs and the sculptured lions in the gateways (whose early date we have already referred to at Boghazköy) were the architectural invention of the Hittites, adopted and eventually improved upon by the Assyrians, as an alternative to the painted frescoes which had previously been in the rule in Mesopotamian public buildings.

One has at once to admit that the Hittite reliefs are from several points of view unimpressive. In the first place the slabs are small – seldom much more than a metre high – and in the second, the sculpture itself is technically immature and the designs poorly balanced. Though the reliefs of the Imperial period are carved exclusively on white limestone of a fairly consistent texture, the fashion became prevalent in Syro-Hittite times, of alternating the material and consequently the colour of the slabs, preferably from black to white. The darkest stone available was the coarse black basalt, which is so plentifully available in north Syria, and this came into such general use, that both masons and draughtsmen were clearly compelled to adapt their technique to its unresponsive character, and one gains the impression that the possibilities of greater refinement in carving offered by other materials were eventually forgotten. Any aesthetic interest, therefore, which the Syro-Hittite sculptures may possess, is greatly outweighed by the archaeological and documentary importance of their content, the latter being again greatly enhanced by the liberal addition of hieroglyphic inscriptions over and among the relief representation of human or divine figures. But before going into any further details regarding the subject of these sculptures and the stylistic evidence which they afford for purposes of comparative dating, it may be well to make some attempt at classifying the buildings in which they appear, availing ourselves at the same time of the opportunity for a general survey of Syro-Hittite architecture.

ARCHITECTURE

Carchemish. The best subjects of study in this respect are Carchemish and Sinjerli. There is nothing very remarkable in either case about their fortifications, which are heavy walls of mud-brick on stone foundations, strengthened in the case of Sinjerli though not of Carchemish, with projecting towers. In the citadel walls at Sinjerli, these take the form of semi-circular bastions, a feature otherwise rather uncommon in Hittite architecture generally. The gateways generally follow the Assyrian model, with flanking towers and, inside the line of the wall itself, a structure containing one or more gate chambers, through which one passes on their cross-axis. At Carchemish the old Water Gate had two extra pairs of lateral chambers and, as one might well have expected considering the date of its construction somewhere about the middle of the second millennium, more closely resembled the portals of Boghazköy. Instead of orthostat slabs, this gate was also decorated with sculptured reliefs on the actual blocks of which its stone sub-structure was composed.

The principal group of public buildings excavated at Carchemish was disposed around an irregular shaped *piazza* at the foot of the citadel mound. It was approached from the 'Inner Town' to the south by a processional gateway, and on the east side by a wide street leading up from the Water Gate. To the north, a monumental stairway rose up through a covered gateway to the citadel, and beside it there was a large temple with a curiously irregular plan. Of the two principal groups of sculptures found in this so-called 'Lower Palace' area, one adorned the staircase and the temple façade facing the *piazza*, which came to be known as the 'Long Wall of Sculptures'; the other, a corresponding façade facing north-wards towards the temple itself. This is usually referred to as the 'Herald's Wall'. South of the *piazza* was a substantially built *hilâni* – a type of building about which there will pre-sently be much to say.

Sinjerli. At Sinjerli matters were rather different. In this case the remains at the summit of the fortified citadel were reason-ably well preserved, and it was here that the principal public buildings were excavated. The citadel was approached by an inner and an outer monumental gateway, since the walls were planned to give a double line of defence. Inside, there was an

'Upper Palace' to the north-east, commanding a fine view over the tops of the fortifications to the open country beyond. Below, to the north-west, there was another and more elaborate complex of buildings, known to the excavators as the 'Lower Palace'. The principal sources of sculpture in this case were the gateways, particularly the southern city gate and the outer portal of the citadel. The palace buildings on the citadel itself were also productive. (See Fig. 11)

One interesting feature of building methods at Sinjerli, which distinguished it entirely from Carchemish, was the use of wooden beams as reinforcement in the walls, as we have so continually seen done in Anatolia. At Carchemish the major walls of a building usually rested upon a rather roughly laid rubble foundation. Upon this were laid a couple of courses of regular masonry, and then a structure about a metre or more high, composed of inner and outer shells of stonework with a filling of rubble between. It was to this part of the wall that the orthostat slabs, either plain or sculptured, were applied as facing, and their top edges usually coincided with the upper limit of the stonework. From here upwards the wall was composed of plain sun-dried brick, faced inside and out with mud plaster. At Sinjerli, on the other hand, stout wooden beams were built in as ties for the first course of masonry, and again at the point where the brick upper structure began. Above this they formed a regular framework in the thickness of the wall.

Apart from the many earlier examples of this device which have already been brought to our attention, it is to be seen in the principal buildings at almost every one of the Syro-Hittite sites which have so far been excavated. It occurs for example in the 'Lion Gate' at Arslantepe (Malatya) and is admirably illustrated by the reconstruction of that building, with its original sculptures, at the entrance to the Ankara Museum. Far to the south it was to be seen in a *hilâni* palace at Taynat, the site 'across the road' from Atchana, to which the Iron Age inhabitants of Alalakh moved their abode, and here one may also notice how the wooden beams fed the flames of the fire which destroyed it. There are many other examples.

In noting, therefore, that the builders of Carchemish, like their neighbours in Mesopotamia, would apparently consider no other method of strengthening their walls than that of increasing their thickness, one must consider whether the explanation of this peculiarity may not indeed be connected with this city's geographical situation. The acknowledged advantages of a 'half-timber' construction in a region subject to earthquakes have conditioned building methods for instance in Anatolia up to quite recent times, and one is led to wonder whether, even in antiquity, such a device were not intended to give to a building that elasticity which would increase its power of resistance. Certainly Carchemish is situated outside the area where this particular menace is most prevalent.

The 'Hilâni'. To return to the buildings on the citadel hill at Sinjerli; the 'Lower Palace', in particular, comprises a complex of separate units, linked together by cloisters and open courts. Within this complex and in the 'Upper Palace' above, there are at least five examples of the unit known as a hilâni — by far the most interesting architectural feature of this period. It consists in a standard suite of reception rooms, each of a prescribed shape and having a standard relationship with its neighbours. In palace buildings of this sort it is a circumscribed element which may vary in size, but whose plan may not be radically changed or elaborated, and it can apparently be repeated or duplicated as the demand arises. It consists, first, of a portico open to one side, its façade supported by one to three columns and approached usually by a low flight of steps. From this there is access by one or more doors to a rectangular 'throne-room', whose long axis is also parallel to the façade. At one end of the portico there is a compartment containing a staircase leading to the upper storey, and beside or beyond the throne room there can be a single range of minor rooms, one perhaps having the function of a bedroom and another of a bathroom. In the hilâni of King Bar-Rakkab in the 'Lower Palace' at Sinjerli, the emplacement of a throne could still be recognized at the end of the main chamber, and

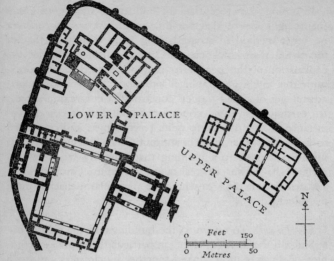

Figure 11. Sinjerli: Palaces in the citadel

before it there was a circular hearth. In a similar throne room at Tell Halaf, von Oppenheim found an iron hearth mounted on bronze wheels which could be moved about as convenient: the same device must have been used in the Upper Palace *hilâni* at Sinjerli, for the grooved stone 'rails' in which it moved could still be seen.

There were other interesting architectural features associated with these *hilâni* buildings. The columns were of wood and had consequently perished, but they had bases, and probably capitals of stone. The bases were of two types: a simple 'cushion' form, composed of three unequal 'torus' mouldings, deeply enriched with carving, or a more elaborately sculptured affair in the shape of paired bulls or lions, sometimes with a smaller figure between. In a unique (and for that matter un-Hittite) example at Tell Halaf, single sculptured beasts formed the bases and the wooden shafts of the columns were replaced by colossal and outlandish human figures in stone, two of them male and one female. A fragment of a stone throne from Taynat gives an impression of what the capitals may have been like: it incorporates a volute form of the type which used to be called 'proto-Ionic'. Finally it is known that these buildings were ornamented with windows in the external façades. (Plate 20)

It seems then that the *bît hilâni* formed an attractive feature of these Syro-Hittite palaces. Certainly the Assyrian kings thought so: for more than one of them is known to have incorporated some arrangement of this sort in his own residence. There is, for instance, the famous paragraph in King Sargon's account of the building of Khorsabad. He says: 'A portico patterned after a Hittite palace, which they call a *bît hilâni* in the Amorite tongue, I built in front of their (i.e. the Palaces') gates. Eight lions, in pairs, weighing 4610 talents of shining bronze fashioned according to the workmanship of Ninagal and of dazzling brightness; four cedar columns, exceedingly high, each 1 GAR in thickness, products of Mount Amanus, I placed on top of the lion-colossi, and set them up as posts to support their doors.'* We have already mentioned in a previous chapter how Sargon's use of the term 'Hittite palace' led to the assumption that the origin of the *bît hilâni* was to be sought in Anatolia – an unwarranted deduction in reality, since for these late Assyrian kings 'Hittite' naturally meant north Syrian. On the other hand, in the successive re-plannings of the Syrian palace excavated by Woolley at Atchana, its evolution can be traced from the early second millennium onwards, and it is not inconceivable that the people of that city were at that time aware of and influenced by contemporary architectural fashions in Anatolia. It should be added that, in the hands of Assyrian architects it tends to lose its true character and to become a mere portico (as Sargon described it), or colonnade between two courtyards.

SCULPTURAL SUBJECTS

We must now turn to the sculptures themselves, which, in quantity if not in quality, take precedence over any other element in our legacy from Syro-Hittite times. In discussing

* Translation quoted from A. R. Luckenbill, *Ancient Records, Assyria and Babylonia*, Vol. II, p. 53.

the cultural affiliations of the city states we have already referred to the influence of a Hurrian-Mitannian element in the population. Such an influence had in fact already been detected during the final years of the Hittite Empire in the sculptures at Yazılıkaya, and it is interesting to observe how increasingly conspicuous it becomes under the new régime. It was in fact through the medium of Mitannian art that many ancient Mesopotamian motives dating from as early as Sumerian times were now added to the Hittite repertoire. It may at this point be asked how, in view of our almost total ignorance of Mitannian art, this can be demonstrated. The answer is that it depends almost exclusively upon the testimony of the designs on Mitannian or Hurrian cylinder seals, a fair number of which have fortunately been recovered. In the present context they are of particular interest since they offer a compendium of the motifs later to be seen in Syro-Hittite sculptures, bronzes, and terracottas. Here are some which can be easily recognized.

One figure, which last appeared a thousand years earlier on the locally carved seals used by the Assyrian merchants at Kanesh, is the Naked Goddess, who was Ishtar for the early Babylonians and evidently identified by the Hittites with the Anatolian fertility cult. In the seals she holds a curious garland resembling a skipping-rope, and she is usually associated with two different gods. One of these, wearing a horned crown, carrying a mace or lituus and standing upon mountain symbols, is the Hurrian Weather God, Teshub; the other, with mitre-shaped head-dress, fur-edged robe and carrying an axe, her son, the 'Young God' of the Hittites. There are other motifs reminiscent of Yazılıkaya, such as the files of small running or marching figures and subsidiary gods mounted on appropriate animals. But the opposed beasts and banqueting scenes with minstrels and attendants are reminiscent of Sumerian times, as also is the figure of Gilgamesh, mythical hero of the famous Mesopotamian epic, and his half-human companion Enkidu.

Carchemish. Now let us see how these figures and scenes occur in the serial pictures composed by the orthostats. Take, for instance, the 'Great Wall of Sculptures' at Carchemish. Here is a procession with deities in front and human warriors behind, obviously celebrating a military victory. It has even been suggested that the gods in this case are returning to their temple from which they have been evicted by the enemy. First comes Teshub, carrying an axe and lituus, then a goddess with a pomegranate and ears of corn, followed by another god carrying a spear head-downwards 'at the slope'. Then, after a gap, there is the great limestone relief of the Naked Goddess, her body here framed in a veil, which hangs behind her, and provided with wings. Beside her is a seated figure, wearing a garment like those of the priestesses at Yazılıkaya, covering the head-dress and wrapped about the body. She also is described as – "... a priestess, certainly a mortal and a member of the royal family". Then there are the battle scenes with chariots and most of the remaining slabs depict foot-soldiers bringing in prisoners. A long hieroglyph inscription doubtless recording the victory of a Carchemish king over his enemies, completes the story.*

In contrast to this series the 'Herald's Wall' is an example of the haphazard arrangement of slabs, having apparently no relation to one another. There is an interesting picture of an armed man riding a camel side by side with a god and a hero killing a winged bull†: rampant sphinxes and winged monsters interposed between quite different scenes in which human figures are naturalistically depicted. This could, of course, be due to the re-use of older reliefs simply as decoration, without regard to their meaning; one need hardly add that it is aesthetically a great deal less satisfying than when the sequence is animated by some unity of purpose or meaning. At Sinjerli an example of this sort is to be seen in the sculptures of the outer citadel gateway, where isolated figures from a hunting scene alternate with real and mythical animals, the

---

* For the sequence of illustrations, see *Carchemish*, Part III. *The Excavations in the Lower Town*, by Sir Leonard Woolley (1952), Plate B37 and ff.

† *Op. cit.*, Plates B50, B52.

participants in a banquet, and various gods and goddesses. Only the archaeological content of the pictures can in these cases be considered as of any great interest.

STATUES

Of the sculptures other than relief carvings, the most conspicuous are perhaps the free standing (or sometimes sitting) statues. These are usually mounted, like the larger portico-columns, on sculptured bases composed of paired animals. One would quote as the best example the seated statue of a god from Carchemish, were it not for the fact that, owing to the vicissitudes through which Woolley's finds passed during the years following their discovery, the statue itself has completely disappeared and in the Ankara Museum only the base remains. One is left to gather from photographs that the god was seated on a square throne, shaped like an armchair, his fists which rested upon his knees holding a mace and a double axe. He was bearded and wore a horned head-dress. The head of one of the lions is in the British Museum and has been replaced by a plaster cast, but one is at least able to observe the small relief-figure of a kneeling genius which holds the two beasts by the neck* (Plate 16a). At Sinjerli such a base carried a standing figure of much more impressive proportions.

Malatya. But perhaps most striking of all these figures in-the-round is the statue of a king, found in the gate chamber of the 'Lion Gate' at Malatya (Plate 15). It is a colossus over three metres high and cut from a single block of limestone. The king wears a voluminous pleated overmantle, one corner of which returns over his right shoulder and is held in his left hand: the right arm is missing. He has no head ornament save for his own elaborately dressed hair and beard. In the restored setting at the entrance to the main salon of the Ankara Museum, the figure stands in approximately its original position, but the circumstances in which it was actually found were most curious and interesting. Its base still stood before a niche in the north wall of the chamber; but from this it had fallen face-

* Woolley, *Carchemish, The Town Defences* (1921), Part II, Plate B25.

downwards on the stone pavement, losing in the process its projecting right arm and damaging its face. It had not, however, remained as it had fallen. Pious hands had rolled it over into a more decorous position on its back and then built around it a sarcophagus of stone slabs, as though it lay in a tomb. The nose, which had become detached, was found by the excavators, but, having unfortunately been mislaid in transport to Ankara, has now had to be re-modelled from photographs. The head of the sceptre which had been held in the right hand was also found lying in the corner of the room where it had been placed for safety.*

The relief sculptures in the Malatya gate are extremely small – hardly more than half a metre high – and occupy a rather unusual position, level with the tops of the guardian lions. For the most part they represent scenes of worship in which libations are being poured to various gods, but there is also one picture, now rather famous, in which a god and his divine assistant are in combat with the Great Serpent of Hittite mythology. The coils of the multi-headed creature are also being belaboured from above by homunculi who reach downwards from among the symbols of falling rain.

Dating the Sculptures. We have mentioned, for example in connexion with the 'Herald's Wall' at Carchemish, the possibility of old relief slabs being re-used side by side with freshly carved sculptures in the decoration of a new building. This applies equally to the 'Long Wall of Sculptures', where the slab bearing the Naked Goddess and the seated priestess is clearly an intrusive element in the victory procession. The problem thus arises as to how the earlier sculptures can be distinguished from the later, and this brings us face to face with the complicated subject of chronology in general. It is a vexed question, but there are at least three different forms of evidence provided by the setting in which sculptures occur;

* L. Delaporte, *Malatya*, Fascicule I, 1940. Plate XXVI illustrates the statue in its 'tomb' and cf. Plates XXVIII, XXIX, and XXX for detailed photographs. The reliefs are also illustrated in the same volume. For details of the colossus cf. Bossert, *Alt-Anatolien*, Nos. 794, 795.

their relations for instance with a building of which the date has already been determined. Next there is a form of evidence which has only recently become effective, namely the hiero-glyphic inscriptions associated with the carvings. And thirdly, there is the evidence provided by the sculptures themselves on purely stylistic grounds.

At Carchemish, where the excavations took place before the science of Hittitology had reached maturity, it was at first necessary to rely exclusively upon archaeological evidence in constructing a tentative scheme of chronology for the history of the site in general. In the early stages of the investigation one imagines that the material remains must have presented a picture of almost bewildering confusion. Throughout the Bronze and Iron Ages, public buildings had been repeatedly rebuilt or enlarged, new sculptures being occasionally pro-vided to fill gaps in an existing series, or reliefs from old buildings incorporated in a new sequence of ornaments. In addition, the remains of the Hittite palaces had often been interfered with by foundation trenches cut in Roman times, and the sculptures which were thus brought to light used as building material for structures of the classical period. Finally, in the historical levels there was little stratification which could be relied upon, and the excavators consequently could seldom even profit from the valuable testimony of pottery shapes.

Cemeteries at Carchemish. But to this last generalization there was one important exception. Both on the mound itself and at widely separated points in its vicinity they were able to locate and afterwards to make test excavations in a succession of cemeteries. In these the contents of the graves – pottery and small objects accompanying the dead – were widely differen-tiated in accordance with the period in the history of the site during which the cemetery had been in use. It was in terms of these graves and the cultural evidence provided by their contents, that the successive cultural periods in the history of the site might eventually be distinguished and set in order.

It would be tedious here to enter into details of the external parallels and other forms of reasoning, by which a place in the sequence could finally be attributed to each type of grave. Of greater importance are the chronological conclusions which consequently became possible.

First, there was the Chalcolithic painted pottery associated with the kilns adjoining the 'Yunus' cemetery. This is the 'Tell Halaf ware' of the early fourth millennium, which has since been made too familiar by excavations in northern Mesopotamia to be any longer of great interest. After this comes the Early (and perhaps Middle) Bronze Age, which seems at Carchemish to be solely represented by the tombs known as 'Champagne' cists. These were shaft graves, lined and sealed over with limestone slabs and containing in almost every case, beside the burial, a surprising number of small, narrow-stemmed clay goblets, resembling (though only approximately) the shape of a champagne glass. In the absence of any other evidence, one has to consider the so-called 'Champagne' period at Carchemish as lasting from the end of the Chalcolithic to the beginning of the Late Bronze Age, for it was not until a date which Woolley estimated at 1750 B.C. (but which by more recent calculation might be a century and a half later), that a new type of grave took the place of the Champagne cists. These, for brevity we must simply refer to as the 'Amarna' graves, and note that they continued in use until the beginning of the Iron Age. The Iron Age itself is represented by the Yunus Cemetery already referred to.

Woolley, on this basis, divides the history of Carchemish into three main periods; an Old Hittite period, corresponding to the 'Champagne' graves; a Middle Hittite, matching the 'Amarna' burials, and a Late Hittite in the Iron Age. For us, the first of these periods would correspond to the Early and Middle Bronze Age, up to the beginning of the Old Hittite Kingdom in Anatolia; the second to the Old Hittite kingdom itself and the Hittite Empire, and the third to the Syro-Hittite.

If this discussion of terminology seems now to have been unnecessarily prolonged, it must be pleaded that without it no argument for the dating of the sculptures would be comprehensible.

Conclusions. It was by the graves, then, that Woolley was initially able to date the old 'Ring wall', which enclosed the citadel at Carchemish. He found 'Champagne' burials 'in niches or pits scooped out under its foundations'* and (more convincingly) dug down into the contemporary filling behind it. At one point also there was a postern or sally-port, like those at Boghazköy, leading to the river, and he found a 'Champagne' grave in the earth filling above it. The 'Ring' must accordingly be assigned to the 'Old Hittite' period. He had already assumed that the inner enclosure wall around the town would have been built at a later date. Sure enough he discovered 'Champagne' burials directly beneath it but 'Amarna' graves both in association with its foundations and dug into its remains after it had become ruined. He was therefore able to date it to the transition from the 'Old' to the 'Middle' Hittite periods (i.e. by his calculation to 1750 B.C.). And here comes the crux of the whole argument, for the Water Gate forms an integral part of the Inner Town wall and its sculptures are carved on the actual structural elements of which it is built. The Water Gate *reliefs*, therefore, Woolley dates to the eighteenth century B.C. – by our own reckoning, that is, to the Middle Bronze Age. This would make the Water Gate sculptures by far the oldest Hittite reliefs in existence, and though he argues the high standard of sculpture elsewhere in Syria at that period, other scholars are unable to accept the existence at Carchemish of characteristically Hittite reliefs so many centuries before the first examples appear in Anatolia.

For to-day, forty years after the excavations at Carchemish took place, there is in fact a good deal of comparative material to assist us in fixing more reliably the chronology of the 'Champagne' period. Stylistic comparisons, for instance, with the contents of the famous Til Barsip tomb;† indications of Sumerian metal styles and funerary practices, developed and prolonged beyond the Third Dynasty of Ur, and other evidence would suggest 2250–2000 B.C. as a fair span for the Carchemish cist graves. Affinities of the pottery from the

* *Carchemish*, II, p. 40.
† F. Thureau-Dangin and M. Dunand, *Til Barsip*, p. 96 ff. (Paris 1936).

Amarna graves on the other hand suggest a date between 1800 and 1600, leaving a gap of two centuries which might be filled by the later cist graves of Woolley's El-Hammam cemetery (not previously mentioned).

The Amarna graves are in fact only interesting for their vital function as evidence to date the Water Gate sculptures; and here finally it is necessary to reconsider the excavator's conclusions. For few other scholars to-day would be prepared to date, for instance, the famous banqueting scene (*Carchemish* II, Plate B30) earlier than the IX-VIIIth century B.C. Woolley's integrity as an archaeological observer is unrivalled; and it is possible that in this case his observation has proved more correct than his conclusion. For his own recording of the contents of the graves in question (*Carchemish*, II, p. 133) must unmistakably suggest that their contents were *re-burials* of earlier remains, unintentionally disturbed – a practice not uncommon at that period.

Woolley dates several other groups of Carchemish sculptures to the 'Middle Hittite' period, including those of the South Town Gate and the greater part of the Herald's Wall.* The remainder belonged to the 'Late' or Syro-Hittite period, which we must now consider. And here we are on safer ground, since the second of the three classes of evidence already mentioned can now be brought to bear. The hieroglyphic inscriptions, absent from the Bronze Age sculptures, are here liberally applied to the background of the reliefs. They do not, indeed, as one might perhaps have hoped, comment on or explain the scenes depicted, but they record their dedication or identify the individuals represented.

The Hieroglyphs. Both at Carchemish and at Sinjerli, when the testimony of the hieroglyphs was added to that of the Assyrian records, it became possible to reconstruct genealogically at least one dynasty of local rulers during the Syro-Hittite period. The Carchemish sequence starts with a king called Luhas in

---

* Again a much lower date is to-day generally accepted for the Herald's Wall sculptures. Reliefs such as the 'Camel-rider' in particular suggest a period as much as five centuries later.

about 960 B.C., and continues right up to the annexation of the city by Sargon in about 716 B.C. Most of the Iron Age sculptures, such as those in the 'Long Wall', can be attributed to one or other of these kings. Similarly, at Sinjerli, during the final years before its annexation, there was the family of Bar-Rakkab (*c.* 730 B.C.), already client-rulers under the authority of Assyria, to whom individual monuments and even buildings can be positively attributed, and good evidence for dating others to earlier periods. The southern city gate, for instance, with its reliefs of mythical animals and hunting scenes, belongs probably to a period in the twelfth century, soon after the fall of the Empire; those of the Citadel Gateway, including a nice representation of the god Teshub as a warrior, to a date perhaps a little later; while the statue of a god on a lion base, already referred to, belongs probably to the tenth century.

Style. Finally, as to the stylistic peculiarities of the sculptures, which constituted our third category of evidence, Woolley has made a number of important generalizations. The earliest category is typified by the 'Water Gate' sculptures,* which are all cut in limestone and therefore show no signs of the limitations later imposed on Hittite sculptors by the harder basaltic material. They are also, he says, softer in modelling, and higher in relief than the later examples, giving even the effect of 'carving in the quarter round'. He draws one important distinction between the 'Middle' and 'Late Hittite' reliefs. In the former, 'the figures are part of a single scene and only have meaning when the slabs are in proper juxtaposition'; whereas in the latter each slab is complete in itself, the sequence appearing arbitrary and meaningless. He also observes that, whereas the 'Late Hittites' have a preference for historical scenes and human activities, the earlier sculptors prefer mythical or religious subjects. In dealing with the 'Late Hittite' period, he finally draws attention to the increasing evidence of Assyrian influence, which, at Sakjegözü and elsewhere eventually reduced Hittite Sculpture to an inferior imitation of Assyrian style and craftsmanship.

* *Carchemish* II, Plates B28–31.

But the most recent and also perhaps the most competent analysis of the Syro-Hittite sculptures has been made by E. Akurgal, whose methodical assemblage of stylistic evidence to supplement that provided by the details of their archaeological content, enabled him to divide the 'Late Hittite' period into three chronological sub-divisions, to one or other of which almost every well-known group could reliably b assigned. Akurgal's reasoned analysis contributed, among others, to the tentative dating of the famous group in the Lion Gate at Malatya (see p. 169). The content of these sculptures had conspicuous points of resemblance to those in the sanctuary at Yazılıkaya; but, rather disconcertingly the gate itself was dated fairly conclusively by archaeological evidence to a late stage in the Syro-Hittite period. Akurgal's attribution of the sculpture on stylistic grounds, at the latest to the tenth century B.C., had already suggested that some explanation of this discrepancy must be sought, when the French excavator, C. Schaeffer discovered that the building stood upon the ruins of an earlier gateway, from which the sculptured decorations were significantly missing. Assuming therefore that they are in secondary use, the close resemblance of the Malatya reliefs to those of Imperial times at Boghazköy may be more than a mere coincidence.

Akurgal himself has distinguished some of the Malatya reliefs as belonging to the second of the three phases into which he divides 'Late Hittite' sculpture (cf. p. 142 of his book, e.g. the 'Lion-hunt relief' and 'Genius', Plates XXIV and XXVa), and further, he has assigned one relief (Plate XXVb), the Assyrian 'Weather God'), to the third phase (730–720 B.C.). To this last phase also he attributes the statue of the King (see p. 168 above and p. 144 of his book), and here his contention is supported by evidence supplied by the famous Nimrud ivories, attributable to the reign of Sargon II, and by Vannic ivories of about the same date. It is the peculiar rosettes in the headdress which find such startling parallels; and if one compares the details of the king's statue illustrated in Bossert, *Alt-Anatolien*, Nos. 794 and 795, with the Nimrud figures in *Iraq* XIII, Part I, Plate VI, No. 1, or with the Vannic ivories in *Iraq* XII, Part I, Plate XIV,* one will find no difficulty in agreeing that the Malatya colossus should be attributed to the final decades of the eighth century B.C. (Plate 29b)

The subject of Syro-Hittite sculpture is naturally not exhausted by this necessarily superficial discussion of the principal excavations. There are innumerable isolated monuments, such as stelae and memorial sculptures, from sites some of which have not even been identified. There are also rock reliefs, like the famous carving at Ivriz on the northern side of the Taurus, whose hieroglyph inscription has recently shown it to be a dedication to the god Tarhundas by Urpalla, a prince of Tabal in about 740 B.C.; and many more. (Plate 21) It is indeed a wide subject, and if in the preceding paragraphs problems of dating have been dwelt upon at the expense of other aspects, it is because their partial elucidation is a more recent attainment and a less familiar subject than the discovery of the material itself.

* Compare also the head-dress of the king in the Sakjegözü relief, Plate 19b.

CHAPTER 10

Karatepe and Urartu

IN the realm of Hittite archaeology, a single group of antiquities remain to be mentioned. These are the discoveries of the Turkish expedition at Karatepe in Cilicia; and if their discussion has been postponed until now, it has been with no intention of belittling their importance, but rather in consideration of their aptitude to serve as a postscript to the whole subject. During the decade which has elapsed since the first rumour of a new 'bilingual' text galvanized the philological world, the revelation of the setting in which it was found and the abundance of new material provided, has served in a sense to revitalize the whole field of Hittite studies. The growing volume of literature on the subject shows that no other contemporary discovery of texts, the Dead Sea Scrolls, the Ras Shamra or the Mycenaean tablets, has made a greater impression on the mind and imagination of the scholar or the intelligent layman.

THE BILINGUAL

First, then, as to the famous bilingual itself, part of which had survived in each of the two citadel gateways. On entering the city, the inhabitants were able (always assuming, as one reviewer remarks, that they were familiar with literate habits of any kind), to read the building inscription of their king, on the right in Hittite hieroglyphs and on the left in Phoenician, since the writing in either case covered the sculptured surface of the portal lions and extended on to the orthostat slabs beyond. The left-hand inscription was not, as was first thought, Aramaic, but what has been described as 'the purest known Phoenician'.* There were reasons for understanding that the original version had been in Hittite, and Phoenician was the language into which the king had chosen to have it translated.

* M. J. Mellink, *Bibliotheca Orientalis*, VII, 5, 1950, p. 145.

The translation, perhaps for political reasons, had been given separate consideration, and included at least one line which did not appear in the Hittite. Yet the two versions have proved sufficiently close to serve the purpose of the epigraphist, and there is no suggestion that the great expectations which their discovery at first aroused have been disappointed. Only some popular misapprehensions induced by the first wave of publicity, regarding the whole subject of the hieroglyphs, have required correcting. The discovery was, for instance then spoken of as a 'new Rosetta Stone'. This comparison has recently been rejected by I. J. Gelb, as a philologist, on the grounds that the basic decipherment of Hittite hieroglyphs was achieved between 1930 and 1935, many years before the discovery of Karatepe. The 'Rosetta Stone' in this case, as he says 'grew out of the sweat and toil of all those scholars who in those years contributed to the unveiling of one of the great mysteries of antiquity'. He explains that – 'while the Karatepe bilinguals add nothing to our knowledge of Hittite hieroglyph grammar, and little – if anything – to our knowledge of the writing, they do add greatly to our knowledge of the vocabulary. Knowledge of the writing permits the reading of signs and words: knowledge of grammar enables us to interpret the general structure of an inscription and guess at its general meaning; but only fully established meanings of individual words make a full translation of an inscription possible. Therein', he says, 'probably lies the greatest single contribution of Karatepe.'

Gelb qualifies this opinion with the necessary reminder that, at the time of writing it depended on a limited knowledge of the Hittite text. The practice, understandably adopted by the excavators after the inscriptions had been copied, was to make the Phoenician version available as soon as possible to scholars in the field of Semitic languages, in order that its meaning should be in no doubt when it came to be used as a basis of comparison with the hieroglyph text. The transcript of the latter was published gradually and in instalments, to allow time for its primary editing by its finder, Bossert himself, the final instalment appearing in 1953.

To return to the actual content of the inscription, when stripped of its verbose rendering, the plain facts which emerge are few in number but of considerable interest. The king is not, as it proves, a Phoenician, but bears the Anatolian name Asitawad. He records the foundation of the fortress at Karatepe, which he named after himself, and then gives the additional information that he is ruler of the Danuna and has been 'made great by', or in other words owes allegiance to Awarikus, a king of Cilicia. In addition he makes it clear that his own kingdom includes the plain of Adana and certain minor principalities not previously subjugated by the 'House of Mopsus', to which he apparently belongs. He mentions the name of a second city with which he is closely associated, perhaps to be equated with the neighbouring site of Domuztepe, and finally invokes the names of various gods, among whom the Ba'al of the Old Testament is included. Regarding the date to which the inscription should be attributed, Awarikus has been identified with a king, whose submission to Tiglathpileser in 738 B.C. is mentioned in the Assyrian records. Palaeographic evidence from the Phoenician text also points to a date late in the eighth century B.C.

THE DANUNA

One of the first important inferences made from the inscription was that the Danuna could only be the Dananians, listed among the 'Peoples of the Sea', who invaded Egypt in the twelfth century B.C. Since they are described at Karatepe as 'People of the City of Adana', they may now also be identified as true Anatolians. Another possible link, which has created some interest is with the Homeric Danaoi. R. D. Barnett, who has been partly responsible for developing this line of thought says – 'Historians had long linked the Danuna with the Danaoi, a name used in Homer for the Greeks at Troy, and one which Greek tradition explained by deriving it from a dynasty of oriental origin which had established itself at Argos. Danaos, its eponymous founder, was said to be the son of Belos, the Babylonian god Bel, i.e. an oriental. For this modern identification of Danaoi and Danuna the Karatepe bilingual brought some unexpected confirmation.' He then recalls the claim of the Karatepe king to belong to the house of Mopsus, the semi-legendary Greek hero, and founder of Mopsuestia (Misis), a city also on the banks of the Jeyhan river. The name of Mopsus is known in both Anatolian and Greek mythology, and if his existence as an historical figure could be substantiated, the stories of his journeys through Anatolia shortly before the fall of Troy and the end of the Hittite Empire would acquire new significance as illuminating for a moment the period of Achaean immigration and the early Iron Age generally. It is perhaps too much to expect that we shall ever be in a position to follow the details of genealogical succession accounting for the gap of five centuries between this problematical Achaean and the princeling who founded Karatepe, or to see in the latter more than a local Anatolian aspiring to associate himself with a distinguished tradition. Certainly, if the Danuna had once been Achaeans, by the eighth century there was little which remained to distinguish them from the indigenous Cilicians, for all trace of the Greek language had disappeared. Archaeologically, too, where it would be logical to think of Mopsus and the companions of his adventures as using Late Mycenaean pottery of the sort which Cilicia has produced in plenty, the Iron Age dwellings of Karatepe could boast no more than crudely painted wares.

THE SCULPTURES

The remarkable interest of the Karatepe inscriptions, both from the linguistic and from the historical point of view, seems rather to have eclipsed the subject of the sculptures, and even to have denied them their fair share of public attention. It is possible to suspect that this may have been in some measure due to their unpretentious character from an aesthetic point of view and general low standard of craftsmanship. (The reliefs have been described as 'among the crudest ever produced in the field of neo-Hittite sculpture, which can never boast of artistic refinement'.*) Yet, aesthetic considerations

* M. J. Mellink, op. cit.

apart, there can be no doubt that much is to be learnt from them archaeologically and that, considered as a group, they have a peculiar significance. The whole subject has been most competently dealt with by H. Çambel, one of the Turkish excavators, in an early report, where her first concern was to emphasize the stratigraphic peculiarity of Karatepe. The lifetime of the citadel, from its foundation by Asitawad to its destruction in some great fire occupied an extremely short period. No public building existed on the site before, and it was not afterwards reoccupied. In the normal sculptures, therefore, as Mrs. Çambel points out, we have a circumscribed body of material, in the analysis of which no distinctions may be made on the basis of age. This being so, it is the more surprising to observe the extraordinary diverse elements of which it is composed – 'finished and unfinished slabs, well and poorly carved ones, utterly heterogeneous styles represented in the same context.'

The installation of some slabs in an unfinished state must be taken to imply that the construction of the citadel was to be completed by a certain date, and that the builders were consequently working against time. The fact that the opportunity to have the carving finished *in situ* seems not to have occurred, has been taken as confirming the shortness of the period during which the buildings survived. The omission from our own point of view has been providential, since it allows us to study the method and technique of the carvers. (One can hardly call all the Karatepe stone-cutters artists.) 'They incise the scene on the orthostat and chisel off a layer of the background. If the sculptor has any artistic ambitions, this preliminary flat blocking out of the figures is followed by a reworking in modelled relief, and a number of details may be also added in incision within the finished figures. The makers of the poorer products do not even succeed in achieving preliminary sketches of tolerable proportions. This fact definitely proves that the sculptural decoration of Karatepe was not designed by one or even a number of good artists. Poor cutters had to do all of their job by themselves, and were given a responsibility which they were unable to carry. On the other hand it looks as if in some of the slabs a master hand gave some touches to show the possibilities of a proper use of the tools. The general division of labour and its deplorable results point to haste and careless production.'

Finally, Mrs. Çambel attempts a stylistic analysis of the reliefs, citing at the same time, as an example of the difficulties with which she is faced, the banqueting scene depicted in the upper gate, which is made up of slabs not only totally different in technique and competence of execution, but of varying shapes and sizes. Eventually, however, she is at least able to isolate the work of a single 'master', whose work, mostly to be seen on the right-hand or 'Hittite' side of the lower gate, is distinguished by some feeling for modelling and suggestion of movement. Yet she is compelled to turn from style to subject for an indication of the ethnological background against which the mentality of the Danuna must be considered. In this respect she is able to distinguish three separate influences: first, the Anatolian Hittite culture, now adapted to its Iron Age 'diaspora'; secondly traces of an increasing familiarity with Assyrian ideas, and thirdly evidence of Egyptian influence through the medium of Phoenician art. Mrs Çambel points to the larger and smaller slabs composing the banqueting scene from the Upper Gate (*Karatepe*,* Plate XI, Nos. 55, 56) as illustrating the first and second styles respectively, though the relief showing a sea battle (Plate XIX, Nos. 95, 96, 97) is an even more striking example of the Assyrian influence. The Egypto-Phoenician style is best seen in the Bes figure (Plate XVIII, No. 89) and the goddess suckling a boy under a tree (Plate XIV, No. 71, second from left). An incoherent synthesis of such diverse elements is presumably to be seen in the hybrid style of the Karatepe sculptors (Plates 22–26).

THE SITE

But there is another side to the Karatepe discoveries to appreciate which one need be neither an antiquarian nor a philologist. The place in which they were made is a very beautiful

* H. Th. Bossert *et al.*, *Karatepe Kazıları*, (First preliminary Report). Ankara, 1950.

and also very remote recess of the hills which break down towards the Cilician plain. The 'Black Mound', a wooded knoll perched high above the swift stream of the Ceyhan, had remained for many centuries unvisited save by an occasional goat-herd or charcoal-burner, and become familiar rather with the restless movements of wild pigs and the noisy flight of chikor partridges than with human voices. Few, in fact could have suspected that, in times almost beyond the horizon of historical memory, a king had chosen it as his place of residence and that, beneath the brambles and scrub-oak, the symbols of his authority still lay buried among the ruins of his castle. Yet such was indeed the case, and in the revelation of discovery, something of his dignity could yet be restored. For here, before the excavators' eyes, were carefully worded sentences which he had composed himself in two languages and the crudely drawn images of a world in which he lived. Among these tumbled galleries of small stone pictures, his people also were to be seen; a graceless folk with sloping foreheads and receding chins, such as are known to have inhabited large areas of Anatolia in his time. Pausing in their various activities, they regard each other as though in wonder at the strange turn of fortune which has disrupted the tranquil obscurity of their long interment. Finally, as though some further circumstance were necessary to assure them the full consideration of posterity, here also is the tenuous thread of their connexion with the Homeric Greeks.

URARTU

Reference has already been made to the fact that in 738 B.C. Awarikus, the overlord of Cilicia, was brought permanently into subjection by Tiglath-pileser III of Assyria. This was the sequel to a succession of insurrections among the small states of North Syria, instigated in the first place by Urartu, whose influence in the west had very greatly increased during the preceding century. To turn, therefore, directly from the archaeology of Cilicia to that of the Vannic state so remotely situated in the mountainous provinces of eastern Turkey is rendered less incongruous by the fact that its most considerable group of antiquities may be dated to the time of an Urartian prince who fought side by side with the Karatepe king against the Assyrians.

Toprakkale. The great cuneiform inscriptions through which first the existence and then the history of the Urartian nation came to be known in the last century, owed nothing of their disclosure to excavation, for they were carved on conspicuous rock faces of the citadel at Van. But the revelation of Urartian art and craftsmanship had to await the discovery, some miles to the east, of the hill called Toprakkale, whose earthen summit concealed the remains of an eighth-century acropolis. This event appears to have taken place sometime in the year 1877, and, as it proved, could profitably have been postponed for another half century.

At about that time Layard had become Queen Victoria's ambassador at the Sublime Porte, and it was to his study in Istanbul that the first chance finds from Toprakkale found their way; bronze objects for the most part, cast in the round or repoussé, apparently the ornaments from some large piece of furniture, which had also borne a cuneiform inscription. Layard bought some of them for the British Museum, and afterwards set about obtaining a *firman* for excavation at the spot where they had been found. From Van the objects had been sent to Istanbul through the initiative of Hormuzd Rassam, Layard's Chaldean assistant of Mesopotamian days, who had become British vice-consul at Mosul, and the permit to excavate was therefore obtained in his name. But for the two years which followed Rassam was engaged elsewhere, and the task of making the first trenches in Toprakkale was jointly entrusted to a British artillery officer, serving in a consular capacity at Van itself, and an American missionary, neither of whom had any specialized knowledge of antiquities. This in itself was an unfortunate circumstance, since the picks of their workmen began at once to 'encounter' a succession of increasingly valuable and increasingly fragile works of art. There were parts of six large bronze shields, ornamented with animals in relief in concentric registers and having cuneiform inscriptions on the rim; more bronze ornaments from furniture inlaid with gold; large bronze vessels decorated with lions' heads and other animal figures; a fairly large collection of human figures carved in ivory in the Phoenician manner, some of them having been clothed in garments of precious metal or other material and presumably a number of smaller and less ostentatiously elegant objects.

Rassam, finally arriving at Van in person in 1880, was able to take stock of these discoveries, but reported to Layard that in his view the results of the work were 'disappointing'. He mentioned for instance that they included 200 lb. of copper in the form of fragmentary vessels and other objects – 'but most of it was so corroded that it would be quite impossible to make any use of it or to distinguish the shape of the article it was made into'. He then proceeded to apply his own methods of excavating in a short but energetic campaign, which he describes in his own words as follows.

'I found on arriving in Van, that the excavations had been stopped owing to the illness of Dr Raynolds and the absence of Captain Clayton on duty. I forthwith took steps to resume the exploration on a large scale, as I was pressed for time on account of my researches in Assyria and Babylonia. The mound being narrow and long, I tried it in three different places by digging right through it to see if I could hit upon any ancient structure; but, though I penetrated it from side to side by tunnelling, I could find no indication of any building, but only discovered other shields, some bronze bulls' heads, and other small objects. On the southern outskirts of the mound we found the remains of a tesellated pavement of three chambers; but there was not a stone to be seen of the walls. The whole mound seemed to consist of nothing but the débris of some ancient building with an abundant quantity of charcoal mixed up with the rubbish, which showed that the palace or temple or whatever it might have been had undergone a tremendous conflagration. The only remains that existed were the base of the temple at the eastern limit of the mound, with a large platform in front of it, paved with limestone.' He then refers to a plan, which he did not in the end remember to publish. The whole excavation had taken little more than a month.

Since Rassam kept few notes and made no drawings, the above account is virtually the only surviving clue to the provenance and interrelation of the objects which were eventually sent to the British Museum. Judged, in fact, by the ethical standards of modern archaeology his procedure was grotesque and the whole episode highly discreditable. It can only be said in extenuation that these were the days before Koldewey, Petrie and others had demonstrated the possibilities of systematic excavation, and that Rassam was merely fulfilling the instructions which he had received; namely to obtain antiquities for a museum. Yet the damage which he had done did not unfortunately end with his departure from Van in 1880, Soon afterwards Raynolds, the American priest, mentions in a letter, 'Yesterday a working man who has been doing some excavating on his own hook in the vicinity of the trenches Mr Rassam opened when here, brought a bronze image in very perfect preservation. ...' The period of illicit excavating had in fact begun, and it continued at Toprakkale until 1890, when Budge relates that 'a whole gateway of great archaeological interest was removed, presumably by stone robbers ...' It was not in fact until 1898 that the expedition properly organized by Belck and Lehmann Haupt brought some order out of the confusion and revealed just how remarkable the contents of Toprakkale might have been had they received proper treatment.

BELCK AND LEHMANN HAUPT

Toprakkale is not an isolated mound, but a prominent shoulder of the hills, looking northwards over the orchards and plantations of modern Van to the old citadel rock and the waters of the lake beyond. Its lower slopes abut against an outcrop of rock with almost vertical sides, which must have made the fortification of the summit easy and provided an excellent emplacement for an acropolis. In fact, at the time with which we are dealing it appears that the only means of access to it was by a wide staircase passing through an artificial tunnel in the rock with a single narrow entrance. Directly inside the latter there was also a spacious rock chamber, which has sometimes been described as a water-cistern, but which seemed to the writer to have appointments of a temple.

The ancient name of the acropolis appears to have been Rusahina and it was founded probably by the Urartian king, Rusas I (c. 733–714). The building mentioned by Rassam (he could hardly have missed it, since several courses of massive limestone blocks still remain standing), was a temple dedicated to the Urartian god Haldis, and probably built by the same king. It is now assumed that the conflagration of which early excavators found traces was that by which the whole place was destroyed in 585 B.C., when the Medes under Cyaxares conquered the buffer-state of Urartu (and thereby found themselves face to face with the Lydians).

The Temple. The temple itself was a building 20 metres long by 13½ wide, with the sub-structure of a plinth for the cult statue still visible in the centre. On the south-west side the sloping rock was built up to a level terrace with an elaborately inlaid pavement. Elsewhere in the surrounding precinct were various large mud-brick buildings which may have been administrative or residential and there were long magazines each containing '20 to 25 vast *pithoi* capable of holding 500–600 litres of wine or corn'. Beneath the main terrace of the temple the ground had been made up to form a second, and the filling behind the retaining wall in this case seemed to consist partly of human bones. Since no skulls could be found among them, Lehmann Haupt took them to be those of decapitated prisoners, sacrificed to Haldis, as they were known to have been from contemporary inscriptions.

Lehmann Haupt's own finds, in addition to a considerable collection of cuneiform tablets, included a magnificent bronze candelabrum, lamps and other ornaments, which could be identified as appointments of the main shrine; remnants, in fact, of the treasure which had been plundered or destroyed by the earlier excavators. Once this was realized it became imperative to reconsider the accumulated results of all these earlier enterprises, in the hope of recovering any clues to their original shape and disposal. But in addition to the official discoveries which were now lodged in various European museums, there were the prizes carried off by clandestine excavators. These remained for the time being in the hands of dealers, and it was in some cases many years before they could eventually be located in private collections. It was not in fact until 1950 that R. D. Barnett of the British Museum finally found himself in a position to review the material as a whole.

Temple Furniture. It was by then possible to see that many items of ornament in bronze and gold, dragged from their setting by the depredations of early diggers, were component parts of the temple furniture. It had in fact long been known that elaborate thrones and beds, with their accessories, such as tripods and stools, figured among the appointments of sanctuaries in Mesopotamian temples and that it was the profane counterparts of these which appeared as the attributes of royalty in the Assyrian reliefs. In this case a throne and a stool seemed to have been the main items surviving, and on the basis of the Assyrian representations these could now be reconstructed with some certainty. Their sumptuous appearance alone would be sufficient to impress one with the magnificence of the Haldis sanctuary; but there are other details which may legitimately be included in the picture. There are the ornamental shields which undoubtedly hung upon the walls, the ivory statues and the great brazen cauldrons on their tripods, whose bulls' head ornaments were no doubt rescued from Rassam's 'two hundred pounds of copper'. (Plates 27 and 29.)

Added to all this is the remarkable circumstance that, for once, we are not at a loss to reconstruct the appearance of the temple itself. It has already been mentioned that the building is to be dated to the time of King Sargon II (or a little earlier), and Sargon is indeed one of the Assyrian kings who fought against Urartu. In the annals of his eighth campaign he records

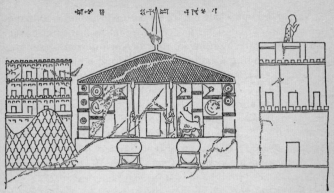

Figure 12. An Urartian palace depicted in an Assyrian relief

an attack upon a city called Musasir, which appears to have
been a protectorate of Urartu, and describes the sacking by
his troops of a temple dedicated to Haldis. One can apprehend
from his account the astonishment of the Assyrians at the
prodigious wealth of this building from the interminable list
of treasures which he removed, and even note that among
them is an 'ivory bed inlaid with silver and precious stones,
which was the god's resting-place'. What is of even greater
interest is that the whole scene is depicted in a relief found in
the king's palace at Khorsabad, in which, thanks to the
pictorial convention of the time, something can be seen both
of the interior and exterior of the building. The concentric
inlays on the walls and the bronze cauldrons, the spear-shaped
finials of the ornaments flanking the door are features which
can easily be recognized from the finds at Toprakkale.

Architecture. Finally, even the appearance of the acropolis
itself can reliably be reconstructed. One of the earliest objects
sent by Rassam to Layard was a fragment of a model castle
carved in stone. As a record of contemporary architecture this
is an almost unique document, for it shows one the façade of a
fortified building with the terminal treatment of its towers and
battlements, as well as the shapes of doors and windows;
information, in fact, which is never provided by the surviving
remains. (Plate 28.)

Van and Toprakkale are by no means the unique source of information about Urartian civilization. A chance discovery was made near Erzincan in 1938 of an important group of bronzes including a cauldron on its tripod which is perhaps the most amazingly well preserved exhibit in the Ankara Museum. Like the sacred throne of Haldis whose reconstruction we have already described, it bore traces of an inscription in hieroglyphs, similar to those used by the Hittites, but embodying what one must assume to be a peculiarly Urartian system. (Plate 27.) There are also preliminary reports of a Russian expedition at a site near Erivan, where an Urartian fortress palace has been found and is at present being excavated.

One purpose which all these discoveries have served was to emphasize the remarkably high standard of craftsmanship attained by the artisans of Van, particularly in the realm of metallurgy. This being so, it is regrettable to find how little remains to be said about the possible source of their artistic predilections and cultural background generally. Their style of ornament and design is an adaptation, only slightly modified, of contemporary Assyrian tradition, and it is hard to detect those features which in the past have been considered as linking it with Anatolia. Of earlier origins in fact nothing is known save that linguistically at least the Urartians were allied to the Hurrians, whose close neighbours they must have been in the later part of the second millennium.

CHAPTER 11

Iron Age Anatolia

ANOTHER and more formidable people to whom the King-dom of Urartu found itself occasionally allied in its wars against Assyria were the Phrygians. In the early centuries of the first millennium, they had extended their frontiers east-wards to Taurus and the upper reaches of the Euphrates, incorporating in their new empire the Anatolian territory not only of the Hittites themselves, but of sundry other states whose names have become familiar through the Hittite records. To return for a moment to the rather scanty historical facts upon which our chronology must be based in considering Phrygian archaeology, the following brief recapitulation may be of value.

THE PHRYGIANS

Within a century of the destruction of the Hittite Empire we are afforded a first clue to the identity of the people who brought it about, by an Assyrian account of how Tiglath Pileser I routed a 'Muski' army of 20,000 men, under five kings which had invaded northern Mesopotamia. After this there is a lapse of 200 years, ending in the ninth century with a further Assyrian reference to the 'Muski,' who can now definitely be identified with the Phrygians of Greek tradition, and understood to have founded a state on the débris of the Hittite Empire. In the second half of the eighth century they are in alliance with Urartu against Assyria, but the pattern is then broken by the first wave of Cimmerian invaders, whose inroads deprive them of their possessions in eastern Anatolia and end with the suicide of the contemporary king Midas at his capital, Gordium. Early in the seventh century, a second Cimmerian invasion culminates in the final destruction of Phrygia as an independent power (*c.* 680 B.C.) and the substi-tution as paramount authority in Anatolia of the state of

Lydia, previously a Phrygian dependency. Yet still, rather confusingly, there continue to be Phrygian princes at Gordium and Phrygian culture survives side by side with that of Lydia. Let us now, therefore, review the sources from which archaeological evidence is available, to supplement this inadequate skeleton of events and clothe the Phrygian character in some semblance of reality.

Archaeological Sources. The archaeology of Phrygia, like that of the Hittite peoples, depends in fact on two classes of evidence; the results of excavations and the interpretation of monuments surviving above ground. They should perhaps be dealt with in this order, since the former have in some cases contributed to the dating of the latter. First and foremost, then, in the realm of excavation, are two cities which must have fallen within the eastern division of Phrygian possessions, namely Boghazköy and Alishar. The Phrygian remains at these two sites showed a marked similarity.

By the time the first reference to the 'Muski' appears in the Assyrian records, the old Hittite capital already shows signs of having been reoccupied, though the settlement was now confined to the summit of citadel hill (Büyükkale). The German excavators found the remains of a modest fortification and the residence of a local ruler, with stratigraphical evidence to show that it had been destroyed and rebuilt at about the time of the Cimmerian invasions. Thus at Boghazköy two separate phases (Levels I and II) of Phrygian culture can be distinguished, the later of the two surviving into a period which politically should be described as Lydian.

ALISHAR

The situation at Alishar was in many ways similar. After being abandoned for a period which in this case must have amounted to five or six centuries, the site was once more partially occupied in the final years of the second millennium. Again it was the ruins of the old pre-Hittite citadel on the central mound which were adopted as an emplacement for the new fortress of some Phrygian feudal lord (Level IVc). His castle was again rebuilt a century or so later and a new fortress-wall provided to protect the settlement which had begun to accumulate on the western slope of the citadel mound (Level IVb). With only minor changes this small community also survived into times which should more correctly be called Lydian.

These two sites are well documented archaeologically, owing to the continuity of occupation from their moment of resettlement onwards. Their stratigraphy has made it possible to date other Phrygian communities, more isolated in time, such as the comparable settlement at Gâvurkalesi, 60 kilometres south-west of Ankara. Here a hilltop is crowned by the ruins of a typical Hittite sanctuary, a platform being created by retaining walls of massive masonry, and a projecting rockface adorned with relief figures of two Hittite gods approaching a seated goddess. (Plate 14b) Once more in after years a Phrygian lord had used the now-deserted platform as an emplacement for his château and thrown an arc of fortifications around the lower slopes of the hill to protect the houses of his dependants. There are other sites in plenty in eastern Anatolia where archaeologists, primarily in search of Bronze-Age remains, have first recorded deposits or buildings testifying to a prosperous occupation in Phrygian times. Alaja Hüyük is one such case, Pazarlı another, and there are many more.

GORDIUM

In the west of Anatolia the most significant site, and one which may in the coming years provide a solution to many problems connected with Phrygian history, is Gordium the capital itself. The mound, which has long been associated with the name of the city, stands on the right bank of the Sangarius (Sakarya). This river, which is narrow but of great depth, here winds a serpentine course through an open valley and in its period of flood creates wide areas of reedy marsh, haunted by wildfowl. Near the mound it divides into three branches which can be crossed successively by log bridges, and there can be little doubt that this must in the past have been the site of an important road crossing. Where the modern village stands, a stony spur of the adjoining hills is studded with earthen tumuli of varying sizes, beneath which the more distinguished inhabitants of Gordium seem to have been interred. Dominating the whole necropolis is a single tumulus rising to the immense height of over 150 feet and locally known as the 'Tomb of Midas'.

Previous to the arrival of the American expedition now working at Gordium, excavations had been confined to a couple of soundings in the summit of the city mound and the investigation of five minor tumuli, to which the Körte brothers were able to attribute dates ranging from the late eighth to early fifth centuries B.C. The earliest remains which they encountered in the city mound were provisionally dated to the eighth century B.C.; but from the evidence of more recent excavations it seems that they had not actually reached the levels which represent the true Phrygian period. We shall return presently to discuss their discoveries in greater detail.

THE ROCK MONUMENTS

The only remaining large-scale excavation of a Phrygian site in western Anatolia has been undertaken by the French Institute at a place which has come to be known as the 'Midas City'. This brings us automatically to the subject of our second class of archaeological evidence, namely, the monuments surviving above ground. For the ruined city takes its name from the great sculptured rock façade, traditionally known as the 'Tomb of Midas'. Tomb and city form the focal point of a geographical area containing a large group of rock monuments attributed to the Phrygian people. This is a geologically peculiar and still rather inaccessible piece of country south-east of Eskişehir, occupying the triangle formed by main roads leading from that industrial centre to Afyonkarahisar in the south and Sivrihisar to the east. There are two principal concentrations of monuments, one in the north around the headwaters of the Sakarya, accessible from Seyitgazi, and the other in the south, reached from Egret on the Afyon road. The two are separated by a range of hills which can only be crossed by ox-cart or on horseback.

The monuments themselves have been rightly described as

among the most impressive in Turkey and Ramsay, who discovered the southern group, gives the following account of the setting in which they are found. 'The country', he says, 'may be described as series of winding level valleys, varying in breadth between a hundred yards and a mile, and bounded by perpendicular cliffs or rocky plateau. Both the valleys and plateaux are frequently covered with pine trees and occasionally with dwarf oaks. The height above sea-level is 3,500 to 4,000 feet. In the cliffs that bound the valleys the tombs are cut, and the soft rock, a volcanic conglomerate, lends itself readily to the work.'* It should be added that, like the volcanic country around Ürgüp, which provides a setting for the famous rock-cut churches of Cappadocia, the landscape is given a most unusual character by the grotesque shapes into which the rocks are carved by fissure and erosion.' Ramsay's description of the monuments as 'tombs' may serve as a first indication of their character, though, as will presently be seen, it may in fact represent an erroneous conclusion as to their purpose.

THE MIDAS CITY (Plate 32)

The limestone cliffs in which the Midas monument is set, return upon themselves to create a citadel of natural rock with a flat oval top about 500 metres long, and it was upon the summit of this rocky plateau that the 'Midas City' stood. The settlement, which the French archaeologists have excavated, was founded some time after the middle of the sixth century B.C. and abandoned before the end of the fourth. Its foundation must therefore again have taken place in a period more properly called Lydian, and its occupation must have been uninterrupted by the Persian conquest. In certain places the houses are built over the filled-up entries to underground stairways, which in an earlier age must have led down to springs or wells at the base of the cliff, and there are other indications to suggest that an older city must have occupied the summit of the rock in the days before the Cimmerian invasions. Few remains of this period have yet been found.

* *Journal of Hellenic Studies*, III (1882), p. 3.

If then, we are to study the united results of such excavations, seeking first the archaeological documentation of the period during which the Phrygians were extending and consolidating their power, it is to those in eastern Anatolia to which we now must once more turn. At most of the sites in question the Phrygian remains lie directly upon those of the Hittite Empire, yet one of the first things to be observed is the conspicuous change in the form and character of ordinary domestic accessories. The contrast is emphasized rather than modified by the survival of one characteristic feature of Hittite life. This is the use of hieroglyphs, which are still to be found on seals or scratched in the form of graffiti on pottery. For the rest, one has only to glance, for instance, at the pottery in order to understand the change which has taken place, both in taste and technology, since the time of the Hittite kings.

PHRYGIAN POTTERY

During Phrygian times in eastern Anatolia one finds both plain and painted pottery simultaneously in use, but the decorated wares are preponderant (Plates 30 a and b). Furthermore, the character and elaboration of the decoration is something which until now would have been considered totally alien to the Anatolian tradition. One would have been compelled to seek its origin in the Mediterranean or Aegean islands. It is indeed a thousand years since such pottery appeared in Cappadocia or the Halys country, and it is hardly surprising that the Phrygian painted wares have occasionally been confused with those of Kültepe. But here again we are faced with a repertoire of variations on the double theme of shape and decoration, of which it is impossible to convey in words any visual picture. The ornament, we may say, is usually in reddish brown on a 'slipped' surface of a neutral colour, and typical motives are stags in combination with concentric rings and trees, often arranged in panels and seldom covering more than the rim, neck and upper part of the vessel. But if, by following the excavators' report as it proceeds in precise and unequivocal terms from decoration to shapes, we are expecting to obtain a true impression of the beautiful objects among which an average Phrygian family lived, there will be some risk of disappointment. 'Typical forms', it tells us, 'are flat bowls with either thickened or flaring rims, cups with high handles, flaring orifices, and pronounced demarcation between neck and body, and large jars with sharply profiled rims, orifices about as large as the greatest body diameter and two or four handles.'* At this point some readers would doubtless turn with relief to the photographic or drawn illustrations. They will there obtain a clearer impression of the coarse but effective technique which characterized the work of Iron Age potters almost everywhere in Anatolia.

ARCHITECTURE

Neither Alishar nor Boghazköy yielded much information about Phrygian architecture. There were of course fortress walls in both cases, but their treatment was undistinguished, and the towered gateway which the American excavators were able to reconstruct, apart from its dressed stone architraves and flat lintel, much resembled any similar Hittite structure. The only relevant finds of any great interest are the architectural terracottas discovered by Koşay at Pazarli (Plate 31) and again by the Körte brothers at Gordium. It is possible to understand from the rock monuments that a feature characteristic of Phrygian buildings was a sloping roof, and to see that the formal treatment of its gable-ends foreshadowed the Greek pediment. The most striking element among the terracottas is panels ornamented with figures in relief, painted and glazed, which seem likely to have formed a frieze beneath the pediment. Both their subject and their style are of the greatest possible interest, as representing a collateral branch of Greek ancestral art. There are processions of warriors with circular shields and plumed helmets, domestic or wild animals sometimes arranged in heraldic groups, and in one case an unmistakable centaur. On the basis of the rock façades the Körte brothers attempted the restoration of a temple, incorporating the many architectural items of this sort which they found scattered about the site. Unfortunately, however, it can

* *The Alishar Hüyük, 1930–32*, Part II, p. 350.

now be demonstrated that these were derived from buildings of several different periods, and that no building of the sort actually existed in the area which they excavated. The stratification of these objects at Gordium in fact shows that only by inference can they be taken to throw light on the architecture of the true Phrygian period, since none of them was made earlier than the Cimmerian invasions. It remains for the American excavations, which are still in progress, to reveal the Gordium of the Phrygian kings. Already a huge monumental gateway has been discovered and further details are awaited with great interest.

THE TUMULI

Another feature ordinarily considered characteristic of the Phrygian period is the tumuli burials. There must be some hundreds of them scattered about the countryside from Cappadocia to the Black Sea and from Ankara to the Aegean coast, but they again usually cover remains dating at the earliest from the end of the eighth century B.C. At Gordium, during the first two seasons' work of the American expedition, eleven new tumuli were opened, and R. Young, who was in charge, has been able to report on the types of burial represented. It seems that from the eighth century onwards, several different methods of interment were practised by people of the poorer classes. Cist graves or urns were used with equal frequency, and in either the body could be cremated or otherwise (the term 'unurned cremation' is used in the report). Considering the immense expense of heaping up a barrow over the grave, one must assume that the tumuli represented the graves of well-to-do individuals. And for these the system of inhumation was fairly rigidly prescribed, though it changed with the passage of time. In the seventh century, for instance, it was the fashion to construct a wooden burial chamber and cover it with stones, before heaping up the tumulus above it. Here, for example, is what the Americans found, after cutting trenches into the centre of 'Tumulus B'.

'A wooden chamber of large beams carefully mortised at the corners had been erected in a shaft and the space between the chamber and the pit walls had been filled in with large stones. The chamber contained two burials, one in a wooden coffin, the other on the floor beside it. The chamber had been roofed with large logs and big stones piled over it to a depth of nearly two metres. Apparently offerings, including bronze cauldrons and two small painted jugs, had been thrown in with the stones on top of the grave. A tumulus had been carefully piled over the grave, its centre being marked by the intersection of lines of rough stones.' Young goes on to mention a case where similar lines of stones were used to mark a false centre, some metres from the point where the grave itself was actually located: a practice which was no doubt intended to mislead tomb robbers.

In the sixth century the practice of cremation became more popular. In 'Tumulus A' – 'a laid floor of white clay about three metres in diameter was covered with the remains of the funeral pyre, a mass of cinders and charred logs, mixed with pottery and objects of bronze and iron, all affected by the fire. A small pit cut through the floor contained the burnt bones of the dead, apparently a young woman, together with jewellery of gold and electrum, some of which was fused while other pieces, together with pottery and stone objects, had apparently been thrown on to the pyre after the fire had been quenched. The grave goods included an intact gold bracelet (a most beautiful object, ending in opposed bulls' heads, finely modelled), and a burnt one, a silver mirror with carved ivory attachment at the base of the handle and fragments of other carved ivories.' The richness of materials and high standard of craftsmanship to which the contents of these graves testify, must in fact be taken to imply a period of peace and prosperity preceding the Persian invasion. Imported objects also suggest extensive trade relations. The same grave contained an Egyptian alabastron, a plastic vase of an East Greek type, and an amphora with geometric decoration, perhaps Cypriot.

In burial customs one sees an aspect of human behaviour which depends too much upon environment to be changed often or easily, and in the cemetery at Gordium (which, indeed, had evidently been in use since the Copper Age) there are many obvious survivals. At Boghazköy, for instance, we have already traced back the practice of cremation to the beginning of the second millennium B.C., while the wooden tomb chambers beneath the Gordium tumuli bring memories of the 'Royal Tombs' at Alaja. Their resemblance to the latter is even strengthened by the animal bones deposited in the filling above them.

CHARACTER OF THE ROCK SCULPTURES

We must now return to the rock monuments, which, having become familiar before ever the excavations began, are still often thought of as the most notable manifestation of Phrygian culture. If, in seeking to establish their character and purpose, they are to be treated as a group, it is first important to eliminate from among them those to which in fact a date in Hellenistic or even Roman times should be attributed, and whose inclusion in the past among Phrygian works has caused some confusion. Among them, for example, are monuments at Ayas İni, Gördük Kayası and that of Solon at Kümbet, which can indisputably be identified as tombs of a late date. Of the truly Phrygian monuments then, to begin with there is the 'Tomb of Midas' itself at Yazılıkaya. Here at once we may see the most common form taken by these rock sculptures, namely the gable-end façade of an imaginary building, formally decorated with fine geometrical ornament in relief. It has an inscription mentioning the name of Midas and there is a subterranean chamber beneath it, approached by a long passage. A minor façade nearby, sometimes called the 'Tomb of Midas' Wife', has an imitation of shuttered windows, another common feature of these architectural monuments, which also occasionally have doors, represented as opening inwards. The rock-cut chambers behind or below them are sometimes arranged like the interior of a house with benches on three sides (the 'Broken Tomb') or a carved bed ('Lion Grave' or 'Pyramid'). There are also heraldic or religious motives in the decoration of the façades: two colossal lions rampant and roaring towards each other over a pillar or other symbolical object (Büyük Arslan Tash, Arslan Kaya, etc.):

two opposed warriors or colossal lions (the 'Broken Tomb'): and many representations of Cybele, the Great Goddess of Phrygia (Arslan Kaya, Berber İni, etc.).

There has been much discussion of the architectural details revealed by the rock monuments. The decoration, for instance, of large surfaces, with an overall geometrical pattern is an unusual feature, and it has been pointed out that the character of the patterns is of a sort more suitable for glazed tiles (like those found at Pazarlı), or even carpets. For a parallel to the gabled façade, one has to look no further than Urartu, where the Musasir temple, to whose representation in an Assyrian relief we have already referred, bears a striking resemblance. As at Musasir, the wide span of the gable could have been reduced by supporting pillars, which would explain a sculptured column base found in a Phrygian setting at Pazarlı, and another, decorated with lotus buds and palmettes, in the Ankara Museum. It is to Urartu also that one must turn for a parallel to the voluted ornament to be seen in the monument at Bahshayish (Bakshish) for it appears as a common motive in Urartian furniture. This would in fact appear to be one of the only sound links which we have so far been able to observe between Urartu and western Anatolia. The disparity of some centuries in date could be explained by our ignorance of architecture in the intervening period.

Their Purpose. Finally, as to the purpose of the monuments; R. D. Barnett has recently made a strong case against their having any of them had the function of tombs or memorials, and even ventured the suggestion that 'the custom of burying the dead in rock-cut tombs did not enter Phrygia before the fifth century B.C.' In 1951 A. Gabriel, the excavator of the Midas City, pointed out that the 'Midas Tomb' was definitely the site of a cult, and that it contained next to it a cult building in which certain mystery rituals were performed. Barnett goes further. As has been done already in the case of the Hittite rock monuments, he falls back upon the theory of religious cults to explain the whole group of Phrygian monuments. In support of this theory, and in order to refute the contention that the monuments were tombs, he rightly points out that the piece of country in which they are all concentrated is not only geologically peculiar, but agriculturally extremely unproductive. He doubts that the Phrygians, whose habitat was in the fertile valleys of the Sangarius and other river systems, and whose normal custom, as we know, was to be buried beneath barrows of earth, should for any reason have sought a final resting-place for their kings among these remote and inhospitable rocks.

Barnett then draws attention to a circumstance in connexion with the location of these monuments, which has till now escaped notice, namely that the area in which they are located, covers the sources of all the principal rivers of Phrygia: the Sangarius (Sakarya), Tembris (Porsuk), Cayster (Akar Çay), Glaukus (Büyük Menderes) and several others. He shows, furthermore, that almost without exception the monuments stand near to, if not actually facing, springs of fresh water. The question is of course at once raised as to whether this was a characteristic peculiar to the Phrygian monuments, and the answer, on consideration, is emphatically negative. If all the Hittite rock monuments which we have mentioned or described in an earlier chapter be again called into account, it will be recollected that almost every single one of them, from Yazılıkaya beside its dried-up spring at Boghazköy to the Sirkeli relief overlooking the waters of the Jeyhan river in Cilicia, is in some way closely connected with a supply of fresh water. Finally, when one recollects that the Younger Storm God of Hittite mythology was 'a god of rocks and waters', it becomes more and more hard to regard this as a coincidence, and one is driven to the conclusion that, both by the Hittites and later by the Phrygians, a bare vertical rock beside or near a source of water was deemed holy and a cult set up there, served by an open-air shrine.

Barnett goes on to consider how the monuments with their internal chambers (often too small to accommodate a body in an extended attitude), could have been adapted to the ceremonial associated with such a cult, and finds that niches for images and cells for sacred offerings would be well suited to known rituals connected, for instance, with the worship of Cybele. He concludes finally that the designation of the Phrygian monuments as tombs should now be forgotten.

If, then, we are to see in the Hittite rock monuments the symbols of a fresh-water cult, of the sort which in classical times can still be seen reflected in religious association with the source of the Marsyas or Adonis river, and if the Phrygian reliefs are to be regarded as a link between the two, we shall then find ourselves contemplating one of the most striking phenomena of Anatolian archaeology – the extraordinary vitality of local religious beliefs and practices, in the face of all social and political changes. One has only to think of the great Asiatic Mother-Goddess, first recognizable in the steatopygous figurines of the Chalcolithic Age, who is still to be found at Pessinus and elsewhere in Roman times, playing the central role of a divine drama whose symbolism is that of earthly life. In Ramsay's word 'she is the expression of a religious belief, which regarded the life of God as embodying and representing the life of nature, and proceeding according to the analogy of the natural world. ...' To-day it is clear to us that this was as true for the earliest inhabitants of Anatolia as it was for the Hittites or Phrygians, and eventually for the priestly zealots in the Artemisium at Ephesus.

*

Lydian remains in Anatolia reach westwards from the region of the rock sculptures to the ruins of Sardis, and beyond to Mount Sipylus and the spur of hills which extends towards the Bay of Smyrna. Here, dating, as one imagines, from the same period, is an interesting group of monuments – an acropolis with sanctuaries and a great many stone-faced tumuli, of which the largest is the great conical Mausoleum, known as the 'Tomb of Tantalus'.

As one looks down from this strange necropolis towards the sea, the very landscape reflects and symbolizes the vicissitudes of Anatolian history, and affords a glimpse of events beyond the horizon of our present study. At the head of the bay, where its rivers once flowed out through shallow estuaries, their burden of alluvium has created a fertile plain. Rising above it in the foreground is a little hill called Bayraklı, once an island connected to the shore by a stone causeway. There had been a village on it throughout the Bronze Age, and sometime in the early centuries of the first millennium it was adopted as their home by a party of Greek colonists. Here on this island, with their ships still ready for emergencies in the little harbour behind, they could postpone for a while the hazard of actual contact with the perils of the interior and peacefully consolidate a small trading centre. It was not until some centuries later that lack of living space and the silting up of their anchorage made a move desirable to a new site on the other side of the bay. It was thus that the Greek colony of Smyrna was founded.

Camping in tents among the olives and vines on Bayraklı hill in the early 1950's, a party of archaeologists – British from the Athens School and Turks from Ankara – set themselves to examine the remains of the old settlement. Founded upon the ruins of the Bronze-Age village was a primitive stone building, foreshadowing the appointments of a Greek temple, and houses with the beautiful Corinthian or Orientalizing pottery of the archaic period. Then, nearer to the surface, and symbolizing a climax of cultural attainment with which this book has no concern, the polished elegance of classical 'black-' and 'red-figure' vases. With this foretaste of the historical process, whereby the Anatolia of Hittite times was eventually transformed into a westernized Asia Minor, our survey of its early archaeology may well end.

A Short Review of the Anthropology of the Ancient Inhabitants of Anatolia, from the Chalcolithic Age to the End of the Hittite Empire*

BY

DR MUZAFFER ŞENYÜREK

*Professor of Anthropology and
Chairman of the Division of Paleoanthropology,
University of Ankara*

As is well known, some writers had formerly supposed that the earlier populations of Anatolia were brachycephalic. Subsequently W. M. Krogman, now Professor of Physical Anthropology at the University of Pennsylvania, in his excellent study on the crania from Alishar Höyük clearly showed that at Alishar the Mediterranean dolichocephals had antedated the brachycephals (see Krogman, 1937). In a later study published in 1941, based upon a larger series of crania from various parts of Anatolia, I was able to show that the majority of the Chalcolithic and Copper Age inhabitants of Anatolia were dolichocephals of Eurafrican and Mediterranean racial types, and that the brachycephals, probably representing invaders, were relatively rare in these periods (see Şenyürek, 1941).

Of the available adult male and female Chalcolithic crania from Anatolia a vast majority are dolichocephalic and mesocephalic, only a relatively small percentage of them being brachycephalic (for figures, see Şenyürek, 1951). In this connexion it would be worth while to say a few words regarding the situation at Kumtepe, a Chalcolithic site in the vicinity of Troy. A study of the skulls from Levels Ia, Ib, and Ic at Kumtepe has shown that the dolichocephals had clearly preceded the arrival of brachycephals, a brachycephalic skull appearing only at level Ic, which represents the last phase of the Chalcolithic period at this site. (See Şenyürek, 1949.)†

* This paper is in main a summary of an earlier study of mine (see Şenyürek, 1951).

† For the antiquity of the two dolichocephalic types, viz., the Eurafrican and Mediterranean racial types, see Şenyürek, 1954.

Of the available 51 adult male and female Copper Age crania, 44 (86·27 per cent) are dolichocephalic and mesocephalic, only seven (13·72 per cent) being brachycephalic (see Şenyürek, 1951). As I have shown in my earlier study, the Copper Age skulls tend to have on the average, a shorter length, a slightly larger breadth, and a somewhat higher cranial index than the Chalcolithic skulls, although the differences in these measurements and the cranial index are not significant statistically (see Şenyürek, 1951). Thus the native Copper Age population of Anatolia appears to be a continuation of the Chalcolithic population. However, the slightly higher cranial index of the Copper Age skulls, on the average, is probably due to a wave of predominantly brachycephalic invaders which appears to have reached Anatolia in the Copper Age.

Of the Early Bronze Age we have unfortunately only four skulls, of which one is brachycephalic. It is likely, but by no means certain, that the Early Bronze Age population of Anatolia was physically the same as the succeeding Hittite population, but because of the lack of a sufficient series of skeletons it is difficult to make a definite statement on this point.

Of the 35 adult male and female Anatolian skulls dating from the time interval between 2000 B.C. and 1200 B.C., 12 (34·28 per cent) are round headed. Of the males 27·27 per cent. and of the females 46·15 per cent are brachycephalic.* Thus it is quite clear that in the Hittite Empire times, in the sites studied, the proportion of the brachycephals had tremendously increased.

When the Anatolian skulls from 2000–1200 B.C. are divided into central and peripheral Anatolian groups, it is seen that in the central group 42·85 per cent of the males and 66·66 per cent of the females are brachycephalic. In the peripheral group there are no brachycephals among the male skulls, whereas 40 per cent of the females are roundheaded. This comparison shows that a large percentage of the Hittites proper, represented by the central Anatolian group, were brachycephalic. On the other hand, in the peripheral Anatolian group there is a conspicuous difference between the sexes in the cranial index, the females showing a large percentage of brachycephals, while the males are long headed. A comparison of the crania of the females from central and peripheral Anatolian groups shows that they are almost identical in average length, breadth, and cranial index. Thus the craniological evidence

* Of the combined series of children and adults, consisting of 37 crania, 35·13 per cent are brachycephalic (Şenyürek, 1951, Table 14).

suggests that the women of the peripheral Anatolian groups were Hittites. As I have stated elsewhere, it seems probable that some men in these peripheral sites had married Hittite women (see Şenyürek, 1951).

In this discussion of the skulls from 2000–1200 B.C. a brief reference should be made to the skeletons from Kültepe. A study of the skulls shows that the cranial index increases in passing from Level III to Level II in Kültepe, and that at the latter level the measurements and indices of the skulls, particularly those of the females, come close to those from the central Anatolian area, that is to those from the Hittite area (see Şenyürek, 1952). Thus, the craniological evidence suggests that the Hittites had probably already arrived in Anatolia at the time when the Assyrian trading colony was flourishing in Kültepe, at the beginning of the second millennium B.C., and that some of these Assyrian merchants had probably married Hittite women.* It should be mentioned in this connexion that S. Alp has already concluded from an analysis of the names of some native Anatolians that the Hittites were established in Anatolia at the time of the Assyrian trading colony at Kültepe (see Alp, 1949, 1950–1 and 1952 and Bilgiç, 1953). In this respect, the craniological evidence is in harmony with the philological and archaeological evidence (for archaeological evidence see Bittel, 1950).

CONCLUSION

The majority of the Chalcolithic and Copper Age inhabitants of Anatolia were dolichocephals mainly of the Eurafrican and Mediterranean racial types, whereas the brachycephals, probably representing invaders, were rare in these periods. This study further supports the conclusion that the earliest known inhabitants of Anatolia were longheaded, and that the brachycephals came in subsequently.

The craniological evidence indicates that an invasion of brachycephals into Anatolia took place during the Chalcolithic period and that it was followed by a second invasion, bringing the brachycephalic elements to Alaja Höyük and other Copper Age sites,

* As I pointed out in my earlier reports (Şenyürek, 1951, p. 610, and 1952, pp. 338–9), it must not, however, be supposed that all these Assyrian traders married Hittite women, as some had definitely married Assyrian women (see Bilgiç, 1951, p. 241) and some may have married the descendants of the longheaded Copper Age inhabitants of Anatolia, who were conquered but not annihilated by the Hittites (see Şenyürek, 1941, p. 245: 1951, pp. 605 and 610).

probably about the middle of the Copper Age. The next invasion of brachycephals, which was more important and extensive than the previous ones, occurred roughly at about 2000 B.C. The craniological, archaeological, and philological evidence, taken together, indicates that this invasion was made by the Hittites who were predominantly of the Alpine type.

LITERATURE CITED*

Alp, S. 1949. 'Hititlerde sosyal sınıf Nam. Ra'lar ve ideogramın Hititçe karşılığı.' *Belleten*, Vol. XIII, No. 50, pp. 245–70.

Alp, S. 1950–1. 'Die Soziale Klasse der Nam. Ra-Leute und ihre hethitische Bezeichnung.' *Jahrbuch für Kleinasiatische Forschung*, Vol. I, Heft 2, pp. 113–35.

Alp, S. 1952. 'On the occasion of a new book concerning the Hittites.' *Ankara Üniversitesi hil ve Tarih-Coğrafya Fakültesi Dergisi*, Vol. X, Nos. 3–4, pp. 249–56.

Bilgiç, E. 1951. 'Die Originellen Seiten im Eherecht der Vorhethitischen Bevölkerung Anatoliens.' *Ankara Üniversitesi Dil ve Tarih-Coğrafya Fakültesi Dergisi*, Vol. IX, No. 3, pp. 239–50.

Bilgiç, E. 1953. 'Kapadokya metinlerinde geçen yerli appellatifler ve bunların eski Anadolu dilleri içerisinde yeri.' *Ankara Üniversitesi Dil ve Tarih-Coğrafya Fakültesi Yayınları*, No. 88.

Bittel, K. 1950. 'Hethiter und Proto-Hattier. Eine archäologische Betrachtung. *Historia*, Vol. 7, Heft 2, pp. 267–86.

Krogman, W. M. 1937. 'Cranial types from Alişar Hüyük and their relations to other racial types, ancient and modern, of Europe and Western Asia.' In von der Osten's: *Alishar Hüyük, Seasons of 1930–1932*, Part III. OIP, Vol. XXX, Researches in Anatolia, Vol. IX, pp. 213–93.

Krogman, W. M. 1949. 'Ancient cranial types at Chatal Hüyük and Tell Al-Judaidah, Syria, from the late fifth millennium B.C. to the mid seventh century A.D.' *Belleten*, Vol. XIII, No. 51, pp. 407–77.

Şenyürek, M. S. 1941. 'A craniological study of the Copper Age and Hittite populations of Anatolia.' *Belleten*, Vol. V, No. 19, pp. 237–53.

Şenyürek, M. S. 1949. 'A note on the skeletons from Kumtepe, in the vicinity of Troy.' *Ankara Üniversitesi Dil ve Tarih-Coğrafya Fakültesi Dergisi*, Vol. VII, No. 2, pp. 300–04.

Şenyürek, M. S. 1951. 'Fluctuation of the cranial index in Anatolia, from the fourth millennium B.C. to 1200 B.C.' *Belleten*, Vol. XV, No. 60, pp. 593–632.

* For a fuller bibliography on the palaeoanthropology of Anatolia, see Şenyürek, 1951, 1952, and 1954.

Şenyürek, M. S. 1952. 'A study of the human skeletons from Kültepe, excavated under the auspices of the Turkish Historical Society. The skeletons from the excavation season of 1948.' *Belleten*, Vol. XVI, No. 63, pp 323–43.

Şenyürek, M. S. 1954. 'A note on the skulls of Chalcolithic Age from Yümüktepe.' *Belleten*, Vol. XVIII, No. 69, pp. 1–25.

Beycesultan

DURING the time that this book has been in preparation, a new and determined attempt has been made to remedy the situation discussed on p. 153 f., which has left us in almost total ignorance concerning the western neighbours of the Hittites. Two seasons of excavating under the author's direction at Beysesultan near the headwaters of the Meander river, have brought to light the remains of a second millennium city, which, in addition to its impressive size, gains special significance from the fact that it must lie within the historical territory of Arzawa. Archaeologically therefore it should create a connecting link between Hittite Anatolia and the distinctive remains of the sixth and seventh settlements at Troy.

At the new site, six main building-levels have so far been investigated, covering a period of about a thousand years, from the end of the Early Bronze Age to the twelfth century B.C. Most interesting of all is the Middle Bronze Age occupation (Level V), which must correspond approximately to the beginning of Troy VI and to the time of the *Karum* at Kültepe. During this period, the city seems to have been the capital of a considerable state, for there are everywhere signs of the kind of luxury which depends on political prosperity. The architecture in particular is remarkable and of a character which has no exact parallel in Anatolia. The eastern half of the mound was at this time completely occupied by a public building almost as large as the palaces of Minoan Crete, which in minor respects it curiously resembles. In its construction both stone rubble and sun-dried brick are used, reinforced with an elaborate framework of timber: but cut stonework is absent, and one gains the impression that its builders were carpenters and metal-smiths rather than stonemasons. The palace is formerly planned on a broad scale and its appointments are most sophisticated. Halls supported by wooden columns are ornamented with painted plaster, and there seems to have been some system of sub-pavement heating. Unfortunately the building had been deliberately burnt to the ground, and the looting which preceded the fire had been so thorough that few objects could be found among its ruins. Even its date remained in some doubt until the end of the 1955 season, when part of an unburnt building of the same period was uncovered elsewhere, and its content of pottery and objects could be studied.

After a long period of material poverty and evident political obscurity, the city once more became the seat of a local ruler in the thirteenth century B.C. Though reduced in size, this occupation (Level II), which must have corresponded in time to the period of the Hittite Empire, showed signs of considerable individuality and cultural distinction. The eastern hill was once more occupied by an enclosed palace-compound, much of which has now been excavated. It has revealed an interesting range of administrative buildings; the residence of the ruler (a *megaron* of the type now known as far afield as Kültepe), with its dependent offices, a food-store and private wine-shop; and finally, as one might have expected from the finds in Troy VI, elaborately equipped stabling accommodation. The pottery and objects have details in common both with Troy and with Hittite Anatolia; but the bulk of the material is completely unfamiliar and individual. Predominant among local vessels are 'champagne-glass' and 'fruit-stand' shapes, and almost all show traces of the metal originals from which they must have been copied. Strangely enough Mycenaean finds were extremely few; mostly weapons, which might have been discarded by an attacking force.

Here then at Beycesultan are the material remains of a second-millennium people, who represent a distinctive culture which has little in common with that of the Trojans or the Hittites. Time will show whether they may in fact be identified as Arzawans.

BIBLIOGRAPHY

*Those entries marked with an asterisk will provide
a basic reading list for the English student*

I. EXCAVATION REPORTS

1. ALISHAR

*OSTEN, H. H. von der. *The Alishar Hüyük. Seasons 1930–32.* Parts I, II, and III. Chicago, 1937.

*OSTEN, H. H. von der. *Discoveries in Anatolia 1930–31.* Chicago, 1933.

SCHMIDT, E. F. *Alishar Hüyük. Seasons 1928–29.* Parts I, II. Chicago, 1932–33.

SCHMIDT, E. F. *Anatolia Through the Ages. Discoveries at the Alishar Mound 1927–29.* Chicago, 1931.

2. TROY

ANGEL, J. L. *Troy. The Human Remains.* Supplementary Monograph 1. Princeton, 1951.

BLEGEN, C. W., *et al. Troy. General Introduction. The First and Second Settlements.* Vol. I, Parts 1 and 2 (Text and plates). Princeton, 1950.

BLEGEN, C. W., *et al. Troy. The Third, Fourth and Fifth Settlements.* Vol. II, Parts 1 and 2 (Text and plates). Princeton, 1951.

BLEGEN, C. W., *et al. Troy. The Sixth Settlement.* Vol. III, Parts 1 and 2 (Text and plates). Princeton, 1953.

DÖRPFELD, W. *Troja und Ilion.* 2 Vols. Athens, 1902.

GEJVALL, N.-G. *The Fauna of the different Settlements of Troy.* Part 1. Stockholm, 1946.

(KUMTEPE) KOŞAY, H. *'Troad' da Dört Yerlesme Yeri.* İstanbul, 1936.

LAMB, W. *Excavations at Thermi in Lesbos.* Cambridge, 1936.

SCHLIEMANN, H. *Atlas des Antiquités Troyennes.* Paris, 1874.

SCHLIEMANN, H. *Ilios. The City and Country of the Trojans.* London, 1880.

*SCHLIEMANN, H. *Troja.* London, 1884.

*SCHLIEMANN, H. *Troy and its Remains.* London, 1875.

SCHMIDT, H. *Schliemann's Sammlung Trojanischer Altertümer.* Berlin, 1902.

*SCHUCHARDT, C. *Schliemann's Excavations.* London, 1891.

3. YORTAN

COLLIGNON, C. R. 'Note sur les fouilles de M. Paul Gauguin de Yortan en Mysie'. Part 2. *Compte rendu de l'Académie des Inscriptions et Belles-lettres,* (1901) pp. 810–17, pl. 1 ff.

FORSDYKE, E. J. *Catalogue of Vases in the British Museum.* Vol. I, Part 1 (1925) p. xii, pl. 1 ff.

FORSDYKE, E. J. *Corpus Vas. Antiq. Louvre.* Fasc. 4, pl. 1é.

*HUTCHINSON, R. W. 'Uruk and Yortan', *Iraq* II, p. 211.

ÖZGÜÇ, T. *Belleten,* VIII (1944) p. 53 ff., pl. XIX–XXIV.

4. SENJIRLI

Königliche Museen zu Berlin, Mitteilungen aus den Orientalischen Sammlungen,

    Heft xi,   I. *Einleitung und Inschriften*. Berlin, 1893.

* Heft xii, C. HUMANN und R. KOLDEWEY. *Ausgrabungen in Sendschirli II. Ausgrabungsbericht und Architektur. (Bericht über die erste Grabung)*. Berlin, 1898.

* Heft xiii, F. v. LUSCHAN. *Ausgrabungen in Sendschirli III. Thorskulpturen*. Berlin, 1902

* Heft xiv, F. v. LUSCHAN und andere. *Ausgrabungen in Sendschirli IV. (Bericht über die 5. Grabung, 1902.)* Berlin, 1911.

* Heft xv, F. v. LUSCHAN und N. ANDRAE. *Ausgrabungen in Sendschirli V. Die Kleinfunde von Sendschirli*. Berlin, 1943.

5. SAKÇAGÖZÜ

GARSTANG, J. 'First Interim Report'. *Liverpool Annals of Archaeology and Anthropology*, I (1908).

*GARSTANG, J. 'Second Interim Report on the Excavations at Sakje-Geuzi in North Syria. 1911'. *Liverpool Annals of Archaeology and Anthropology*, v, Parts 1 and 2, (1912).

*GARSTANG, J. 'Third Report on Excavations at Sakje-Geuzi'. *Liverpool Annals of Archaeology and Anthropology*, xxiv, Parts 3 and 4 (1937).

TANKARD, E. 'The Sculptures of Sakçe Gözü'. *Liverpool Annals of Archaeology and Anthropology*, xxvi (1939) p. 85.

TAYLOR, J. du Plat, M. V. SETON WILLIAMS, and J. WAECHTER. 'The Excavations at Sakçe Gözü'. *Iraq*, xii (1950), p. 53.

VAUGHAN, D. M. 'Some Notes on the Dado Sculptures at Sakçe Gözü'. *Liverpool Annals of Archaeology and Anthropology*, xxi (1934) p. 37.

WAECHTER, J., S. GÖĞÜS, and M. V. SETON WILLIAMS. 'The Sakçe Gözü Cave Site. 1949'. *Belleten*, xv (1950).

6. MERSIN

GARSTANG, J. 'Explorations in Cilicia'. *Liverpool Annals of Archaeology and Anthropology*, xxiv (1936) p. 52; xxv (1937) pp. 12, 71; xxvi (1938) pp. 38, 89.

*GARSTANG, J. *Prehistoric Mersin. Yümük Tepe in Southern Turkey*. Oxford, 1952.

7. KUSURA

*LAMB, W. 'Excavations at Kusura near Afyon Karahissar'. *Archaeologia*, 86 (1936) pp. 1–64. *Archaeologia*, 87 (1937) pp. 217–74.

8. TARSUS

GOLDMAN, H. 'Excavations at Gözlü Kule, Tarsus'.
    American Journal of Archaeology, xxxix (1935), p. 526 f.
    American Journal of Archaeology, xli (1937), p. 262 f.

American Journal of Archaeology, XLII (1938), p. 40 f.
American Journal of Archaeology, XLIV (1940), p. 60 f.
American Journal of Archaeology, LIII (1949) p. 46 f., pl. XII–XIV.
*GOLDMAN, H. *Excavations at Gözlü Kule, Tarsus*. Vol. I (text and plates); Vol. II in the press.

9. MINOR ANATOLIAN SITES

BITTEL, K. *Demirci-Hüyük*. Berlin, 1939.
BITTEL, K. 'Ein Gräberfeld der Yortan-Kultur bei Babaköy'. *Archiv für Orientforschung*, XII, parts 1 and 2.
KANSU, Ş. A. *Etiyokuşu Hafriyatı Raporu 1937*. Ankara, 1940.
KÖKTEN, K., and T. and N. ÖZGÜÇ. 'Samsun Kazıları'. *Belleten*, IX (1945) pp. 361 ff., pl. LXIII–LXXIV.
KOŞAY, H. Z., and M. AKOK. 'Preliminary Report on Test Excavations at Büyük Gülücek'. *Belleten*, XII (1948) p. 479, pl. LXXXII–CVIII and plan.
KOŞAY, H. Z. *Karaz Sondajı*. Türk Tarih Kongresi, 1943. pp. 164–77, Figs. 1–21 and plan.
KOŞAY, H. Z. *Les Fouilles de Pazarlı*. Istanbul, 1938 and Ankara, 1941.
*LLOYD, S., and N. GÖKÇE. 'Excavations at Polatlı'. *Anatolian Studies*, Vol. I (1951) p. 3.
ÖZGÜÇ, T. *Samsun Hafriyatının 1941–42 Yılı Neticeleri*. Türk Tarih Kongresi. p. 393 ff., pl. 1–10.
ÖZGÜÇ, T. and N. *Karahüyük Hafriyatı Raporu 1947*. Ankara, 1949.
ROBINSON, D. M. 'Sizma'. *American Journal of Archaeology*, XXXI (1927) pp. 26–50.

10. BOGHAZKÖY

BITTEL, K. *Boğazköy. Die Kleinfunde der Grabungen 1906–12*. Leipzig, 1937.
BITTEL, K. *Die Ruinen von Boğazköy*. Berlin, 1937.
BITTEL, K., and H. CAMBEL. *Boğazköy*. (Guide in English). Istanbul, 1951.
*BITTEL, K., and H. G. GÜTERBOCK. 'Boghazköy. Neue Untersuchungen in der Hethitischen Hauptstadt'. *Abhandlungen der preussischen Akademie der Wissenschaften*. Berlin, Jahrgang 1935.
*BITTEL, K., and R. NAUMANN. 'Boğazköy II. Neue Untersuchungen hethitischer Architektur'. *Abhandlungen der preussischen Akademie der Wissenschaften*. Berlin, Jahrgang 1938.
*BITTEL, K., and R. NAUMANN. *Boğazköy-Hattusa I. Architektur, Topographie, Landeskunde und Siedlungsgeschichte*. Stuttgart, 1952.
*BITTEL, K., *et al*. *Yazılıkaya. Architektur, Felsbilder, Inschriften und Kleinfunde*. Leipzig, 1941.
GÜTERBOCK, H. G. *Siegel aus Boghazköy*. Teil I–II. Berlin, 1940–42.

KRAUSE, K. *Boghazköy Tempel V*. Berlin, 1940.

PUCHSTEIN, O. *Boghazköi. Die Bauwerke*. Leipzig, 1912.

WINCKLER, H. *Excavations at Boghaz-Keui in the Summer of 1907*. Washington, 1909.

11. GORDIUM

COX, D. H. *A Third Century Hoard of Tetradrachms from Gordion*. Pennsylvania Museum Monograph, 1953.

KÖRTE, G. *Ergebnisse der Ausgrabungen im Jahre 1900*. Berlin, 1904.

YOUNG, R. 'Gordion 1950'. *Bulletin University Museums, Philadelphia*, Vol. 16, 1 (1951).

YOUNG, R. 'Gordion 1951–52'. *Bulletin University Museums, Philadelphia*, Vol. 17, 4 (1953).

YOUNG, R. 'When Alexander the Great cut the Gordian Knot'. *Illustrated London News*, 3 Jan. 1953.

12. ALAJA

ARIK, R. O. *Les Fouilles d'Alaca Hüyük. Rapport Préliminaire sur les Travaux en 1935*. Ankara, 1937.

KOŞAY, H. Z. *Alacahöyük*. (Guide in English) Ankara, 1953.

KOŞAY, H. Z. *Ausgrabungen von Alaca Hüyük*. Ankara, 1944.

*KOŞAY, H. Z. *Les Fouilles d'Alaca Hüyük. Rapport Préliminaire sur les Travaux en 1937–39*. Ankara, 1951.

13. KÜLTEPE

GENOUILLAC, H. de. *Céramique Cappadocienne*. Vols. I and II. Paris, 1926.

HROZNY, B. 'Rapport préliminaire sur les fouilles Tchécoslovaques du Kültepe'. *Syria*, VIII (1927).

*ÖZGÜÇ, T. *Ausgrabungen in Kültepe 1948*. Ankara, 1950.

ÖZGÜÇ, T. and N. 'Vorbericht über Siegel und Siegelabdrucke'. *Belleten*, XVII, p. 123.

ÖZGÜÇ, T. and N. 'Vorläufiger Bericht über die Grabungen von 1950 in Kültepe'. *Belleten*, XVII, p. 109.

ŞENYÜREK, M.S. 'A Study of the Human Skeletons from Kültepe'. *Belleten*, XVI, p. 323.

14. MALATYA

AKURGAL, E. *Remarques Stylistiques sur les Reliefs de Malatya*. Istanbul, 1946.

*DELAPORTE, L. *Malatya. Arslantepe. La Porte des Lions*. Paris, 1940.

DELAPORTE, L. *Revue Hittite et Asianique*, 2 (1932–33) pp. 129–54, 257–85; 5 (1938–39) pp. 43–56, 85–6.

GARSTANG, J. 'The Winged Deity and other Sculptures from Malatya'. *Liverpool Annals of Archaeology and Anthropology*, VI (1914) p. 116.

SCHAEFFER, C. *Archiv für Orientforschung* XVI, pp. 151–2.

BIBLIOGRAPHY

15. KARATEPE

BOSSERT, H. Th. *Die Ausgrabungen auf dem Karatepe.* (*Erster Vorbericht.*) Ankara, 1950.

*BOSSERT, H. Th., and U. B. ALKIM. *Karatepe. Second Report.* Istanbul, 1947.

*BOSSERT, H. Th., and H. ÇAMBEL, *Karatepe. First Report.* Istanbul, 1946. *Belleten*, passim.

16. CARCHEMISH

*HOGARTH, D. G. *Carchemish. Part I.* London, 1914.

HOGARTH, D. G. 'Carchemish and its Neighbourhood'. *Liverpool Annals of Archaeology and Anthropology*, II (1909).

*WOOLLEY, C. L. *Carchemish. Part II.* London, 1921.

*WOOLLEY, C. L. *Carchemish. Part III.* London, 1952.

WOOLLEY, C. L. 'The Iron Age Graves of Carchemish'. *Liverpool Annals of Archaeology and Anthropology*, XXVI (1939).

WOOLLEY, C. L. 'The Prehistoric Pottery of Carchemish'. *Iraq*, I (1934).

II. GENERAL WORKS

AINSWORTH, W. F. *Travels and Researches in Asia Minor, Mesopotamia, Chaldea and Armenia.* 2 Vols. London, 1842.

*AKURGAL, E. *Späthethitische Bildkunst.* Istanbul, 1949.

BILABEL, F. *Geschichte Vorderasiens und Aegyptens.* Part I. Berlin, 1927.

BITTEL, K. *Die Ruinen von Boğazköy.* Berlin, 1937.

BITTEL, K. *Grundzüge der Vor- und Frühgeschichte Kleinasiens.* Tübingen, 1945.

BITTEL, K. 'Kleinasiatische Studien'. *Istanbuler Mitteilungen*, Heft 5 (1942).

BITTEL, K. 'Prähistorische Forschungen in Kleinasien'. *Istanbuler Forschungen*, VI (1934).

*BOSSERT, H. Th. *Alt-Anatolien.* Berlin, 1942.

CAVAIGNAC, E. *Les Hittites.* Paris, Maisonneuve, 1950.

CHANTRE, E. *Mission en Cappadoce. 1893–4.* Paris, 1898.

CHAPUT, E. *Phrygie I Géologie et Géographie Physique.* Paris, 1941.

CONTENAU, G. *La Civilisation des Hittites.* Paris, 1948.

CONTENAU, G. *La Civilisation des Hittites et des Hurrites du Mitanni.* Paris, 1948.

CONTENAU, G. *La Glyptique Syro-Hittite.* Paris, 1922.

CUINET, V. *La Turquie d'Asie.* Paris, 1894.

DELAPORTE, L. *Les Hittites.* Paris, 1936.

GABRIEL, A. *Phrygie II. La Cité de Midas. Topographie. Le Site des Fouilles.* Paris, 1952.

*GARSTANG, J. *The Hittite Empire.* London, 1929.

GÖTZE, A. *Hethiter, Churriter und Assyrer.* Oslo, 1936.

GÖTZE, A. *Kizzuwatna and the Problem of Hittite Geography.* New Haven, 1940.

*GÖTZE, A. *Kleinasien.* München, 1933.

*GURNEY, O. R. *The Hittites.* London, 1952.

GÜTERBOCK, H. G. *Siegel aus Boğazköy.* 1. and 2. Teil. Berlin, 1940–42.

HAMILTON, W. J. *Researches in Asia Minor, Pontus and Armenia.* London, 1942.

HASPELS, E. *Phrygie III. La Cité de Midas Céramiques et trouvailles diverses.* Paris, 1951.

KRAUSE, K. *Boğazköy Tempel V.* Berlin, 1940.

LANDSBERGER, B. *Sam'al.* Ankara, 1948.

LEHMANN-HAUPT, C. F. *Armenien einst und jetzt.* Parts I and II. Berlin, 1910.

MANSEL, A. M. *Türkiyenin Arkeoloji, Epigrafi ve Tarihi Coğrafyası için Bibliografya.* Türk Tarih Kurumu, Ankara, 1948.

MARI and ORBELI, *Russian Archaeological Expedition to Van.* (Russian) S. Petersburg, 1922.

MESSERSCHMIDT, L. *The Hittites.* London, 1903.

OSTEN, H. H. von der. 'Explorations in Hittite Asia Minor'. *Oriental Institute Communications,* Nos 2, 6, 8. Chicago, 1927–29.

ÖZGÜÇ, T. *Anadolu'da Ölü Gömme Adetleri.* Ankara, 1948.

PRZEWORSKI, S. *Die Metallindustrie Anatoliens in der Zeit von 1700–500 vor Chr.* Leiden, 1939.

SAUTER, M. R. *Préhistoire de la Mediterranée.* Paris, 1948.

*SCHAEFFER, C. *Stratigraphie Comparée et Chronologie de l'Asie Occidentale.* Oxford, 1948.

TEXIER, C. *Déscription de l'Asie Mineure.* Parts 1, 2, and 3. Paris, 1839–99.

RAMSAY, W. M. and G. L. BELL. *The Thousand and One Churches.* London, 1909.

WAINWRIGHT, G. A. 'Asiatic Keftiu.' *American Journal of Archaeology,* LVI, 4 (1952).

III. JOURNAL ARTICLES

BARNETT, R. D. 'The Excavations of the British Museum at Toprak-kale near Van'. *Iraq,* XII, Part 1 (1950), p. 1.

BARNETT, R. D. 'Karatepe. The Key to the Hittite Hieroglyphs'. *Anatolian Studies,* III (1953) p. 53.

BARNETT, R. D. 'The Phrygian Rock Monuments'. *Bibliotheca Orientalis,* X, 3 and 4 (1953), p. 78.

BARNETT, R. D. 'Russian Excavations in Armenia'. *Iraq,* XIV, Part 2 (1952), p. 132.

BARNETT, R. D., and NURI GÖKÇE. 'Urartian Bronzes from Erzincan'. *Anatolian Studies,* III (1953), p. 121.

BITTEL, K. 'Beitrag zu Eflatun Pinar'. *Bibliotheca Orientalis,* X, Nos. 1 and 2 (1953) p. 2.

BITTEL, K. 'Einige Idolen aus Kleinasien'. *Prähistorische Zeitschrift*, XXXIV/V (1949/50).

FRANKFORT, H. 'The Origin of the Bît Hilani'. *Iraq*, Part 2 (1952), p. 120.

GELB, I. J. 'The Contribution of the New Cilician Bilinguals to the Decipherment of Hieroglyphic Hittite'. *Bibliotheca Orientalis*, VII, 5 (1950), p. 129.

GOLDMAN, H., and J. GARSTANG. 'A Conspectus of Early Cilician Pottery'. *American Journal of Archaeology*, LI, 4 (1947), p. 370.

HYSLOP, R. MAXWELL. 'Daggers and Swords in Western Asia'. *Iraq*, VIII (1946), p. 1.

HYSLOP, R. MAXWELL. 'Western Asiatic Shaft-hole Axes'. *Iraq*, XI (1949), p. 90.

KÖKTEN, K. 'Die Bedeutung der Umgebung von Bayburt innerhalb der Vorgeschichte Nord-ost-Anatoliens'. *A.U. Dergi*, III, 5 (1945), p. 487, fig. 1–6 between pp. 468 and 469.

KÖKTEN, K. 'Exploration in East-Anatolia'. (Öncesi Araştırmaları.) *Belleten*, XI (1947), p. 431 ff., pl. LXXVIII–CVII.

*LAMB, W. 'New Developments in Early Anatolian Archaeology'. *Iraq*, XI, Part 2 (1949), p. 188.

*LAMB, W. 'Some Recent Developments in Anatolian Archaeology'. *Anatolian Studies Presented to W.H. Buckler*. Manchester, 1939.

LAROCHE, E. 'Le Panthéon de Yazılıkaya'. *Journal of Cuneiform Studies*, VI, 3, pp. 115 ff.

*LLOYD, S. 'Mound Surveys'. *Antiquity*, XXVIII (1954), pp. 214 ff.

*MELLINK, M. J. 'Karatepe. More Light on the Dark Ages'. *Bibliotheca Orientalis*, VII, 5 (1950), p. 141.

ORMEROD, H. A. 'Prehistoric Remains in SW Asia Minor'. Parts 1–3. B.S.A. XVI, p. 76; XVIII, pp. 80–94; XIX, pp. 48–60.

TAYLOR, J. du Plat *et al.* 'The Excavations at Sakçe Gözü 1949'. *Iraq*, XII (1950), p. 53.

WOOLLEY, C. L. 'Hittite Burial Customs'. *Liverpool Annals of Archaeology and Anthropology*, VI (1914), pp. 87 ff.

YOUNG, R. 'Gordium'. *Anatolian Studies*, I (1951), p. 11, and II (1952), p. 20.

INDEX

Principal page references are printed in bold type

224